The Protestant Experience in America

Christ dispersing a papal conventicle. Harper's Weekly, January 2, 1875. Courtesy of Florida State University.

The Protestant Experience in America

Amanda Porterfield

The American Religious Experience
Philip Goff, Series Editor

GREENWOOD PRESS
Westport, Connecticut • London

Library of Congress Cataloging-in-Publication Data

Porterfield, Amanda, 1947–
    The Protestant experience in America / Amanda Porterfield.
        p.   cm.—(The American religious experience)
    Includes bibliographical references and index.
    ISBN 0–313–32801–3 (alk. paper)
    1. Protestant churches—United States.   2. United States—Church
history.   I. Title.   II. Series: American religious experience (Greenwood
Press [Westport, Conn.])
BR517.P67   2006
280'.40973—dc22   2006015362

British Library Cataloguing in Publication Data is available.

Library of Congress Catalog Card Number: 2006015362
ISBN: 0-313-32801-3

First published in 2006

Greenwood Press, 88 Post Road West, Westport, CT 06881
An imprint of Greenwood Publishing Group, Inc.
www.greenwood.com

Printed in the United States of America

The paper used in this book complies with the
Permanent Paper Standard issued by the National
Information Standards Organization (Z39.48-1984).

10 9 8 7 6 5 4 3 2 1

With appreciation for my colleagues,
John Corrigan, John Kelsay, and Sumner B. Twiss

Contents

Series Foreword

Philip Goff

Some years ago, Winthrop Hudson, a leading religious historian, began his survey book on religion in America with a description of a London street. "When Americans walk down the street of an English city," he wrote, "they will be reminded of home..."[1]

Few would dispute that for many years this was the case. Multiple faith traditions in today's United States trace their roots to English lineage, most notably the Episcopal, Methodist, and Baptist Churches. But that sort of literary device would not hold up under the pressure of today's diversity. Lutherans, Presbyterians, and Dutch Reformed adherents would balk at such oversimplification—and those are just a few among only the Protestant Christians. Add the voices of Jews, Eastern Orthodox, Muslims, Buddhists, and Irish, Italian, and Polish Catholics, and we would have a powerful chorus demanding their stories be told. And their stories do not begin on the streets of London.

Of course, Hudson knew that was the case. His point was not that all significant American religions began in England, but that, "with only a few exceptions, the varied religious groups of America have their roots abroad."[2] But clearly the "abroad" Hudson worked with was predominantly European, even if not entirely English. Today's scholarship has broadened that focus to include African, Asian, Central and South American, as well as Canadian and some "home grown" traditions that are on their way to becoming worldwide faiths. If ever scholarship in American religion has reflected the lineage of its people, it is in the recent writings that have moved beyond conventional ideas of faith traditions to include non-Anglo peoples who, while often existing off the radar screen of the establishment, have nonetheless formed much of the marrow of American religious life.

Although our studies of American religion have expanded to include more migrating faith groups from more areas of the world, the basic question that divided historians early in the twentieth century remained: namely, are traditions of American life (religion, politics, economics, etc.) transplants from the Old World, or did something entirely new and unique form in the New World? That is, should we seek to comprehend America's present religious scene by understanding its roots? Or should we try to understand it by looking at its transformations?

Of course, the truth lies somewhere in between. One cannot understand present-day Methodists or Buddhists by knowing their Old World beginnings in England and China or Japan. Nor can one determine the transformations those faith traditions underwent in America without knowing a good deal about their Old World forms. The American experience, then, is one of constancy of tradition from one angle and continual revision from another. The fact that they may look, think, and sound different than their Old World forms does not negate the fact that they are still recognizably Methodist and Buddhist in their new contexts.

This book series is meant to introduce readers to the basic faith traditions that characterize religious life today by employing that continuum of constancy and change. Each volume traces its topic from its Old World beginnings (when it applies) to its present realities. In doing so, readers will see how many of the original beliefs and practices came to be, as well as how they transformed, remained nearly the same, or were complemented by new ones in the American environment. In some cases—African Americans and Mormons most clearly—the Old World proved important either implicitly or imaginatively rather than explicitly and literally. But even in these cases, development within the context of American culture is still central to the story.

To be sure, each author in this series employed various approaches in writing these books. History, sociology, and even anthropology all play their parts. Each volume, then, may have its idiosyncrasies, as the authors chose which approaches worked best at which moments for their respective topics. These variations of approach resemble the diversity of the groups themselves, as each interacted in various ways at different stages with American society.

Not only do these volumes introduce us to the roots and development of each faith group, they also provide helpful guides to readers who wish to know more about them. By offering resources for research—including published primary and secondary sources—the series presents a wealth of helpful information for formal and informal students of religion in America.

Clearly, this is a series conceived and published with the curious reader in mind. It is our hope that it will spur both a deeper understanding of the varieties of religious experience in the United States and better research in the country's many and always changing traditions.

Notes

1. Winthrop Hudson, *Religion in America*, 4th ed. (New York: Macmillan Publishing, 1987), p. 11.
2. Hudson, *Religion in America*, pp. 11–12.

Introduction: Protestantism as a Political Concept

What is a "Protestant"? Half a century ago, the sociologist Will Herberg thought the answer to that question relatively simple. "Protestant" was one of three "melting pots" that immigrants to the United States joined, the other two being "Catholic" and "Jew." Herberg emphasized the importance of subscribing to one of these identities, calling them "the primary context of self-identification and social location" in the United States. "For being a Protestant, a Catholic, or a Jew," Herberg wrote, is "increasingly perhaps the only way of being an American and locating oneself in American society."

Herberg built his concept of social identity on the premise that America was a nation of immigrants. Newcomers arrived in this country with a complicated array of ethnic and religious heritages—Scottish Presbyterians, Norwegian Lutherans, Sicilian Catholics, Sephardic Jews, to name a few. Members of these particular religious and ethnic groups assimilated to American culture by identifying with one of the three big groups everyone could recognize. Protestant-Catholic-Jew represented something like a typology of super-denominations, and the vast majority of Americans accepted affiliation with one of these three groups. Those who tried to stand outside the paradigm often felt pressured to conform. Herberg recounted the story of a high-church Episcopalian recruited into the U.S. Army who claimed not to be Roman Catholic or Protestant. "Well, if you're not Catholic, Protestant, or Hebrew," his exasperated sergeant supposedly said, "what in blazes *are* you?"

To some extent, "Protestant," "Catholic," and "Jew" were interdependent, relational terms; at least in part, "Protestant" meant "not Catholic" and "not Jew." In the past, Herberg thought, citing the definition advanced by H. Richard Niebuhr, "Protestant" may have referred to a distinctive commitment to "the sovereignty of God, the kingship of Christ, and the coming kingdom." But such forceful theological emphasis could not be counted on in the 1950s, Herberg believed, when 60 million Americans, more than half the total population, identified themselves as Protestant whether or not they attended church or subscribed to a definitive set of religious beliefs. In 1955, Herberg thought it "more than likely that a Yankee turned Buddhist would still be regarded as a 'Protestant,' albeit admittedly a queer one."[1]

Origins of the Term "Protestant"

In its earliest meaning, "Protestant" referred to protests for reform within the Roman Catholic Church. The term originated in the early sixteenth century in northern Germany to describe people who denounced priestly corruption within the church and called for changes in the meaning and celebration of the sacraments. Calls for church reform were nothing new, but in the sixteenth century they were more widespread and far-reaching through their associations with resistance to feudal oppression, conflicts dividing European princes, the organization of new states, the resurgence of classical humanism, the invention of the printing press, and the early development of print culture. In 1529, when a majority of German princes feared that religious reform was disrupting political stability and weakening their ability to withstand military pressure from Turkish forces mounting to the East, the governing federation of princes met to call a halt to church reform. In response to this mandate from the Reichstag, a minority of German princes still committed to reform signed a "Protest." The term "Protestant" stuck as a moniker for those who actively supported religious reform.[2]

In the cities of northern Germany and elsewhere, Protestants demanded greater attention to the transcendent authority of God, surpassing that of all earthly rulers. They also demanded devotion to the sole power of Christ to forgive sin, which meant denouncing popular devotion to Mary and other saints as intercessors for Christ with miraculous powers of their own. Devotion to the sole power of Christ to forgive sin also meant commitment to the priesthood of all believers, elevating the authority of laypeople, and restraining that of clerics. Coinciding with these recalibrations of religious authority, Protestants looked to the coming transformation of human society through Christ's return to earth. Although they disagreed about how soon that transformation might occur and how much political and ecclesiastic upheaval they as faithful servants of God's authority and Christ's transforming spirit should support, all Protestants regarded the Church of Rome as a major obstacle in the way of the full disclosure of divine authority and the transformation of life on earth.

Protestants defined religious life in terms of adherence to biblical teaching, and many groups devoted enormous effort to governing themselves according to rules derived from the Bible. Although earlier Christians also lived in religious worlds defined by biblical symbols, stories, and motifs, the development of Protestant cultures based on the hearing and reading of biblical texts translated into ordinary languages was unprecedented. Printing opened the Bible to laypeople and even made Bible study a key element of religious practice and piety. Preaching also flourished in the context of this new attention to the Bible, spilling out of the mouths of laypeople and ministers of newfound churches outside the bounds of the Catholic Church and priesthood. Protestant preachers took biblical texts as points of departure for sermonizing and often used the Bible to attack Catholic corruption and to call believers to restore the pure faith and primitive religious practices described in the Bible.

Protestant emphasis on the authority of the Bible, the importance of Bible study as a form of religious practice, and the need for preachers to expound on biblical texts in relation to contemporary life had vast implications for the church. With the Bible held up as the supreme authority in matters of religious practice, theological doctrine, and church governance, Protestants not only condemned Catholic traditions not found in the Bible but in many cases also criticized the very existence of the Catholic Church. But if Protestants agreed that the Bible set the standards for how churches should be constructed, they disagreed about what exactly those standards were and how they ought to be met.

Many Protestants believed in a universal church, more or less hidden and unfinished and awaiting completion through the Second Coming of Christ and the meeting of heaven and earth. Because of this tendency to project the universal church into the future and because of their disagreements with one another, Protestants never erected an institutional church that paralleled the Church of Rome. At the mundane level of institutional organization and church politics, considerable differences of opinion existed among Protestants on specific points of doctrine, especially with regard to how radically the implications of the coming kingdom ought to be interpreted. As particular groups of Protestants in different locales developed specific doctrines and forms of liturgical practice, some of these groups became established as state churches; others existed without political support. Some independents wanted their churches to be separate from state government, others were hopeful of becoming established. No single institution ever held

"Protestants" together. What united them (more or less) was hatred of Catholicism and attention to the realities they believed Catholicism obscured, namely, the pristine truths of biblical revelation, the sovereignty of God, the sole power of Christ to save sinners, and the transformation of human society anticipated through the coming of Christ's kingdom to earth.

Denominationalism

Important alliances among reform leaders and their churches did develop, however, resulting in the concept of denominationalism that came to play a major role in American ideas about religious organization. As historian Winthrop S. Hudson explained the origin of this concept, in the midst of the English civil war in the 1640s, when Puritan reformers, eager to further the Protestant cause in England, overturned the British monarchy and established an unstable government, the leaders of independent Puritan churches promoted an understanding of the nature of the church that stressed cordial relationships among an array of different Protestant groups. These independents cherished their fellowship with reformed churches on the continent, where political situations led to different forms of church government than in England, and also wanted to extend respect to Puritan leaders in their own country who wanted a national church.

When the Puritan government convened an Assembly at the Westminster Church in London in the 1640s to reform the Church of England along Puritan lines, the independents spoke out at the Assembly as "Dissenting Brethren"; they did not want a national church, but rather wanted each congregation to be self-governed. As the ironic name "Brethren" suggested, they were mindful of "the danger of rending and dividing the godly Protestant party," and eager to show that "love and unity are Christ's badge." Referring to "the wants and weaknesses that do ordinarily attend men's apprehensions," the independents argued that differences of opinion about church government were inevitable given human nature. The diversity and fallibility of human perception were no reason, however, to require Christians to deny their honest convictions and submit to the will of others in matters of religious belief. Open discussion of differences of opinion might even be God's way of producing new light, they hoped, just as "sparks are beaten out by the flints striking together."[3] According to Hudson, this eagerness for dialogue, cooperation, and respect for different opinions expressed by independent Puritans during the English civil war laid the groundwork for the concept of denominationalism.

The word "denomination" came into use in the eighteenth century, when evangelical preachers in England and America popularized it in the context of their efforts to call people with different (or no) church affiliations to new birth and salvation in Christ. The Scotch-Irish Presbyterian Gilbert Tennant employed the term during the revivals he led in New Jersey in the 1740s. There was "one Church of Christ," Tennant declared, "but several branches (more or less pure in minuter points) of one visible kingdom of the Messiah." These branches or "societies," he explained, "who profess Christianity and retain the foundational principle thereof, notwithstanding their different denominations and diversity of sentiments in smaller things, are in reality but one." Around the same time, the famous Anglican revivalist George Whitefield contrasted differences in church affiliation, doctrinal particulars, and customary forms of worship with the transcendent need for new birth in Christ, preaching that distinctions among denominations would disappear in heaven. Speaking to a crowd in Philadelphia in the 1740s, Whitefield made the point dramatically: "Father Abraham, whom have you in heaven? Any Episcopalians? No! Any Presbyterians? No! Any Independents or Methodists? No, no, no!" he exclaimed. "All who are here are Christians."[4]

While Hudson identified the concept of denominationalism as the defining element behind "the whole structure of American Protestantism,"[5] we can extend his observation further to say that the concept of denominationalism has informed the way many Americans have perceived different religious groups in their midst. By the mid-twentieth century, respect for different forms of religious practice and belief had expanded to include Catholics and Jews as well as members of various Protestant churches. From the perspective of Protestant history, mutual respect among Protestants, Catholics, and Jews represented an amplified version of the concept of the church that the Dissenting Brethren had hammered out in seventeenth-century England. At least to some extent, then, the approach to religious difference that many Catholics and Jews came to share derived from Protestant theory about the denominational structure of church organization.

Purpose and Scope of This Book

This book approaches Protestantism as an important movement within Christianity, concerned with matters of self-government, social order, and politics and closely associated with the development of modern culture, modern forms of government, and modern science. Protestant ideas about the sovereignty of God, the lordship of Christ, the kingdom of God, and the authority of biblical revelation contributed significantly to the development of modern ideas about self-government, social order, and nationhood and also to a confidence that the study of nature would reflect and proclaim the glory of God. Confidence in the ultimate harmony between nature and the Bible contributed not only to enthusiasm for scientific study of nature but also to countless efforts to harmonize religion and science; it also led to fundamentalist criticism of scientific evidence that appeared not to support biblical revelation.

In its focus on Protestant experience in America, the book is concerned with the enormous influence of this religious movement in the history of American culture. The book attends to important differences and debates in the history of this movement as well as to major trends and events that changed perceptions of what "Protestant" meant in relation to American identity, scientific enterprise, and other forms of religion. The book traces the meaning of the term "Protestant" from its origin in efforts to rid Christianity of Catholic influence through subsequent equations with American nationhood to its weaker meaning, after World War II, as a melting pot of American religious and ethnic identity, and to conservative, patriotic reaction against that weakened meaning in the twentieth and early twenty-first centuries.

Although many important events and debates and many different individuals, groups, religious practices, and experiences are discussed here, this book is not a comprehensive history of American Protestant churches, nor is it a guide to the full spectrum of liturgical forms and theological doctrines represented in those churches. A book of that sort would be an important contribution to the history of American Christianity. This book moves away from that worthy undertaking in order to achieve another purpose, that of tracing the underlying history of ways of thinking advanced by people in those churches who applied their experiences of God, Christ, and biblical teaching to the construction and reform of American society. This book shows how Protestant religious experience, thinking, and practice have shaped American life.

Bringing the Kingdom Down to Earth

A key ingredient in American Protestant thinking is the expectation of sainthood as part of Christian life. Protestants believed that all true Christians were saints and that the ordinary lives of all Christians revealed important aspects of God and his teachings. Saints were not mediators between Christ and ordinary Christians who could help ordinary Christians obtain forgiveness or special blessings; ordinary Christians were all saints who had received forgiveness from Christ directly. By removing saints as heavenly mediators and bringing them down to earth as exemplary neighbors, citizens, and housewives, much of the force of Christian life was directed toward manifesting the principles of Christ's teaching at home and in society. Considerable disagreement existed about whether and how Christians were made and recognized by others, and many believers were deeply concerned about problems of hypocrisy and the falsity of people who represented themselves as Christian but were not. For all the disagreement and confusion generated by such concerns about Christian identity, however, American Protestant ideas about sainthood called attention to ordinary human existence as the realm of Christian life and generated expectations about the changes in human self-government that the growing presence of true Christians would bring. While American Protestants often set their sights on heaven as the place where saints would be crowned with glory, many believed that their work on earth reflected their relationship with God and the movement of his will through history.

Visions of Christian saints building God's kingdom on earth expressed a fusion of otherworldly images and this-worldly agendas that united evangelicals from different denominations to work together toward common goals of social reform and missionary outreach. Beginning in the eighteenth century, evangelical Christians in America engaged in countless efforts to construct their society in fulfillment of the plan of redemption that they believed God had designed at the beginning of time. Congregationalists, Baptists, Presbyterians, Methodists, Disciples, and other Christians disputed with one another over questions of baptism, free will, and the exact nature of the conversion process but also joined together in many efforts to promote conversions, revivals, antislavery, temperance, and moral order in America and the world.

In the early nineteenth century, anti-Catholic hostility flared up with renewed intensity among Protestant evangelicals in response to the immigration of thousands of Catholics seeking a better life in the United States. As far as many evangelicals were concerned, these immigrants threatened their sense of ownership of America and their vision of an American destiny flowing forward from the Puritans and the holy commonwealths that the Puritans had established in America.

In *A Plea for the West*, published in 1835, the evangelical preacher Lyman Beecher (1775–1863) expressed alarm at the "rapid influx of foreign emigrants, unacquainted with our institutions, unaccustomed to self-government, inaccessible to education." Alluding to the tortures of the Spanish Inquisition and to rumors of political conspiracies plotted inside the Vatican, Beecher warned of the "inveterate cruelty, and intrigue, easily embodied and wielded by sinister design," to which these immigrants were vulnerable by virtue of their adherence to Rome. He urged fellow Protestants to enlist in vigorous efforts to educate the new immigrant in the values of Protestant culture, asserting that the alternative was to allow him to "fall back into a dark minded, vicious populace—a poor uneducated, reckless man of infuriated animalism."

Beecher hoped this fall into animalism could be avoided. Looking to the American West, where many immigrants were heading, he saw "a young empire of mind, and power, and wealth, and free institutions, rushing up to a giant manhood, with a rapidity and a power never before witnessed below the sun." Claiming that "the religious and political destiny of our nation is to be decided in the West," Beecher called Protestants to send forth their most "learned and talented ministry" to meet the challenge of the immigrant population and its susceptibility to the "sinister design" of the Roman Church. Protestant success in the West would prove that the absorption of foreign immigrants into the American Protestant nation was a crucial part of God's unfolding plan.

Beecher was not entirely confident that Protestants would win the day. "We must educate! We must educate!" he cried, eager for Protestants from different denominations to band together to control the continent. Like Americans in the cold war a century later who feared the Russians, Beecher summoned defenders of American values to action against a common threat, placing special emphasis on the need for education as means of strengthening the nation.

Beecher reminded his readers that the great Puritan theologian Jonathan Edwards (1703–1758) held "the opinion" that "the millennium would commence in America." With that sense of American destiny in mind, Beecher called Protestants to their duty: "if this nation is, in the providence of God, destined to lead the way in the moral and political emancipation of the world, it is time she understood her high calling, and were harnessed for the work." Empowered by "[o]ur alliance of blood, and political institutions, and common interests," Protestant ministers and missionary teachers would bring these newcomers into the American Protestant fold. "We opened our doors wide," Beecher boasted. "Let the Catholics mingle with us as Americans," he wrote. "If in these circumstances the protestant religion cannot stand before the Catholic, let it go down."[6]

Protestant desires for religious supremacy figured importantly in the hopeful vision of history that many nineteenth-century evangelicals shared, and in the fears they shared about foreign plans for overtaking the country. With reference to efforts made by Catholic sisters in Maryland, Louisiana, and Ohio in establishing convents and schools for

Catholic immigrants, the evangelical educator Mary Lyon (1797–1849) informed her supporters in 1837 that Catholics had already established "more than a hundred female schools" in the United States and that, for lack of good alternatives, some Protestant mothers even allowed their children to attend. Alarmed by "the dangers to which our country is exposed" as the immigrant population expanded westward, she warned her supporters that Catholics were spending vast sums to educate female teachers "to lend their aid in converting this nation to the Church of Rome." Convinced that Protestant ministers could not carry forward the work of redemption without the help of female teachers, she stressed the urgency of establishing a new school for training young evangelical women to be teachers. "This work of supplying teachers," she warned, "must be done or our country is lost, and the world will remain unconverted."[7]

In fact, the Catholic sisters who concerned Mary Lyon were far more focused on providing schools that enabled Catholics to retain their faith than with converting Protestants. Protestant teachings permeated the public school system in the United States in the nineteenth century and involved Protestant prayers and singing, lessons in the Protestant King James Bible (a translation not approved by the Catholic Church), and derogatory remarks about Catholics and their church in classroom textbooks. According to historian Ray Allen Billington, nineteenth-century textbooks "took every opportunity to emphasize the corruptions of Catholicism." One public school text described the sixteenth-century reformer Jon Hus as a "zealous reformer from popery" who was burned at the stake as a result of innocently "trusting himself to the deceitful Catholics." Another passage imagined a dialogue between the good Pennsylvania Quaker William Penn and the bad Catholic explorer Hernando Cortez in which Penn exclaims, "A Papist talk of reason! Go to the Inquisition and tell them of reason and the great laws of nature. They will broil thee as thy soldiers broiled Guatimozin," Penn predicted, referring to a Native American leader killed by Spanish soldiers under Cortez's command.[8] Through the zeal of Protestant educators, the public school system in the United States developed as an effective institution for the inculcation of Protestant values. "The nineteenth century was a time when the schoolhouse became the sacred temple of the American nation," according to Catholic historian Jay Dolan. "The school had replaced the family as the principal educational institution," Dolan argued, and through that process, "educators and politicians pushed their campaign forward with the zeal of religious crusaders."[9]

Nineteenth-century evangelicals often cited Jonathan Edwards as an authoritative source supporting the idea that the kingdom of God was dawning in America, and a number of his remarks lent themselves to that interpretation. In *Some Thoughts Concerning the Present Revival*, published in 1742, he described the religious awakening of his day as "the dawning, or at least a prelude, of that glorious work of God, so often foretold in Scripture, which in the progress and issue of it shall renew the world of mankind." Edwards speculated that "the dawn of that glorious day" and "the beginning or forerunner of something vastly great" might be at hand. He reasoned that, since Christ's return and thousand-year reign on earth had long been anticipated, "we can't reasonably think otherwise, than that the beginning of the great work of God must be near." It also seemed reasonable to surmise the location for the commencement of this work: "there are many things that make it probable," he remarked, "that this work will begin in America."[10]

Edwards' *History of the Work of Redemption* was a favorite of evangelicals in the nineteenth century who, like Beecher, encouraged Americans to join new societies and interdenominational ventures for the promulgation of Protestant values. Mary Lyon collected subscriptions for a reprinting of Edwards' *History* and drew inspiration for her plans for building a school for evangelical teachers from the image of God's kingdom on earth described in that book—an enormous building, constructed over the course of history "on the foundation of the prophets and apostles, the Redeemer himself being the chief cornerstone." This edifice, Edwards wrote, was moving toward completion through a revival of evangelical religion and universal Protestant reform. Soon God's plan for history would be accomplished, "with the top-stone laid" in "a time of great light and *knowledge*" and "all the world" brought into the same order and "united in one amiable society."[11]

Edwards' image of the millennium as "one amiable society" built like an enormous church out of the bodies of saints stayed with Lyon through the construction and development of Mount Holyoke Female Seminary, which became world famous in the nineteenth century as an interdenominational school for teachers and missionaries. "The stone and brick and mortar speak a language," Lyon wrote about the laying of the cornerstone for her school on a beautiful fall day in October 1836, "which vibrates through my very soul." The cornerstone image applied to the first thousand dollars contributed to the school and to the place of her school and students in the history of the world. "Another stone in the foundation of our great system of benevolent operations, which are destined, in the hand of God, to convert a world, will then be laid," she proclaimed in a circular promoting her seminary and its commitment to the education of female teachers. Mount Holyoke's first diplomas pictured a palace with a quarry in front, a group of young women standing alongside blocks of stone, with a passage from Proverbs printed below: "That our daughters may be as corner stones, polished after the similitude of a palace."[12]

America as New Israel

Throughout Christian history, preachers explained that Christ fulfilled the promises of the Old Testament, that his sacrifice atoned for human sin, and that those who lived in him would enter the kingdom of heaven. They also blamed Jews for not recognizing Jesus as the Messiah and for putting him to death. These negative perceptions of Jews, rationalized by reference to scripture, had real social effects. In medieval and modern Europe, vicious pogroms scapegoated Jews as the cause of social ills, and in many instances Jews had to choose between conversion or religious disguise on one hand and expulsion or death on the other.[13]

Although American Protestants were not above blaming Jews for Jesus' death or society's ills, religious visions of America as the New Israel contributed to the culture in which Jews participated and worked against anti-Semitism. Protestant ideas about the kingdom of God derived, in part, from Old Testament stories of Israel as the promised land of God's chosen people and of the bounteous fertility and prosperity God promised to bestow on Israel in response to her repentance and obedience to his law. English Protestants brought such visions to America, appealing to biblical stories about God's covenant relation with Israel to express their hopes of being God's chosen people building a New Israel in the wilderness of America. After American independence and the enormous expansion of U.S. territory as a result of the Louisiana Purchase in 1803, evangelicals elaborated upon Puritan images of the New Israel in their efforts to build a Protestant empire in America.

In a highly successful variant of mainstream evangelicalism in the nineteenth century, the Mormons literally built a new Zion in the desert wilderness of Utah, drawing inspiration from ancient Israel in constructing their religious government, communal life, and temple, even referring to non-Mormons as Gentiles. The Mormons were just one example of a larger American fascination with ancient Israel. Caught up in pursuing parallels between Israel as described in the Bible and America as the new promised land, more than a few evangelicals have regarded themselves as authorities on Jewish customs and law.

For Jews themselves, Protestant visions of America as the New Israel had little to do with living Judaism, at least initially; to evangelicals who regarded themselves as having supplanted Jews as God's chosen people, living Jews were anachronisms, holdovers from an ancient era whose final return to Jerusalem would signal the Second Coming of Christ or, in the case of Identity Christians, imposters usurping places rightly held in society by Aryans. While these constructions of their heritage were foreign and offensive, Jews perceived linkages between Protestant idealism about America and policies of religious freedom they wholeheartedly embraced. Isaac M. Wise (1819–1900), the leading Reform rabbi in the United States after the Civil War, believed that being an American enabled him to live freely as a Jew and that being a Jew enabled him to contribute to God's providential role in history in a special way. He appropriated elements of Protestant rhetoric to describe America's providential role in history and to show how America made space for Jews. In an address delivered in 1869, Wise asserted that, "History is Providence realized." Praising America as "the heiress of the civilized world's blood, experience and wisdom, as Greece was in days of yore; the mistress of the vast domain fortified by heaving oceans, really wealthy as none was before her; the favored high priestess of the goddess of liberty, with the diadem of honor and breast-plate of justice," he exulted that religious freedom was America's great contribution to the unfolding of God's plan. "Liberty is our place in history, our national destiny, our ideal, the very soul of our existence." Religious freedom made America home to Jews. As long as that ideal was paramount, Wise could celebrate America as a nation that fulfilled a providential design.[14]

Much as Isaac Wise and other Jewish leaders appropriated the rhetoric of American religious destiny in ways that included them and affirmed their freedom of religious expression, a number of influential Catholic leaders claimed America as Catholicism's best home. Orestes Brownson, a Protestant convert to the Catholic Church, believed that religious freedom in America offered Catholics the opportunity to take up their faith more actively than Catholics did in Europe. He also believed that the power of Catholic sacraments and the communal solidarity they offered was the right antidote for the excessive individualism of American culture. American Catholics, he predicted, would play a major role in America's providential destiny, advancing her progress as a Christian nation.[15]

At the grassroots level, nineteenth-century American Catholics worked to create spaces where their own faith could be nurtured and protected. They also worked to demonstrate their patriotism as Americans. During the Civil War, the diligence and compassion of Catholic nurses proved to be an important breakthrough in disarming Protestant hostility against Catholics. Many Protestant soldiers received comfort from Catholic nurses who respected them as human beings and never asked them to convert.

Christian Freedom Through Science and Government

By the time an official organization called the Evangelical Alliance was formed at the end of the nineteenth century, interdenominational co-operation in the service of the coming kingdom had become more clearly linked to social welfare programs and to the solution of problems caused by industrial capitalism and less clearly associated with the arrival of anything supernatural. The leading spokesman for the Alliance, Josiah Strong (1847–1916), combined theology with sociology, linking an older theological tradition that anticipated the dawn of the millennium in America to a modern faith in scientific methods for analyzing problems of industrialization, immigration, and urban poverty. In his 1893 book, *The New Era, or The Coming Kingdom*, Strong insisted that the kingdom of God be interpreted as a mandate for society and not as something supernatural and otherworldly: "by the kingdom of heaven, or the kingdom of God, of which Christ speaks so often," Strong wrote in 1893, "he does not mean the abode of the blessed dead, but a kingdom of righteousness which he came to establish on the earth, of which he is the king, and whose fundamental law is that of love."[16]

Strong showed no sympathy for the Catholic view that Christians reached the kingdom of heaven through participation in the sacraments. He celebrated Protestantism as a revolutionary protest movement against the conservatism of Catholic doctrine and ecclesiastical control. Protestantism was "a reaction against the absolutism of Rome," Strong asserted, "a development of individualism" that "at length achieved religious liberty." Like Lyman Beecher, Mary Lyon, and other evangelicals earlier in the nineteenth century, Strong feared the strength of the Catholic Church, especially its uniformity as an all-encompassing paramilitary organization, which he vastly overrated. He seems to have perceived the Catholic Church as a sinister version of the smooth-running modern organization he hoped the Evangelical Alliance would become. One hundred years later, the filmmaker George Lucas developed a fantasy along similar lines: a federation of Jedi Knights fighting against the Evil Empire in the blockbuster movie series, *Star Wars*.

Strong believed that, for all their nobility and contributions to progress, Protestants suffered from a "weakness of disorganization and of rival sects," while Catholics boasted "the strength and permanence which spring from a consummate organization." To meet the new problems of industrialization, popular discontent, and "the separation of the masses from the church," Strong proposed new methods of organization and "a committee of the churches" representing laypeople as well as ministers that would "foster co-operation" and "cultivate the fellowship of the churches." This fellowship would rekindle enthusiasm for the social teachings of Jesus, "thus enabling the collective church to undertake its social mission by consciously and intelligently attempting to apply the principles of the Gospel to the entire life of the community." The modernization of society created great problems for the world and the church, Strong admitted, but also opened up new and more scientific ways of thinking about humanity that would enable the people of the church to take up their full responsibility as Christians and finally realize their social mission. "This broader conception of the mission of the church," Strong argued, "has never been grasped by the church herself. She has deemed the world a hopeless wreck, and herself commissioned to save out of it as many as possible, whom she is to land on the heavenly shore. It has not yet dawned on her that she is to save the wreck itself." The moment of that dawning realization, Strong thought, was now at hand.[17]

Rejecting the tendency to divide the sacred from the secular, Strong urged American Protestants to spiritualize the secular realm and make all of life holy. He blamed the "Latin fathers" of the Roman Church for infecting Christianity with a "vicious dualism" that separated sacred from secular and produced monasticism, which he defined as "an attempt to overcome the world by running away from it." He also blamed skeptics in modern America who had lost faith in the ongoing vitality of Christianity and cast aside the sacred to embrace the secular world. Strong believed that only by infusing the secular with sacred meaning would the problems of poverty, crime, and discontent be solved. "It is very difficult to hoe potatoes or build a steam-engine to the glory of God when the occupation of the farmer and that of the machinist are deemed 'secular,'" he argued. Confident that the kingdom of God would become manifest through scientific principles and discoveries as well as through the glorification of human labor, he wanted Christians to see "that the laws of the material world are laws of the kingdom of God," and, "whether pertaining to mind or matter, that every stroke of honest and well-directed work is laying a stone in the upbuilding of the glorious kingdom which shall one day fill the earth."[18]

The establishment of an Evangelical Alliance at the turn of the twentieth century represented an important moment in the history of American Protestant experience. As a real organization with an ambitious agenda, it may have come as close as anything yet had to bringing a universal Protestant Church to institutional reality. Strong's emphasis on the need for laypeople and pastors to take responsibility for building the kingdom carried forward the hope of social transformation that energized many of the reformers in the sixteenth century. At the same time, however, Strong's belief that Christians should not wait for some heavenly event to intervene and accomplish their work drained the supernaturalism out of Protestant visions of the kingdom of God and undercut the hope of life after death and personal immortality in heaven that many Protestants held. The success of Strong's vision depended on people's willingness to let go of their belief in an afterlife and interpret the meaning of the gospel in humanistic terms. It also depended on an optimistic faith in science as a vehicle that would enable Christians to finally bring the kingdom to earth.

The direction of Strong's thinking, and that of other proponents of a "social gospel," did not go unopposed. Defenders of heaven emphasized the miracles of Christ's resurrection, his atonement for human sin through his sacrifice on the cross, his birth from a virgin mother, and their own hopes of bodily resurrection and eternal life. Proponents of the social gospel countered that they understood the power of sin and that Christianizing the social order depended on the transformation of individuals. But defenders of heaven were not convinced. "The beginning of the Christian life," wrote J. Gresham Machen in 1923, "is an act of God." Contrary to the emphasis on humanity as the source of its own salvation, Machen called the new birth that made salvation possible "an act of God and not an act of man."[19]

Protestantism Peaks as an Organizational Movement

American Protestants developed extensive organizational structures in the twentieth century, building on the denominational alliances of the nineteenth century and on the concept of denominationalism that had figured importantly in Protestant ideas about the nature of the church since the seventeenth century. Twentieth-century American Protestants often conceptualized the church as a network of people, institutions, and activities working together in love and faith in the kingdom of God. Lutherans, Methodists, Presbyterians, and Disciples of Christ with somewhat different liturgical styles and traditions of historical development were united in the spirit of Christ, many believed, in much the same way that the ancient churches in Antioch, Corinth, Ephesus, and Galatia were distinctive and yet united in Christ.

The Federal Council of Churches, founded in 1908, and its successor, the National Council of Churches, coordinated the missionary and social service programs for many American denominations, even as these denominations grew larger and larger bureaucracies of their own. Mergers between denominations contributed to the web of organizations. In 1939, Methodists repaired the split over slavery that had divided them into northern and southern churches in the nineteenth century. In 1957, the Methodist Church expanded further by incorporating the Evangelical United Brethren, itself a union of pietist churches of German ancestry formed in 1922 and then expanded in 1946. Unitarians and Universalists joined forces in 1961, overcoming class and regional differences that had separated them in the past to find common ground in their emphasis on inclusiveness and respect for individual conscience. In 1984, northern and southern Presbyterians finally reunited. As the most ambitious of all the denominational mergers in the twentieth century, the formation of the United Churches of Christ in 1957 comprised Congregationalists whose heritage stretched back to the Puritans, Christians whose church originated with Alexander Campbell's effort to restore the organizational structure of the primitive church in the mid-nineteenth century, and members of the Evangelical and Reformed Church, which represented an earlier union of German pietist churches in the United States. Many of the Christians joining the UCC believed that they were leading the way in a bold ecumenical movement and hoped that other churches would join them in forming a vast and united Protestant Church.

Even as the extent of denominational union and institutional cooperation attained new breadth in the 1950s, however, the signs of a disintegrating process within American Protestantism were appearing. On several fronts, the grounds of consensus for the kind of evangelical alliance Josiah Strong had envisioned at the turn of the twentieth century had eroded. Optimism about science and sociology as extensions of Protestant faith that would lead Americans into a new world of harmonious order was in decline, replaced by fear of The Bomb, uneasiness about social engineering, and hatred of communism. For many American Protestants, two world wars had undermined the kind of confidence in humanity that Strong had exuded, along with unquestioning belief in Christian faith as the natural ally of social progress and scientific achievement. At the same time, the doctrinal clarity that Protestants of an earlier generation took more for granted was dissolving, partly as a result of all the denominational mergers, interfaith efforts, and ecumenical dialogue going on. Further loosening the meaning of Protestant identity, growing numbers of Protestants were exploring Hinduism, Buddhism, and Freudian psychology. Increasing respect for and familiarity with Jews and Catholics dispelled perceptions of Jews as curious anachronisms and undermined the long-standing hostility toward the Church of Rome so fundamental to the construction of Protestant identity. In 1952, only one in ten Protestants surveyed in a national poll reported having a negative attitude toward Catholics. By 1979, that number had declined to one in fifty.[20]

Protestant-Catholic-Jew as a Unifying Patriotic Construct

Looking back on Herberg's study today, when identification as a Protestant, Catholic, or Jew no longer seems sufficient or so all-encompassing, we can see how the system of identification worked in the 1950s to enable Americans of different backgrounds to express an enthusiasm for religion that overlapped, to a considerable extent, with enthusiasm for being American. Identification as a Protestant, Catholic, or Jew preserved certain differences while locating people as members of different religious branches of the same nation. An overarching investment in America as a nation of freedom and democracy enabled Protestants, Catholics, and Jews to perceive themselves as different branches of one patriotic family.

American religious life was actually much more diverse and less well organized. In addition to numerous subdivisions among Protestants, Catholics, and Jews themselves, Buddhists, Taoists, and Confucians had resided in the United States since the nineteenth century, especially in California and the Northwest, and Christians affiliated with Orthodox churches in the Northwest traced their origins to the eighteenth century. Native Americans practiced a wide variety of indigenous religions, and Africans brought many different religious traditions to the United States. If Protestant-Catholic-Jew was more of a nationalistic construction of American religious life than a true measure of religious diversity, many Americans in the post–World War II period accepted and identified with it.

The post–World War II division of American society into Protestant, Catholic, and Jew was not a division into equal parts, however. Through their historical dominance and investment in their own forms of cultural unity, Protestants contributed to the structure of American culture in ways that Catholics and Jews did not. Despite the dramatic increase in the numbers of Catholics and Jews during the nineteenth and twentieth centuries and their substantial contributions to American social welfare, education, and cultural life, Protestants represented a religious majority and occupied a privileged place in American society, or so they thought. This assumption of superiority could be seen in the Air Force Academy Chapel in Colorado Springs, opened in 1962 as the federal government's expression of "the democratic ethos accommodating Protestant, Roman Catholic, and Jew."[21] Designed by the architectural firm Skidmore, Owings, and Merrill, the Catholic and Jewish chapels on the lower level were relatively small, dark, and unpretentious, while the huge triangular chapel dedicated to Protestant worship jutted proudly into the Colorado sky. Reading the architecture, visitors might see Protestant,

U.S. Air Force Chapel, Colorado Springs. Courtesy of Skidmore, Owings & Merrill LLP.

Catholic, and Jew as part of the same national church, with Catholic and Jew being lower subdivisions in a triumphantly Protestant design.

In 1962, wealth and political power in the United States were still concentrated in the hands of white Protestants with British and Northern European forbearers, although the election of John F. Kennedy as president in 1960 signaled a major shift in loosening that control. Protestant hegemony in America had a long history, and twentieth-century Protestants often made assumptions about the religious character of the nation and its leaders based on that history. As historian William Hutchison explained, "the unofficial Protestant establishment," which governed the country through the Second World War and controlled most of the wealth and industry, proclaimed a "unitive ideology" with respect to American culture. Through their public presence as political leaders, oversight of resources and production, and network of professional relationships and family friendships, these elite Protestants "fell short as pluralists," Hutchison wrote, "mostly because of a desperate, yet perhaps understandable, desire to re-create the considerable homogeneity of the long colonial era."

During that long colonial era, the colonists were almost exclusively white, Protestant, and English. By the early nineteenth century, Hutchison observed, when the political nation of the United States was still in its infancy, "the dominant European component in this society had had two centuries in which to develop and imprint a common culture." Efforts by colonists to control Native Americans and African Americans helped to define this common culture, as did their efforts to present their causes in England. In addition to shared experiences that united them as colonists, these English people in America shared a common history, a common king, and to a great extent a common religion. However many "internal differences" roiled the waters, Hutchison concluded that "this culture had been, as nearly as one can estimate from this distance, well over 95 percent Protestant Christian. Within that Protestant frame it had been overwhelmingly Calvinist and English-speaking."

In the course of the nineteenth and early twentieth centuries, the population of the United States became much more heterogeneous. The numbers of Catholics and Jews living in the United States multiplied several times over and at much faster rates than that of Protestants, with the number of Catholics in the United States at the end of the twentieth century coming to surpass even the largest (Southern Baptist) Protestant denomination. As Hutchison pointed out, Protestant enthusiasm for religious pluralism did not keep pace with this diversity. In addition to the fear and hatred of Catholics and Jews that infected more than a few Protestants, a profound "concern for unity and social cohesion" worked against hospitality to "outsiders."[22]

Of course, Catholics and Jews made many contributions to American society before the Second World War, and the fabric of American society prior to 1945 would have been much different without their presence. During the nineteenth and early twentieth centuries, Catholics established many hospitals and schools that strengthened American society and the well-being of its citizens, and Jewish philanthropy improved social welfare and cultural life in many American cities. But in the nineteenth and early twentieth centuries, the growing number of non-Protestant immigrants disturbed many Protestant leaders, prompting them to proclaim America's destiny as a Protestant nation. Catholics and Jews often had to confront considerable hostility and misunderstanding as a result of such proclamations. And as a result of the disproportionate influence Protestants exerted in American society, Protestant tendencies and sensibilities saturated the larger culture in which Catholics and Jews participated.

Concern for unity and social cohesion was not exclusive to Protestants after World War II. The tripartite classification of American social identity reflected the orderly discipline, camaraderie, and shared trauma that Americans from different backgrounds experienced in trenches, bombers, battleships, and hospitals in the Atlantic and Pacific theaters during the Second World War and in their war efforts as factory workers and homemakers who accepted gas, tire, and food shortages in a spirit of collective industry and self-sacrifice. The feelings of patriotism, mutual respect, and willingness to cooperate that many Americans associated with their reliance on one another during the Second World War carried over into the 1950s as young couples moved to the suburbs, started families, and joined churches and synagogues. These were the days of the gray-flannel suit, the bouffant hairdo, and the girdle. Despite rumbling against this consensus, leading Protestant, Catholic, and Jewish spokesmen all preached the value of patriotism and the need for positive thinking.

As Catholics and Jews claimed more of a place for themselves in American society in the postwar period, they not only contributed their own points of view and religious sensibilities to the national culture they shared with Protestants, but also enlarged a religious vision of America that had previously been militantly Protestant. In its earlier, militantly Protestant form, this religious vision involved rhetoric about the moral inferiority of Jews and Catholics and celebrated Protestant possession of religious truths that Jews and Catholics allegedly had abandoned or proved incapable of understanding. The spirit of cooperation among Protestants, Catholics, and Jews that emerged in twentieth-century America not only represented a lessening of Protestant hostility toward Catholics and Jews but also reflected considerable success on the part of Catholics and Jews in proving themselves patriots and thus partakers in an essentially religious vision of America as the greatest country on earth.

Amidst unprecedented prosperity, great respect for military alertness and discipline, and fears of being suddenly attacked, Americans stepped into the military industrial economy of the cold war and its anxieties, raising children to compete with the Soviet Union and shoulder responsibility for the preservation of free society under the looming fear of global catastrophe unleashed by The Bomb. In schools, children marched in line out of their classrooms to crouch down in hallways and bathrooms in practice for a nuclear emergency. In October 1957, when the Soviet Union launched the first spacecraft, American families turned out together to look for Sputnik in the night sky and worry that the Russians were getting ahead in the race for command over the earth. For many white American Protestants, the Soviet Union had replaced the Catholic Church as the enemy of religion, morality, and political integrity. The prominence of American Catholics in efforts to expunge Soviet influence in the United States, especially Joseph McCarthy's efforts to hunt down Communists as Chair of the Senate Committee on Un-American Activities, brought conservative Catholics and Protestants together.

Like the Boy Scouts and Girl Scouts that trained many of the nation's children in leadership, self-reliance, and respect for one another, the religious system of identification in postwar America carried vestiges of military organization. During the war, the armed forces had made the Protestant-Catholic-Jew typology popular by using it to assign chaplains to military personnel and to organize religious services for the sick and dead. In the 1950s, the same terminology helped ease people into new living and working arrangements as young adults attended college on the G.I. Bill and joined the business corporations of postwar society. Identification as a Protestant, Catholic, or Jew solidified assent to a national system of social organization as many Americans who participated in the war relocated from rural areas to cities and towns and from inner cities to uptown apartments or bedroom communities in the suburbs, committing themselves to living and working together as Americans while

Red Dawn (1984) by John Milius. Courtesy of Photofest.

preserving certain distinctions among and between themselves through religious institutions and special schools, clubs, and vacation spots.

In the suburbs, church and synagogue memberships grew at a fast pace and Americans poured considerable sums of money into the construction of new religious buildings and recreational centers. Friendship and cooperation among religious groups also ran high, and ecumenical activities were more extensive than ever before as ministers, priests, and rabbis collaborated in numerous interfaith ventures in cities and towns across the country. Befitting their participation in a common culture, Protestants, Catholics, and Jews went through a period of religious growth together in the 1950s. Identification as a Protestant, Catholic, or Jew not only facilitated cordial relations among people of different groups but also contributed to demographic shifts that eroded more specific forms of religious and ethnic identification. Thus historian Robert Orsi described the passing away, in the 1940s and 1950s, of the *festa* in honor of the Madonna of Mount Carmel that set immigrants from southern Italy apart from other Catholics as well as from Protestants and Jews. At the height of the *festa*, Italian American Catholics had paraded through the streets of Harlem with the statue of their beloved Madonna, sent to them from Sicily, and pinned money and jewelry all over her gown in hopes for special blessings. Along with solemn expressions of devotion to their Madonna, people enjoyed days and nights of socializing, singing, dancing, playing games of chance, and eating traditional pastries, sausages, and holiday foods. But the summer *festa* marking this particular community of Italian immigrants and its ties to the old country gradually disappeared, Orsi wrote, "as American-born and -raised young people came to adulthood during and after World War II and claimed more of a place for themselves" in American society, often as residents in suburban communities where they interacted more with Protestants as well as with Catholics from very different cultural backgrounds.[23]

This suburban transformation of American Catholicism in the postwar era coincided with pressure for modernization and theological renewal within the Catholic Church. And the vitality of American Catholicism contributed significantly to that pressure, which culminated in the Second Vatican Council beginning in 1962. Through their activism in building churches, schools, and hospitals, American Catholics embodied an understanding of the church that was centered more on the energy, devotion, and leadership of laypeople than on the authority of the priestly hierarchy. American Catholics proved that the Catholic Church could flourish in a society dedicated to religious freedom, and it was no accident that the chief author of *Dignitatis Humanae Personae* was John Courtney Murray, an American priest and leader of the Jesuit order. In 1965, the Council ratified his declaration, committing the church to religious freedom and to the separation of church and state. Although many at the Council were wary of conceding too much to reformers (and still are), the vitality of the Catholic Church in the United States contributed to the eagerness, expressed by many at the Council, to open the doors of the Church to the modern world and develop more cordial relationships with Protestants and Jews.

Jews also underwent a process of religious change and renewal. As historian Jonathan Sarna showed, Jewish periodicals commented on "vast numbers of Jews, especially young middle-class couples" migrating to the suburbs after World War II. One study found that "between 1945 and 1965, about a third of all American Jews left the big cities and established themselves in suburbs." This move away from urban con-claves required more engagement with non-Jews and new strategies for constructing and encouraging religious life; "outside the protective womb of the urban Jewish subculture," Sarna wrote, "Judaism could no longer be absorbed, like sunshine, from the surrounding atmosphere."[24] New synagogues and Jewish community centers appeared as Jews undertook new efforts to preserve and develop their religious heritage, and to con-struct strong support systems for Jewish participation in American society.

Theological flexibility characterized postwar conceptions of Jewish as well as Protestant identity. As Sarna explained, increasingly little agreement existed on what a person had to do or believe to be Jewish. According to a survey conducted at the end of the twentieth century, 83 percent of survey respondents claimed that "It bothers me when people try to tell me that there's a right way to be Jewish." Considerable flu-idity and tolerance existed inside the boundary defined by widespread agreement that "being a Jew means, at the very least, being 'not Chris-tian.'" Strong consensus on that point, Sarna concluded, coincided with "broad agreement that an identifying but totally non-believing and non-observant Jew remains a Jew."[25]

The Dissolution of Protestantism as a Distinctive Religious Tradition

One of the most influential theologians of the twentieth century, the German immigrant to the United States Paul Tillich (1886–1965), fo-cused on the protest against demonic forces that he perceived to be in-herent in the spirit of Protestantism and on the coinciding desire for spiritual renewal and direct encounter with God. In 1957, Tillich thought that a certain era in the history of Protestantism might be coming to an end. He was confident, however, that "the Protestant principle" was not limited to any era of history; it was an eternal dialectic built into the relationship between God and human beings defined by our discovery, loss, and recovery of God. The "No's" of protest against religious corruption and religious complacency were essential, he thought, to the "Yes" of meeting God. Anyone seriously concerned about life was inevitably in a kind of dialogue with God, he argued further, even if they had doubts about God's existence. Tillich used the New Testament Greek word "kairos," meaning "fullness of time," as a name for "the moment when the eternal breaks into the temporal," and he defined the Protestant principle as the persistent human desire for awakening to the force of creativity, the "ultimate ground" of human existence, which he sometimes referred to as the "God above God."[26]

Tillich associated the Protestant principle with the Reformers' protest against the Catholic Church in the sixteenth century and their criticism of what Tillich believed was the Church's attempt to control the power of grace. He believed the Protestant principle was manifest in other religions at other times in history, and in great expressions of art that lay outside the realm of conventional religion. The popularity of Tillich's theology among liberal Protestants in America during the cold war period coincided with the expansiveness of Protestant organizational structures and the diffusion of Protestant values.

Tillich's theology is vulnerable to many criticisms, not the least of which is the problem of his insistence that serious unbelievers are really believers, an insistence that serious unbelievers could find maddening, silly, and arrogant. Many who consider themselves Christians might also object to Tillich's definition of the Protestant principle as a definition so universal that it includes experiences that have little to do, in any specific sense, with Christ. Nevertheless, Tillich is helpful in conveying a sense of the direction in which many Protestants in America were moving in the 1950s, when interdenominational cooperation was at its peak, and when the boundaries between Protestants and other groups were diminishing.

The Racial Divide and Post–World War II Efforts to Repair It

An ethos of religious coexistence and theological flexibility characterized a good deal of American society in the post–World War II period, and the importance of this ethos for American religious life deserves emphasis. But it is far from the whole story. In addition to being diverse, American religious life was not as harmonious as many would have liked. Racial segregation cut across the postwar society, deeply complicating the interfaith cooperation on which the cohesion of American society rested. The vision of America as an essentially religious nation united in respect for God and religious freedom was open to conservative as well as liberal interpretation, and progressives and conservatives disagreed about whether or not the religious vision of America included racial integration, even as they often shared the belief that God intended a special role for America in world history. Coinciding with the anger black Americans felt about the ways other Americans treated them, divisions among whites about the status of blacks in American society seriously disrupted patriotic religious consensus about America.

President Harry Truman integrated the armed services in 1948, but civilian life was not so quickly changed. The Civil Rights movement of the 1950s reopened the old division among white Protestants over whether the Bible endorsed or condemned white supremacy, along with a related set of divisions over whether the Bible should be read literally or symbolically and whether it warned of apocalypse or encouraged visions of social progress. Proponents of racial segregation were fierce believers in God and religious freedom who believed that the Bible sanctioned racial segregation and that morality and social order depended on it. Fundamentalists in the South teamed up with southerners nostalgic for antebellum culture to defend racial segregation against Yankee pragmatism and what they perceived as self-righteous pushiness about socialistic interpretations of justice.

But even as it divided American society along progressive versus conservative lines, racial controversy contributed to new forms of cooperation among Protestants, Catholics, and Jews. An ideal vision of America as an essentially religious nation united in respect for God and religious freedom encouraged cooperation among progressive Protestants, Catholics, and Jews in the Civil Rights movement, which aimed to fulfill the promise of equality for blacks. Progressive Protestants, black and white, teamed up with progressive Catholics and Jews to fight racial segregation and integrate public schools. In Montgomery, Birmingham, and Atlanta, Jewish rabbis, Catholic sisters, white Protestant ministers, and students from the North marched shoulder to shoulder with Martin Luther King Jr. and his army of nonviolent black protesters.

The Civil Rights movement was not as radical as some of the protest movements that followed in its wake; indeed, black militants condemned it for being too moderate and accommodating to whites. But however pragmatic its leaders were, the Civil Rights movement carried images of the kingdom of God and its coming manifestation on earth that echoed earlier forms of millennialism in American Protestant history. King gave new voice to this long-standing Protestant hope of the kingdom dawning in America in his famous speech in Washington, D.C., in August 1963, when he addressed the crowd that had joined the March for Jobs and Freedom. As part of that speech, he proclaimed, "I have a dream that one day this nation will rise up and live out the true meaning of its creed—we hold these truths to be self-evident that all men are created equal." Alluding to the communion of saints celebrated in the Lord's Supper in anticipation of fellowship in God's kingdom, he identified that communion with integration, envisioning the day when "the sons of former slaves and the sons of former slave owners will be able to sit down together at the table of brotherhood." He imagined the transformation of the world that would take place when children of all colors could hold hands and the justice of racial equality came to pass: "I have a dream that one day every valley shall be exalted, every hill and mountain shall be made low, the rough places will be made plain and the crooked places will be made straight and the glory of the Lord shall be revealed and all flesh shall see it together."[27]

King's speech was a powerful fusion of Protestant visions of the kingdom of God and American idealism about equality. He applied biblical images of justice to an American context in which racists were exposed and brought low, while the saints prevailed through a cooperative effort that renovated the world. However moderate King and his followers were with respect to violence and political process, and however just their cause and overdue their satisfaction, their vision of the coming kingdom carried revolutionary implications that reignited desires for religious consummation and expectations for dramatic social change.

King's leadership of the Civil Rights movement was a significant turning point in American Protestant experience both because of its contribution to racial integration in the United States and because of the way he pushed forward Protestant idealism about the kingdom of God. King took seriously the long-standing Reformed emphasis on the transformation of human society and establishment of divine justice on earth. He also advanced the Protestant tendency to seek political and cultural approaches to social change. His vision of a promised land of racial equality made social interpretations of Christianity real for many people as did his martyrdom in the cause of that equality.

Radical Religious and Political Militancy

The Civil Rights movement stimulated a host of other protest movements in the 1960s, including the antiwar movement, the women's liberation movement, the American Indian Movement (AIM), the environmental movement, and the black power movement. All these movements called attention to the inequities and injustices of American society, and to the unfinished business of American democracy. These movements also carried tendencies toward political radicalism that had been part of American Protestant culture since the seventeenth century. Nurtured by the military ethos of American patriotism on one hand, and by opposition to American militarism in Southeast Asia and at home on the other, these radical political tendencies came to new expression in the late twentieth century.

In some respects, the protest movements of the 1960s and 1970s foreshadowed the religious militancy of the late twentieth and early twenty-first centuries, when conservative Protestant and Catholic activists banded together in protest against abortion, homosexuality, and the permissiveness of American society. The impetus to moral reform persisted, while the direction of social activism shifted in the 1980s from efforts to move further ahead to efforts to restore a social order associated with the past. Radical hopes of revolutionizing society continued to surface alongside more moderate impulses aimed at realizing the promise of a cohesive, moral society.

Today's conservative efforts to rebuild the moral structure of American society differ in many respects from the Civil Rights movement of the 1950s and 1960s. But they both involve expectations of America as a nation chosen by God for a special purpose in history, a nation with special obligation to embody religious and moral principle, and rise above the tyranny and corruption that plague other societies. These religious visions of America are partly rooted in earlier Protestant ideas about the coming kingdom of God on earth; for many people, America is itself a religious vision, however much tarnished by sin and rebellion against God.

From Protestant to Christian Nation

Many changes in twentieth-century American religious life raised questions about what it meant to be Protestant that had not occurred to earlier Congregationalists, Methodists, and Presbyterians. Transparent deployment of conservative religion for political ends along with increasing religious diversity undermined the strength and integrity of the religious structures that earlier American Protestants had worked hard to construct. Even as the number of people in the United States increased greatly between 1950 and 1996, the number of Presbyterian and Lutheran churches failed to grow and the number of Methodist and Episcopalian churches actually declined.[28]

The conservative Southern Baptist denomination defied some of the forces that led more liberal denominations to lower boundaries between themselves and other groups. Baptists continued to increase after 1950 at the fast rate with which they had grown in the first half of the twentieth century, replacing the Methodists as the largest Protestant group in the 1920s and then doubling in size during the 1960s. The takeover of the leadership of the Southern Baptist Convention by fundamentalists forced liberal and moderate professors out of Southern Baptist seminaries, thus ensuring that Southern Baptist churches would be pastored by fundamentalist preachers. Despite the loss of many moderates and moderate conservatives during the 1980s and 1990s, membership in the Southern Baptist Convention approached 16 million at the end of the century.[29]

Conservative and fundamentalist Baptists nurtured the growth of megachurches, characterized by massive auditorium seating, hi-tech audiovisual displays, and multifaceted support groups and services for families, singles, and children. Conservative and fundamentalist Baptists also launched aggressive political campaigns against abortion, feminism, and homosexuality, and in support of their conservative understanding of "family values." As major players in the building of a coalition of politically conservative and militantly religious Americans popularly known as the Religious Right, Southern Baptists became aggressively involved in national politics during the Reagan era and dominated the Republican Party during the administration of George W. Bush. On a number of issues, especially those concerning homosexuality, abortion, stem cell research, and the end of life, conservative Protestants join forces with conservative Catholics to advance conservative agendas and defeat political candidates and legislation they opposed.

Although the tone of their rhetoric differs considerably from that of earlier Protestants who formed the Evangelical Alliance and the National Council of Churches, Southern Baptists and other Protestants associated with the Religious Right carry forward the gusto for organization and social activism that has long been a hallmark of American Protestantism. They also carry forward the belief that America has been and should continue to be a Christian nation, and that as such, she has a special role in the world to play as an instrument of God and expression of God's will. Last but not least, the Religious Right carries forward the spirit of protest for which Protestants originally acquired their name.

But for members of the Religious Right, the object of protest is no longer the Catholic Church; indeed, the Religious Right includes conservative Catholics in many of its political efforts. Liberalism, relativism, and the supposed moral corruption of secular culture are the evils the Religious Right intends to combat. The Religious Right does carry forward an earlier and powerful religious vision of American nationhood, but its animus is directed against some of the democratic gains that earlier Protestants sought to obtain and that many Americans from a variety of different religious backgrounds continue to seek.

Notes

1. Will Herberg, *Protestant-Catholic-Jew: An Essay in American Religious Sociology* (Chicago: University of Chicago Press, 1983; orig. 1955), quotation from p. 123, referring to the chapter titles and main themes constituting the Protestant movement identified by H. Richard Niebuhr in *The Kingdom of God in America* (New York: Harper & Row, 1937), and from pp. 39–40.

2. Euan Cameron, *The European Reformation* (Oxford: Oxford University Press, 1991), pp. 341–342.

3. Winthrop S. Hudson, *American Protestantism* (Chicago: University of Chicago Press, 1961), quotations from pp. 40–41.

4. Hudson, *American Protestantism*, quotations from pp. 45, 46.

5. Hudson, *American Protestantism*, quotation from p. 33.

6. Lyman Beecher, *A Plea for the West* (Cincinnati: Truman and Smith, 1835), quotations from pp. 49, 60, 31, 24, 9–10.

7. Mary Lyon, *General View of the Principles and Design of the Mount Holyoke Female Seminary* (Boston: Perkins & Marvin, 1837), quotation from p. 8.

8. Ray Allen Billington, *The Protestant Crusade, 1800–1860: A Study of the Origins of American Nativism* (Chicago: Quadrangle Books, 1964; orig. 1938), quotations from pp. 144–145.

9. Jay P. Dolan, *The American Catholic Experience: A History from Colonial Times to the Present* (Garden City: Doubleday, 1985), quotations from p. 262.

10. Jonathan Edwards, *Some Thoughts Concerning the Present Revival of Religion, Works of Jonathan Edwards* (New Haven: Yale University Press, 1972; orig. 1742), quotations from vol. 4, pp. 353–358. Also see George Marsden, *Jonathan Edwards: A Life* (New Haven: Yale University Press, 2003), pp. 264–266; and Gerald McDermott, *One Holy and Happy Society: The Public Theology of Jonathan Edwards* (University Park: Pennsylvania State University Press, 1992), pp. 50–92.

11. Jonathan Edwards, *The History of the Work of Redemption; Comprising an Outline of Church History* (Boston: American Tract Society, 1774), quotations from pp. 22, 128, 47, 479.

12. Quotations from "Mary Lyon to Zilpah P. Grant, October 9, 1836," and Mary Lyon, "Dear Madam" (South Hadley, MA: M. Lyon, 1836); Edward Hitchcock, *The Power of Christian Benevolence Illustrated in the Life and Labors of Mary Lyon* (Northampton: Hopkins, Bridgman, 1852), pp. 201, 311. Also see Amanda Porterfield, *Mary Lyon and the Mount Holyoke Missionaries* (New York: Oxford University Press, 1997).

13. Not until the Second Vatican Council in the 1960s, after the extermination of 6 million Jews by the Nazis in World War II, did the Roman Catholic Church acknowledge Judaism as a legitimate religious tradition and declare that the Jews, as a people, are not responsible for the death of Jesus.

14. Isaac M. Wise, *Our Country's Place in History* (Cincinnati: Theological and Religious Library Association, 1869).

15. Anne C. Rose, *Transcendentalism as a Social Movement, 1830–1850* (New Haven: Yale University Press, 1981), pp. 210–211; Joseph P. Chinnici, ed., *Devotion to the Holy Spirit in American Catholicism* (New York: Paulist Press, 1985), p. 8.

16. Josiah Strong, *The New Era, or the Coming Kingdom* (New York: Baker & Taylor, 1893), quotation from p. 231.

17. Strong, *The New Era*, quotations from pp. 26, 203, 319, 236.

18. Strong, *The New Era*, quotations from pp. 222, 248.

19. J. Gresham Machen, *Christianity and Liberalism* (Grand Rapids: William B. Eerdmans, 1923), quotations from p. 141.

20. Robert Wuthnow, *The Restructuring of American Religion: Society and Faith Since World War II* (Princeton: Princeton University Press, 1988), p. 93.

21. Allan Temko, "The Air Academy Chapel: A Critical Appraisal," *Architectural Forum* 117 (December 1962): 75, quoted in William R. Hutchison, *Religious Pluralism in America: The Contentious History of a Founding Ideal* (New Haven: Yale University Press, 2003), p. 210.

22. Hutchison, *Religious Pluralism*, quotations from pp. 7–8.

23. Robert Orsi, *The Madonna of 115th Street: Faith and Community in Italian Harlem, 1880–1950* (New Haven: Yale University Press, 1985), quotation from p. 217.

24. Jonathan Sarna, *American Judaism: A History* (New Haven: Yale University Press, 2004), quotations from pp. 282–283.

25. Sarna, *American Judaism*, quotation from p. 367.

26. Paul Tillich, *The Protestant Era* (Chicago: University of Chicago Press, 1957), quotations from pp. xi–xxix; Paul Tillich, *The Courage to Be* (New Haven: Yale University Press, 1952), quotation from p. 186.

27. Martin Luther King Jr., "I have a dream," in *The Autobiography of Martin Luther King, Jr.*, ed. Clayborne Carson (New York: Warner Books, 1998), quotations from p. 226.

28. Edwin Scott Gaustad and Philip L. Barlow, *New Historical Atlas of Religion in America* (New York: Oxford University Press, 2001), p. 390.

29. Nancy Tatom Ammerman, *Baptist Battles: Social Change and Religious Conflict in the Southern Baptist Convention* (New Brunswick: Rutgers University Press, 1990); Peter Williams, *American Religions: From Their Origins to the Twenty-first Century*, 3rd ed. (Urbana: University of Illinois Press, 2002), p. 386; Gaustad and Barlow, *New Historical Atlas*, pp. 375, 390.

Chapter 1

A Holy Commonwealth

The history of American Protestant experience begins in Europe. Before the first Protestant settlers set foot in North America, images of a New World, free of the corruptions of Europe, shaped Protestant expectations. The New World was an idea as much as a reality, and one determined by biblical stories and utopian imagery. Biblical stories about Israel, the promised land of God's chosen people, and expectations of a New Israel dedicated to the glory of Christ contributed significantly to Protestant ideas about America, and to hopes of a new social order that could be established there.

European and British Heritage

Seeds of these Protestant hopes for America were planted in the burgeoning cities and towns of sixteenth-century Europe and Britain. In Germany, Switzerland, and France, images of a New Jerusalem and New Israel helped fuel civil unrest and demands for increased self-government among peasants and growing numbers of artisans, shopkeepers, lawyers, and preachers. Sermons and religious pamphlets poured out of these cities and towns, filled with longing for a new era in Christian life in which justice, grace, and redemption would become manifest in real time, in the lives of ordinary families. This religious excitement reflected conflict and change occurring in Europe, and hopes that the spirit of Christ would transform society there. The religious reform movements of sixteenth-century Europe laid the groundwork for expectations about Christian society that Protestant settlers brought with them to the New World.

Of course, the desires expressed in sixteenth-century Europe for a purified and rejuvenated Christianity were not entirely new. Demands for moral and ecclesiastical reform, and longing for a new society that conformed to the spirit of Christ had been building for centuries. The twelfth-century Cistercian, Bernard of Clairvaux (1090–1153), complained that wooden priests with golden chalices stood in his own day in place of the golden priests with wooden chalices of old,[1] and his much-quoted lament expressed a perennial desire for religious reform within Christian history. New Testament demands for moral purity stimulated this desire, as did Old Testament admonitions about Israel's backsliding and need to reaffirm its covenant relation with God. Stories about God's promises to Israel, the miracles performed by Jesus and his saints, the coming kingdom of God, and the final days of violent upheaval described in the book of Revelation inspired numerous movements of religious renewal and reform among medieval Christians.

A host of deep frustrations and high expectations made these stories especially relevant to sixteenth-century Christians, and contributed to the buildup of pressures for religious and social reform in Europe. As urban centers of population and commerce developed, disease and social unrest increased, as did disparities between rich and poor. In this volatile context, no institution came under greater criticism than the Roman Church, whose cathedrals, pageants, and prelates grew in splendor even as the disjuncture between its worldly wealth and the mean conditions in which many people lived grew more apparent. Late-medieval reformers criticized the hypocrisy associated with the church's accumulation of wealth, which seemed antithetical to the virtues of poverty and spiritual purity preached by many followers of Christ. They also criticized the church's exploitation of popular fears of hell and purgatory through the sale of indulgences, or reprieves against sin. As an expression of mounting desires for spiritual purity, new orders of mendicant monks and nuns gained adherents, and mystical forms of interior spirituality flourished as alternatives to the external pomp of churchly rituals. Women contributed importantly to this culture of spiritual renewal. In addition to growing numbers of women's religious orders recognized by the church, communities of pious laywomen sprang up in many cities, exalting the sufferings of Jesus, and ministering to the sick and poor who reflected his humanity.[2]

Interior spirituality and devotion to the suffering humanity of Jesus reflected growing investment in subjective experience and analysis of personal feeling and desire. Religious symbols and worship mediated this fascination with interior life and helped facilitate the development of what we now think of as modern selfhood and individualism, with their emphases on individual conscience, analysis of emotional feeling, and resistance against arbitrary impositions of external authority. For many Christians swept up in the reform movements that gathered momentum in early-sixteenth-century Europe, rising commitment to individual inspiration coincided with visions of new social order in which individual voices would come to expression in choirs of saints singing praises to the glory of God. Of course, the harmony of many individuals expressing themselves was a heavenly ideal requiring a vast infusion of supernatural grace; and even then, hypocrites, heathens, and infidels would have to be separated out and thrown into the bowels of hell. Depictions of the Day of Judgment in woodcuts, etchings, and sermons represented the violence necessary to cleanse the earth of sin so that the harmony latent in all the voices of individual Christians could be heard.

The religious reform movements of the sixteenth century drew from a variety of sources, including the humanistic spirit of the Renaissance and its recovery of classical literature and philosophy. While reformers were cautious about celebrating the pagan writers of antiquity, their idealization of ancient Israel paralleled the idealization of ancient Greece and Rome expressed by Renaissance humanists, and their devotion to biblical narratives was part of a more general enthusiasm for classical texts current among scholars of the time. Religious reformers were often deeply invested in the recovery of biblical texts in their original languages, and in the writings of the early church fathers.

Like so many other aspects of early Protestant reform, reverence for the classical texts of Christianity contained different, even conflicting impulses. On one hand, the impulse to go back to the original texts of scripture and church fathers was an effort to restore Christianity to its original simplicity and purity. On the other hand, this effort to recover the primitive truths of Christianity coincided with new and forward-looking impulses of individual self-expression associated with increasing literacy and the growth of a middle class, increasing analysis of subjective experience, and increasing demand for individual liberty and freedom of expression. Early Protestants joined these quintessentially modern trends to their reverence for the ancient, primitive truths of Christianity.

Luther and Calvin

Many of the early leaders of Protestant reform worked to contain these potentially conflicting elements in coherent visions of a stable society that provided room for expressions of pure conscience while harshly punishing threats to civil order. The most famous religious writer, talker, and Bible reader of the sixteenth century was Martin Luther

Martin Luther's triumph over the monk's devil. From *Mattheus Gnidius' Dialogi,* a Reform pamphlet against the Papists Murner and Weddel, Germany, 1521.

(1483–1536), a dedicated student, translator, preacher of Holy Scripture, and enthusiastic interpreter of the fifth-century church father, Augustine of Hippo. Building on Augustine's distinction in *The City of God* (413–427) between the divine city represented through the church and the temporal cities on earth, Luther argued that Christians live in two kingdoms, church and state, both of which were under divine rule and responsible to God. Defense of the gospel could justify certain acts of resistance against the state, as it justified protest against the Catholic Church for distorting and corrupting the gospel. But Christians were obliged to submit to the authority of the state under all other circumstances, since the authority of God stood behind that of the state.

The son of a German miner, Luther entered the Augustinian order after making a vow to St. Anne in the midst of a terrifying thunderstorm to become a monk if she protected him. In fulfilling his vow, Luther outdid other monks in heroic efforts of penance and prayer. But he failed to rid himself of the gnawing sense of sin and unworthiness before God. Finally realizing that he could not save himself no matter how hard he tried, he threw himself on the mercy of Christ, where he found forgiveness of sin and faith in a redeemer whose sacrifice justified believers, making them right with God. Luther renounced his vow of celibacy, along with the other means he had tried to work his way to salvation (including his veneration of St. Anne, whose cult he now opposed), and proclaimed his freedom to live fully as an imperfect creature in the promise of forgiveness and redemption in Christ.

Luther married a former nun, Katherine von Bora, and embraced domestic life for the spiritual lessons it taught. He never doubted men's superiority over women, or men's authority as fathers of their households, and he found parallels to men's dominance in Christian homes in Old Testament stories about the patriarchs of ancient Israel and their families. He also found reminders of Christ in familial affection, and in the sweet subordination of wives and children. For example, he invited Christians to "meditate on the Nativity just as we see it happening in our own babies." Nothing better represented the happiness and freedom from fear that Christians enjoyed: "there is no greater consolation given to mankind than this, that Christ became man, a child, a babe, playing in the lap and at the breasts of his most gracious mother. Who is there whom this sight would not comfort? Now is overcome the power of sin, death, hell, conscience, and guilt, if you come to this gurgling Babe and believe that he is come, not to judge you, but to save."[3] Luther's appreciation of family life as a proper context for Christian living filtered through many forms of Protestantism, and contributed to the emphasis on well-ordered households so important in Puritan New England, and in other American Protestant contexts as well.

Luther never thought that sanctification, or holiness, was completely possible in human life, but the prospect of the spirit of God descending from on high to transform humanity excited him, as it did more than a few of his followers. In 1525, during the tumult and bloodshed of the Peasants' War, Luther thought the Second Coming of Christ, and the end of time, might be near. But he condemned extremists who took up swords to hasten the apocalypse, and he warned that the devil would stir up the worst of human behavior as the day of final judgment came closer. Against Luther's trust in social hierarchy and the need for obedience to kings and princes, Thomas Müntzer (before 1490–1525) embraced apocalyptic rhetoric with headlong enthusiasm, preaching that God's people were already one with the angels, honing their sickles for the harvest cutting.[4] Müntzer taunted the city fathers of Allstedt in northern Germany, after he was expelled from there, with the kind of disdain for civil authority that horrified more moderate Protestants. "Stir it up, my dear lords, let the muck give out a good old stink," Muntzer wrote. "I hope you will brew a fine beer out of it, since you like drinking filth so much."[5]

In addition to his reputation for inciting revolution among the poor and disenfranchised, Muntzer originated the idea of a holy common-wealth, which crystallized hopes for a total renovation of society based on biblical principles. One variant of this idea found expression in seventeenth-century New England, where Puritan leaders attempted to create a society based on a covenant relationship with God, much like the one God established with Israel. Although Muntzer was not some-one New England Puritans ever wanted to be associated with, they were similar to him in their hopes of election as God's chosen people and in their intention to build a holy commonwealth whose ordering principles were biblical authority and glorification of God.

A more direct inspiration for New England Puritans was John Calvin (1509–1564), the son of a cathedral administrator in Picardy, France, who created what he hoped was a holy commonwealth in the city of Geneva. While visiting Geneva in 1540, Calvin found leadership of the city thrust upon him, along with the responsibility for averting civil war. When Calvin stopped in the city on his way to Strasbourg, Guillaume Farel, an older leader of the reform movement in Geneva, pressed him to stay, warning Calvin that God would "curse" him if he left. Farel's threat had its intended effect and says much about the fear of God that Calvin lived under: "I was so stricken with terror," Calvin later wrote, "that I desisted from the journey I had undertaken." In the decades that followed, Calvin maintained a tight working relationship between the city's governing council and the reformed church, and saw to it that anyone not approved by the church was banished from town. Governed by his interpretations of biblical authority, the city under Calvin's leadership served as a model for reformers in France, England, and America, even though its reputation for strict rule and harsh im-plementation bothered more than a few observers.

Calvin's interpretation of redemption owed much to his legal back-ground, as did his ability to translate biblical precepts into city ordinance. While studying for the law as a young man at the University of Paris, he experienced "a taste of true godliness" that drew him away from "the superstitions of the papacy" and "set [him] on fire" with "a desire to progress" as a Christian and as a reformer. Later on, he interpreted this taste of godliness as a sign of God's contract with him, and went on to implement his desire for progress in political and legal form, fairly con-fident that he had a contract with God to implement God's will.[6]

The Papist Devil. "Ego sum Papa (I am the Pope)." From a Reformation hand-bill against Pope Alexander VI, Paris, late fifteenth century.

Like others of his generation studying in Paris, Calvin was inspired by Luther's understanding of the need to depend solely on Christ for forgiveness and grace, and by Luther's celebration of the presence of Christ in the lives of ordinary Christians. But he went beyond Luther in insisting that Christian faith was always manifest in good work and a progressively sanctified life. He agreed with Luther that no one could attain salvation on his or her own merit, or by means of his or her own work. But he also believed that grace made work good and that everyone chosen by God to receive grace was predestined to lead a morally productive life.

Religious Reform in England

Calvin's emphasis on the work of God's saints in the world fell on fertile ground in England, where a growing middle class was beginning to build what would eventually become the British Empire. Against otherworldly concepts of religious vocation as a call to leave the ordinary affairs of the world behind, Calvin defined vocation as a calling from God to step vigorously into an ordinary walk of life—as a husband, wife, merchant, ship's captain, or soldier—with a sense of divine purpose animating one's work. His call to work dovetailed with England's growing sense of nationhood, with the enterprising spirit of Britain's emerging middle class, and with zeal for a holy commonwealth modeled on the pattern of ancient Israel. Of course, this sort of enterprising commonwealth did not entirely square with the social agenda that British monarchs and aristocrats had in mind, nor did it sit well with English folk whose commitment to life centered more on food, shelter, merriment, theater, and other forms of worldly life.

In England and in Europe, Calvin's thought became intertwined with powerful political forces and new expressions of nationalism. When Henry VIII (1491–1547) broke with Rome in 1534 to establish a national church with himself as supreme head, the English Reformation developed as a political as well as religious event in which the formation of a national church reflected a consolidation of political alliances and institutions, and a stronger construction of national identity. Old Testament stories about the nation of Israel prompted hopes for England as a new political and social order dedicated to Christ. References to Israel did more than conjure up images of a biblical kingdom whose achievements lay in the past; they also provided inspiration and justification for patriotic idealism about England and, later, inspiration and justification for patriotic idealism about America.

As part of establishing a national church independent of Rome, Henry confiscated church properties and closed down shrines and pilgrimage centers. He severed institutional and economic ties to Rome and allowed English translations of the Bible to be used in local parishes. He did little to alter the liturgical practices of the church, however, or to support the movement for spiritual renovation. Among Calvin's admirers, frustration over these failures of reformation escalated when Henry's Catholic daughter Mary (1516–1558) ascended the throne in 1553, and reestablished England's ties to Rome. Mary executed some reform leaders and forced others into exile. An influential group fled to Geneva, where they observed Calvin's holy commonwealth firsthand. These exiles revered the Protestant martyrs put to death during Mary's reign, and viewed the papacy's return to England as God's wrathful judgment against their nation. Inspired by the Geneva Bible and John Foxe's *Book of Martyrs*, the Marian exiles and their supporters at home harbored fervent hopes that England's covenant relationship with God might be renewed.

The succession of Henry's Protestant daughter Elizabeth (1533–1603) in 1558 enabled the Marian exiles to return to England, where they resumed their efforts to renovate England, hailing Elizabeth as the "restorer of Israel" and comparing her to Deborah, the warrior and leader of ancient Israel described in the Old Testament. Not everyone in Shakespeare's England wanted to be renovated, however, and numerous critics mocked the strict interpreters of the Bible who preached against gambling, dancing, and the theater. Things came to a head in 1566, when Elizabeth, alert to any threat to her sovereignty, pressed her reluctant Archbishop Matthew Parker to enforce a dress code for clergy that involved wearing the surplice, a white ceremonial robe with big sleeves. Acquiring their name from their critics, Puritans (also known as Precisionists) emerged to protest the surplice as a vestige of papal idolatry. Plain dress was only one of the reforms Puritans wanted to institute in their efforts to draw the Church of England further away from Catholicism, and bring all aspects of English life under biblical rule. Although the queen resisted reforms she thought might undermine her authority, the Puritans acquired allies in Parliament and controlled important posts at Oxford and especially Cambridge, where most of the first generation of New England Puritan leaders were educated.

When the Stuart kings James I (1566–1625) and Charles I (1600–1649) took over, Puritans endured increased harassment—even having their ears cut off in some cases. Suppression of Puritan reform became more systematic when Charles appointed William Laud (1573–1645), a staunch opponent of Puritanism, to be Archbishop of Canterbury in 1628. Those committed to a plain style of worship and to the wholesale renewal of civil and domestic life found themselves at an impasse. In these straitened circumstances, one adventurous group looked to the New World as a place where their dream of a holy commonwealth might be realized. In 1629, the vanguard of this group set off to found a colony around Massachusetts Bay. They hoped to live there as a community in a covenant relationship with God like that of ancient Israel. Only in their case (unlike that of Israel), the ability to maintain this covenant would come through grace-given faith in Christ.

The Holy Commonwealth in America and Its Protesters

On board the flagship *Arbella*, the governor-elect, John Winthrop (1588–1649), delivered a sermon that laid out his expectations for the kind of Christian community he hoped the group would build. Warming to the idea of a covenant between God and his people that involved a mutually loving relationship as well as a legal contract, Winthrop declared, "Thus stands the cause between God and us. We are entered into covenant with him for this work. We have taken out a commission, the Lord hath given us leave to draw our own articles." If their ships landed safely, Winthrop asserted, that would be God's sign that he had sealed the covenant. Should the people betray their promises in the course of establishing their community, God would punish them as he had punished the people of Israel: "the Lord will surely break out in wrath against us, be revenged of such a perjured people, and make us know the price of the breach of such a covenant." The means of averting such catastrophe were simple: the people should endeavor "to follow the counsel of Micah, to do justly, to love mercy, to walk humbly with our God." That would require living together in peace and harmony, or as Winthrop put it, "we must be knit together as one man." Godly community would involve much more than the restraint of wickedness: "We must delight in each other, make others' conditions our own, rejoice together, mourn together, labor and suffer together, always having before our eyes our commission and community in the work, our community as members of the same body." If the members loved God and one another in this way, God in turn would "delight to dwell among us as his own people." This relationship between the Puritans of New England and their God would bring strength as well as happiness and prosperity. Indeed, Winthrop prophesied, "We shall find that the God of Israel is among us, when ten of us shall be able to resist a thousand of our enemies."[7]

The Puritans who settled around Boston with John Winthrop were not the first or only Protestants in seventeenth-century America. Earlier Protestant explorers and entrepreneurs established several outposts in the Chesapeake region, the most famous of these being the settlement of Jamestown, the site of the first Anglican church in America, as well as the destination of America's first African slaves. But the English population in Virginia (a huge territory, stretching to the Mississippi, named for the Virgin Queen Elizabeth) was considerably smaller and less well organized than the English population in New England, and contained a much higher percentage of young, unmarried men bent more on profit and adventure than on settlement. Anglicans were even fewer and less firmly planted in seventeenth-century Carolina and Georgia.

Other Protestant colonies existed in seventeenth-century North America, but they, too, were much smaller and less well organized than those in Puritan New England. Calvinists from the Netherlands settled in the middle colonies, especially in New York along the Hudson River. These Dutch Reformed Protestants established a successful trading center and stable religious community in Albany that stayed intact well into the eighteenth century.[8] English Quakers and German Protestants found freedom from persecution in Pennsylvania, where Quakers exerted considerable influence on government and economic life, and instituted policies of religious tolerance that later Americans heralded as an important forerunner of the freedoms guaranteed in the Bill of Rights and Constitution of the United States.[9]

Still, the strength of the Protestant culture that Puritans established in New England was unsurpassed elsewhere in North America during the seventeenth century. Most of the early immigrants to New England arrived in families, intent on settlement and the construction of a holistic social order. Although churchgoers deemed worthy of partaking in the Lord's Supper were a minority, all of the elected officials in Massachusetts Bay during the seventeenth century belonged to this influential minority. Punishment of moral offenders as threats to civil order and disturbers of peace was often severe. Church attendance was mandatory in the early years of settlement, and when that proved impossible for the state to enforce, churches relied on their members to bring others to church. Life in seventeenth-century New England was often harsh and strident. Nevertheless, in very short order, the Puritans who settled there established a relatively stable and self-perpetuating religious culture of long-lasting influence. From Boston and its environs, Puritans spread west across western Massachusetts, upper New York, the Ohio River valley, and south into the Hudson River valley and Chesapeake Bay region, meeting and mixing with people who practiced other forms of Protestant expression as well as with many others without any church affiliation.

The Puritan vision of a holy commonwealth had a lasting impact on American culture, and contributed to the idea of America as a nation under God with a special destiny to fulfill. It coincided with equally powerful tendencies to individualism and factionalism that constantly challenged civil order. If belief in the compatibility between communal harmony and individual freedom attracted people, failures to realize that compatibility fueled protests against injustice, corruption, and suppression of individual conscience. From the beginning, the idea of America as a holy commonwealth and place where religious freedom enables a strong, peaceful, and coherent society has inspired millions of people. At the same time, this idea of America has obscured the real diversity of American life and contributed to the suppression of religious minorities and dissenting opinion.

The idea of America as a holy commonwealth harked back to the religious tumult and political conflicts of sixteenth-century Europe. It also had antecedents in medieval movements of religious reform and before that in the utopian visions of the kingdom of God embraced by the early followers of Jesus and, before that, in Judean visions of Israel as a nation of God's chosen people. Thus Puritan idealism about America was rooted in ancient history while at the same time profoundly influenced by early modern forces of individualism, economic modernization, and scientific and technological development. Linkages between biblical inspiration and modern reform and social change informed visions of America as a holy commonwealth and prompted many new efforts to bring heaven to earth.

The Plymouth Separatists (or Pilgrims)

The small but famous group of English Separatists who helped found New Plymouth in 1620 had intentions somewhat different from the larger group of Puritans who began to settle nine years later around Boston harbor and moved out from Boston to found numerous towns. The thirty-five Separatists on board the *Mayflower* in 1620 were Puritans of a more radical stripe who had renounced the state Church of England to establish a church independent of the state. Jailed and persecuted in England, they had fled to Leyden, in the Netherlands, in 1608, where the Dutch policy of religious tolerance enabled them to meet freely as a congregation. Although they found freedom to worship in Holland, they also found their children being lured away from religious life by attractions of a cosmopolitan city. Faced with the decline of their community if they stayed in Holland, and with persecution if they returned to live in England, a core group of these religious Separatists determined to move to America.

A great deal hinged on the meaning of "Separation." It may be difficult, today, to appreciate how seriously seventeenth-century English people took the issue of Separatism and other matters of church governance. In understanding why these disputes aroused such passion and concern, it is important to see that they were not simply matters of narrow theological interpretation but in fact carried implications about social order and how it should be constructed and maintained. In forming churches independent of the state in a country where church and state were officially united, Separatists raised the specter of political insurrection; the English crown viewed Separatism as a form of sedition.

The crown had difficulty restraining Separatism, not least of all because the English church herself had separated from Rome. Henry VIII's break with the Church of Rome and establishment of a Church of England was a decisive step in political history that set England on its way to becoming, in the eighteenth century, the world's most fully developed modern nation-state. But the road to such political strength was paved with violence and insurrection. The 1640s saw a proliferation of radical religious sects, the eruption of civil war, the beheading of Charles I, and convening of the Long Parliament and the election of Oliver Cromwell as head of an unstable Puritan government. As tensions leading to civil war built during the 1630s, when the Great Migration of Puritans to New England occurred, disputes over church governance were part of a larger culture of mounting political unrest. They were part of larger questions about how society should be organized, what a Christian's responsibility to society should be, and what role churches should play in the world.

The English Separatists who fled to Leyden in 1608 had influential supporters in Europe, including Refomed clergy, who tried to ease their persecution in England. But compared to the Puritans of Massachusetts Bay, they were a small and fairly isolated group with relatively modest expectations about the role their community might play in building a New Israel. In contrast to the Massachusetts Bay Puritans, who had their own company and charter from the Crown that supported the emigration of several thousand people and empowered them to elect magistrates and establish a government, the Separatists got to Plymouth by joining up with "adventurers & planters" who set the conditions of plantation. Representatives of those adventurers on the *Mayflower* were members of the Church of England hired by an investment company in London to secure and protect a colony. The thirty-five Separatists permitted to travel with them simply hoped to settle their religious community in a place removed from both worldly distraction and state persecution. They had "a great hope & inward zeal" for their community in the New World, and imagined themselves "as stepping-stones unto others," and as "laying some good foundation, or at least to make some way thereunto, for propagating & advancing the gospel of the kingdom of Christ in those remote parts of the world."[10]

Originally headed for the warmer region of Virginia, the *Mayflower* came to ground on December 21, 1620, on Cape Cod. During that first winter in a rude settlement nearby, which they named Plymouth, half of those who had sailed on the ship died of starvation, exposure, or disease. The colony survived a second winter thanks to Indian corn, and celebrated their harvest before that winter with a feast of venison and fowl joined by Indians who were, temporarily, their friends. The Plymouth Colony persisted as a separate entity until 1691, when it was absorbed by the larger colony of Massachusetts Bay.

The original Separatists who founded Plymouth Colony were less ambitious in their plans for building a holy commonwealth than the Puritans of the Massachusetts Bay Colony. Mainly intent on escaping worldly snares, the Plymouth Separatists were less concerned than their Puritan neighbors with reforming the church or constructing a civil polity. While John Winthrop imagined his Puritan community of Massachusetts Bay as "a city upon a hill"[11] (a bold reference to the beatitude of Matthew 5:14, in which Jesus says to his followers, "You are the light of the world. A city built on a hill cannot be hid"), the Separatists of Plymouth Colony pictured themselves more modestly as stepping stones under the feet of others.

In a bicentennial speech in 1820, Daniel Webster (1782–1852) coined the term "Pilgrim Fathers" to commemorate the religious heroism of the Plymouth Separatists. He picked up the word "pilgrim" from the journal written by the first governor of Plymouth, William Bradford (1590–1657), who described the "Saincts" who ventured with him to the New World as "pilgrims." These wayfarers were traveling through this earthly world on their way, as Bradford put it, to their true resting place "in the heavens, their dearest cuntrie." In the early nineteenth century, Webster overlooked the difference, so obvious in the seventeenth century, between these Separatists and the larger group of New England Puritans. He celebrated the Pilgrim Fathers as founders of America whose quest for religious liberty foreshadowed the independence of the United States and its guarantee of religious freedom. As the Civil War of the 1860s loomed closer, the Pilgrim Fathers and their First Thanksgiving acquired even more importance. In her popular magazine, *Godey's Lady's Book*, Sarah Josepha Hale promoted a nationwide celebration of Thanksgiving Day to commemorate the Pilgrim's First Thanksgiving that would unite the country around its religious heritage. In 1863, in a similar effort to promote national unity, President Abraham Lincoln declared Thanksgiving Day a national holiday.

Roger Williams (1603?–1683) Challenges New England's Covenant Theology

Committed to planting a holy commonwealth in New England, the Puritans of Massachusetts Bay faced challenges that would not have arisen if they had not conceptualized their settlement as a holy commonwealth. Even as the Great Migration of Puritans to New England in the 1630s was underway, and optimism about realizing the vision of a New Israel still on the rise, Roger Williams criticized the whole endeavor as deeply misguided. He challenged the idea of a holy commonwealth, claiming that it would inevitably lead to violence. He also argued that hopes for a holy commonwealth were based on a misreading of scripture, and a misunderstanding of what adherence to biblical authority ought to entail.

It took several years for other Puritan leaders to grasp the full force of Roger Williams' ideas and the radical implications of his point of view with respect to New England society. At first, the young preacher impressed people with his learning and piety, and soon after his arrival in February 1631, the church in Boston called him to be their minister. He declined on the grounds that the church had not officially separated from the Church of England.

Most Puritans in Massachusetts insisted they were non-Separatists, who retained their affiliation with the Church of England, even though they believed the church needed reform. They thought that a plain style of worship should replace the ritual pomp of the Anglican Church, and disagreed with the policy of appointing bishops to oversee local churches on the grounds that scripture mandated a congregational form of church governance. But if they rejected certain aspects of Anglican polity, these Puritans hardly wanted to appear disloyal. Far removed from England, and with a charter from the king in hand, the Puritans of Massachusetts Bay enjoyed considerable powers of self-governance. Why raise suspicions of radicalism in the minds of authorities in England who had the power to revoke the charter granting them land and governing authority?

Even more important, the policy of non-Separation resonated well with the principle of religious uniformity that most of the Puritan leaders in New England wanted to enforce, and understood to be essential to social order. Although they believed each congregation should be free to organize its own leadership, worship, sacraments, teaching, and discipline without interference from meddling bishops, most Puritan leaders in New England assumed that each congregation would be a loving sister to the others, bound together as loving communities of saints dedicated to implementing God's will on earth. Many Puritan leaders in New England perceived their self-governing churches as part of a larger, holistic plantation in the New World in which all aspects of life were directed toward the common religious end of upholding a covenant relationship with God.

Roger Williams thought differently. With Christ's appearance on earth, he argued, God's connection with humanity had shifted to the individual. Stories about God's covenant relationship with the nation of Israel and the guidelines for community life laid out in the Old Testament had become irrelevant in the new era instituted by Christ, and should not be taken as models for social order. In light of the new covenant of grace inaugurated by Christ, he insisted, the Old Testament descriptions of God's commitment to Israel had no bearing on any political group or nation; God had established a covenant with one and only one nation—ancient Israel—and that had come to an end with the appearance of Christ. Attempting to create a New Israel, a society based on the principles of social order and religious uniformity prescribed for the people of the Old Testament, was nothing less than a failure to grasp the meaning of Christ, and the radical break with the past that Christ inaugurated. Saints of the new covenant might gather together to establish covenants with each other for the purpose of worship and teaching, Williams believed, but to remain true to the new covenant of grace established by Christ, such congregations should be set apart from the world, and removed from profane entanglements.

This interpretation of scripture led Williams into conflict with the Puritan leaders who tried to enforce church attendance in New England and who believed it was their duty to punish religious dissent as a threat to social order. Writing against the assumptions about religious authority these leaders viewed as essential, Williams argued that Christians should read the Old Testament stories about God's covenant relationship with Israel not as directives about how to erect Christian societies, but rather as guides for how to conduct their lives as individual Christians. The spiritual benefits that Christians enjoyed were unsurpassed, but not to be confused with worldly recognition, Williams believed, or with authority to legislate religious conduct or belief for others. "God's people are now in the Gospel brought into a spiritual land of Canaan," Williams wrote, "flowing with spiritual milk and honey, and they abound with spiritual and heavenly comforts, though in a poor and persecuted condition." Given this Canaan of the spirit, scattered and often persecuted as it was throughout the profane world, any imposition of religious uniformity was inappropriate. In contrast to standard operating procedure both in England and Massachusetts Bay, Williams believed that the state should not require citizens to support any type of clergy: "[A]n enforced settled maintenance is not suitable to the Gospel as it was to the ministry of priests and levites in the law."[12]

Between 1631 and 1635, when he was banished from Massachusetts as a threat to civil order, Williams spelled out further implications of his rejection of the Puritan ideal of a holy commonwealth. In sermons delivered to the Separatist church of Plymouth, and to the church of Salem—which considered Separatism and decided against it—he appealed to the qualitative difference between the religious life reserved for saints and the civil laws that applied to everyone, regenerate or not, who lived under civil authority. Magistrates had no right to require any person to swear a sacred oath, he argued, since they had no authority, as magistrates, to discern who was a saint and who was not, or to impose any form of religious obligation.

This strict interpretation of the principle of separation of church and state derived from Williams' reading of the New Testament, especially the parable of the wheat and the tares in Matthew 13, which he understood to mean that the elect and the damned should live together in the world until the final harvest on the Day of Judgment. Misunderstanding of that point frequently led to catastrophe, he believed: "[T]oo oft the world laid upon bloody heaps in civil and intestine desolations" because civil authorities had arrogated religious authority to themselves, and hounded people on religious grounds. "All which would be prevented—and the greatest breaches made up in the peace of our own or other countries— were this command of the Lord Jesus obeyed: to wit, to let them alone until the harvest."[13] In Williams' mind, religious persecution was politically disastrous as well as antithetical to the Christian gospel.

Commitment to a government policy of religious freedom was a logical consequence of these beliefs. Under the new covenant of grace, God's chosen people were scattered through the world, dispersed among all nations. And since saints were hidden, like wheat among the tares, religious freedom was the only reasonable policy earthly governments could adopt. As President of Rhode Island, Williams put his belief into practice, arguably creating the world's first secular government as the logical means of respecting the religious freedom mandated by Christ's new covenant of grace.

Williams' insistence on the disconnect between Christianity on one hand, and national, cultural, and ethnic identity on the other, enabled him to make some realistic appraisals of English behavior and some unusual comparisons between English and Native peoples. He thought the English had little reason to claim moral or cultural superiority over Native peoples. Indeed, English people needed to be especially concerned lest their own deafness to the gospel lead them to damnation, while Native people, who had many fewer opportunities to hear the gospel, leapt ahead of them in grace.

Boast not, proud English, of thy birth and blood,
They brother Indian is by birth as good.

Of one blood God made him and thee and all,
As wise, as fair, as strong, as personal.

By nature, wrath's his portion, thine no more,
Till grace his soul and thine in Christ restore.
Make sure thy second birth, else thou shalt see
Heaven ope to Indians wild, but shut to thee.[14]

Adding fuel to the fire of opposition against him, Williams claimed that the civil authorities of Massachusetts Bay had no right to take over land in the name of their king and his divine right. As far as political sovereignty and civil authority went, Williams maintained, there was no such thing as divine right. Consequently, the colonists were obligated to purchase any land they wished to live on from its Native American inhabitants. Williams followed this policy after being exiled from Massachusetts, founding Rhode Island with land purchased from Narragansett Indians.

Anne Hutchinson (1591–1643) and the Question of Assurance

While Roger Williams challenged the Puritan ideal of a holy commonwealth, another troublemaker emerged to challenge the authority ministers had to supervise religious experience and control biblical interpretation. Williams found the covenant of grace a point of departure for criticizing the Puritan effort to build a holy commonwealth; Anne Hutchinson found it a point of departure for celebrating the inspiration saints received through the Holy Spirit. Williams thought the New England Puritans had gone way too far in arrogating authority to themselves as a group. Hutchinson believed they had not gone far enough in acknowledging the authority of individual conscience and inspiration.

In 1633, Anne Hutchinson and her husband followed their minister, John Cotton (1585–1652), to Boston. Cotton was an eloquent preacher famous for his descriptions of the spiritual satisfactions involved in union with Christ. His sermons depicted a "sealing of the Spirit" beyond conversion, through which Christians found assurance of salvation and a foretaste of eternal life in heaven. Like other Puritan preachers, Cotton employed images of betrothal and marriage to describe the pleasures of union with Christ, comparing Christ to a bridegroom and husband, and depicting the Christian saint as the bride and wife of Christ. While Cotton's chief rivals in New England, Thomas Hooker (1586–1647) and Thomas Shepard (1605–1649), used some of the same tropes, or guiding images, to warn their listeners about infidelity or unreadiness for Christ, Cotton dwelt more on the privileges the saint enjoyed in her betrothal and marriage to Christ. Many of Cotton's most devoted followers were women, and in the early years of settlement in Boston, a small but influential cadre of these women considered themselves fully united with Christ.

Chief among them was Anne Hutchinson, a nurse and midwife whose kitchen became a center of religious instruction in Boston. After tutoring a circle of women on the fine points of sermons delivered by Cotton and her brother-in-law John Wheelright, she broadened her instruction to include a mixed group of men and women. Governor John Winthrop and other prominent Puritans became alarmed at the disruption of social order entailed in a woman lecturing to men—as Winthrop complained, she acted more as "a preacher than a hearer" and "more as a husband than a wife" in presenting herself as an authority on religious matters. Even worse, she criticized certain ministers for the lack of spirit in their sermons, measuring the insufficiency and misguided nature of their preaching against the inspired sermons of Cotton and Wheelright.

In Hutchinson's view, uninspired ministers tended to equate assurance of salvation with outward conformity to moral law. With Cotton and Wheelright, Hutchinson argued that true assurance of salvation came through an experience of union with Christ conveyed by the Holy Spirit. To suggest that salvation might be conveyed through a person's ability to lead a virtuous life was to lapse back into the covenant of works, which Christ had condemned and destroyed. After the Roman Church had allowed it to infiltrate and corrupt Christianity, Protestant reformers had put reliance on works down again and restored the covenant of grace, but now reliance on works was creeping back within Protestant churches founded in New England as sanctuaries of purity. Since all Puritans denounced the covenant of works, and indeed took that denunciation as fundamental to the gospel they proclaimed, the leaders of New England were hardly pleased to hear the attack on works aimed at themselves.

In Puritan parlance, the covenant of works originated with the agreement God made with Adam, which stipulated that Adam and Eve could live in Eden so long as they did not eat fruit from the Tree of Knowledge. Because they ate the forbidden fruit, Adam and Eve were expelled from paradise and condemned, along with all their progeny, to toil and suffering. From these first parents, all human beings inherited original sin, a kind of diseased or disabled state making it impossible to love and obey God fully. Despite their human propensity to sin, God revealed himself further to Israel, his chosen people, through Abraham,

Moses, and other holy men and prophets. Israel received God's commandments, honored God's law (more or less), and preserved the promise of a future redeemer who would establish God's kingdom over the world. The sinless life and sacrificial death of Jesus Christ, which the Puritans believed the Old Testament had foretold, led those who believed in Christ to eternal life in heaven, and paid off their accumulated debt of sin.

Salvation from sin and punishment in hell occurred through the operation of grace, which Christ imparted to his saints through the Holy Spirit. Over the centuries, the Roman Church had obscured the true nature of this redeeming power of grace, the Puritans believed, substituting works of penance, acts of indulgence, superstition, and priestly rigmarole for the pure gospel of salvation through faith and grace. Following earlier reformers, Puritans condemned the corrupt practices of the Roman Church and denounced the false belief that works of piety and penance would lead to salvation. The rediscovery of biblical principles by Luther, Calvin, and other reformers played a major role in world history, Puritans believed, but the work of redemption was still very much a work in progress and Christians who aspired to salvation remained vulnerable to the seductions of Satan.

Impatient with the incomplete state of religious reform, many on the radical side of the Puritan spectrum believed that some of those identified with the Puritan cause had fallen into a misguided reliance on works, mistakenly confusing an outwardly virtuous life with the grace of salvation. Christ brought the new covenant of grace to free his people from the old covenant of works, and those who reverted back to the old covenant while espousing allegiance to the new stood doubly condemned—as souls bereft of grace and as hypocrites who posed as saints.

New England Puritans agreed with each other on the main points of this history of redemption. Especially in the early years of Puritan settlement in America, hope ran high at the prospect of living in harmony with fellow members of Christ's new covenant. Separatists aside, many Puritan leaders hoped to establish a holy commonwealth composed of members of the new covenant. But while the first generation agreed about the plan of salvation, disputes arose over the question of what constituted assurance of salvation, with those on the more radical end of the spectrum calling for a "sealing of the Spirit" beyond conversion that brought union with Christ. More conservative types thought that hope of salvation, coupled with the implied presence of redeeming grace within a virtuous life, was all a saint should ask.

In the process of exerting their authority over radicals during the late 1630s, the relatively moderate cohort of first-generation New England leaders became shriller and less moderate. With animosity toward Anne Hutchinson never far from mind, Thomas Shepard in Cambridge and Thomas Hooker in Hartford were adamant about the need for guidance and preparation in the work of salvation. For them, Christian experience meant working through life with the hope of salvation as a constant guide in the struggle against pride, a steady ray of light to keep weak Christians from falling into despair. While Cotton and Hutchinson emphasized mystical union with Christ as a privilege of election, Shepard and Hooker concentrated more on the dangers of sin and the need for constant vigilance and insight into the subtle dynamics of sin. For Shepard and Hooker, the chief form of sin was pride, manifest in many forms and disguises. Even despair, in Hooker's analysis, amounted to prideful rebellion against God. Rather than complain about one's lot in life or fall into despondency, Hooker argued, the Christian should regard difficulties, limitations, and failures as opportunities to develop one's spiritual life and prepare for union with Christ.

By 1636, conflict had developed over the status of preparation, which Shepard and Hooker equated with the Christian's journey to salvation, but which Cotton, Wheelright, and Hutchinson claimed was insufficient. Tempers erupted over the charge Hutchinson allegedly leveled against Shepard for teaching the covenant of works, which was her interpretation of his emphasis on the need for preparation. This impertinence, and Shepard's angry defensiveness, drew the governor, John Winthrop, into the fray. Shepard and his allies accused Hutchinson and her friends of "antinomianism," a position they caricatured as so radical in its insistence on the contrast between grace and works that self-proclaimed saints set themselves above all forms of law.

In November 1637, after ordering her not to hold meetings in her home, the magistrates hauled Hutchinson in before the General Court to hear and respond to charges of having "troubled the peace of the commonwealth and the churches." She had persisted, the court charged, in holding "a meeting and an assembly in your house that hath been condemned by the general assembly as a thing not tolerable nor comely in the sight of God nor fitting for your sex." There were also serious questions about what she taught at these gatherings, and about the ground of religious authority upon which she presumed to stand. Pressed by the Deputy Governor, Thomas Dudley (1576–1653), as to how she knew which ministers were true exponents of the covenant of grace, and which ministers were not, Hutchinson responded that God had spoken to her by "an immediate revelation" just as he had revealed himself to Abraham. "By the voice of his own spirit to my soul," she declared, much to the court's amazement. Putting herself on a par with Abraham in this way, and claiming for her own opinion the same status as biblical revelation, proved the case against her as far as the court was concerned, as did the grievous nature of her charges against upstanding ministers of the gospel. Dudley compared the trouble she had stirred up in Boston to the Peasants' War a century before in Germany, when religious radicals "stirred up their hearers to take up arms against their prince and to cut the throats one of another." He declared himself "fully persuaded that Mrs. Hutchinson is deluded by the devil." Governor Winthrop concurred.[15]

The court condemned Hutchinson to exile and kept her under house arrest until a second trial the following March, this one conducted by her church for the purpose of her excommunication. Now pregnant and more deeply in trouble as a result of making religious pronouncements over the winter, Hutchinson tried to explain herself as confused and mistaken. But the tide of ecclesiastical opinion was decidedly against her and she was banished from communion as a religious leper.

When Hutchinson miscarried, Winthrop called the fetus a "monstrous birth" after corresponding with the physician who had examined it. Following up on that ghoulish appraisal, Cotton delivered a pair of sermons linking each of the fetus' particular deformities to errors espoused by the mother. In exile, Hutchinson enjoyed more freedom to preach, but she and her few followers lived on the margins of English society. In 1643, having taken up residence among the Dutch in New York, Hutchinson and sixteen of her family and friends died in an Indian raid.[16]

Family Life

If she overstepped the accepted bounds of wifely authority by turning her kitchen into a meeting place for both women and men, and went further to criticize the sermons of recognized ministers in her discussions with people gathered there, Hutchinson nevertheless represented, at least before her trials, the kind of religious and social status that godly women in Puritan society received. Puritan women could not vote in public elections, and did not enjoy the same legal rights as men, but they found important elements of spiritual status and authority through their relationships with God. Indeed, after the first decade when they joined churches in more or less equal numbers as men, Puritans recognized more women as visible saints than men. In addition to celebrating the piety of godly women, and admitting more women to the Lord's Supper than men, Puritans viewed the domestic environments in which women lived and worked as centers of Christian life.

Although Puritans conceptualized the family in ways that emphasized the authority of fathers and husbands, their emphasis on the importance of family life provided a context for female religious expression and influence. Families bore many of the same responsibilities that churches did as places of religious instruction and guidance. Family devotions often focused on sermons and Bible readings heard in church, and ministers expected the messages they delivered in church to be rehearsed at home. Along with their constant attention to discipline, Puritans understood love, affection, and tenderness to be characteristics of Christian virtue. As many sermons, diaries, and letters indicate, wives and mothers often exhibited these Christian traits more readily than men.[17]

Family relationships served as models for relationships with God, and vice versa. Marriage, parenting, adoption, and servitude were proving grounds for religious life, providing the social contexts that supported individuals as they worked out their personal relationships with God. At the same time, Puritans held images of God as husband, father, and master that, to some degree at least, shaped their expectations about earthly husbands, parents, and masters, and how wives, children, and servants ought to behave toward them. In sermons and guidebooks, Puritan writers described family households as important religious environments where individuals exercised the habits of authority and submission central to the Puritan way of life.

A number of Puritan ministers wrote guidebooks for family life that defined a "well-ordered household" in terms of paternal and parental authority, and emphasized the importance of domestic order for Christian life. Familial relations were a frequent theme in Puritan sermons, both as topics of moral instruction in their own right and as metaphors for the Christian's relationship with God. America's first published poet, Anne Bradstreet (1618–1672), followed these themes in her personal writings, offering religious guidance to her children and reflecting on the interplay between her religious and domestic roles. In a poem, titled "In my Solitary houres in my dear husband his Absence," Bradstreet captured both the similarity and the difference between her love toward her husband and her love toward God:

Tho' husband dear bee from me gone,
Whom I doe love so well;
I have a more beloved one
Whose comforts far excel.[18]

In this poem, Bradstreet turned to God for solace, extending to him the kind of love she felt for her husband Simon, and implying that her love for Simon shared the quality of her love for God. That implication is even clearer in her famous love poem, "To my Dear and loving Husband," in which she described her love for Simon, and Simon's love for her, as true gifts freely offered. Just as the covenant of grace operated above and beyond the covenant of works, so the love that Anne and Simon exchanged was above and beyond calculation. As the last part of the poem reads:

> My love is such that Rivers cannot quench,
> Nor ought but love from thee, give recompence,
> Thy love is such I can no way repay,
> The heavens reward thee manifold I pray.
> Then while we live, in love lets so persever,
> That when we live no more, we may live ever.[19]

Church Life

As places where preachers applied lessons from the Bible to everyday life and pastors guided Christians toward salvation, churches were essential to Puritan life. The authority Puritans invested in ministers played a crucial role in the organization of New England society. The victory over Anne Hutchinson and her supporters achieved by Shepard, Hooker, and their colleagues only enhanced this authority. That victory also helped to establish the kind of firm guidance Puritans could expect ministers to exercise.

Ministerial authority resonated with and reinforced the authority of fathers, husbands, masters, and magistrates on one hand while reinforcing belief in God's authority on the other. However much they affirmed a priesthood of all believers and opposed Catholic beliefs about priesthood as a holy office that imbued clerics with divine power, Puritans accorded great respect to the ministers who devoted their lives to religious study and the supervision of souls in their congregations. The social consensus that Puritans generated around God, ministers, and other authority figures depended on the minister's success in winning and maintaining the respect of the congregation who called him and could also vote to relieve him of his duties. It also depended on the willing submission of parishioners, citizens, wives, children, and servants to ministerial authority. In many places, people willingly granted such submission. Indeed, Puritans achieved a fair degree of consensus in seventeenth-century New England towns and villages as a result of the cultural value placed on willing submission. Spats occurred, to be sure, some of which were serious and even life threatening, and dissension grew as the century wore on. Nevertheless, the dynamics of ministerial authority shaped much of the ethos of seventeenth-century New England society, and defined the nature of both salvation and social order in Puritan culture. Although resentment often festered beneath the surface and erupted off and on in many towns and villages, respect for ministers and church authority contributed significantly to the stability of Puritan social life.

The Sacraments

As part of the cluster of symbiotic relationships between church and home, the sacraments celebrated at church drew families together in a worshipping community and strengthened the interplay between family and religious life. Puritans recognized two sacraments—baptism and the Lord's Supper. Some on the radical end of the spectrum rejected infant baptism as biblically unfounded, and insisted on adult baptism as a sign of conversion or "new birth." Roger Williams embraced that radical idea after leaving Massachusetts, and Rhode Island was one place in New England where Baptists were free to worship. But infant baptism was common practice in seventeenth-century New England, as it was and still is among the majority of American Protestants today. Then as now, infant baptism emphasized commitments by parents and church to prepare a new child for grace. Baptism represented the child's entrance into the church community, the parents' commitment to instruct and raise the child as a Christian, and the church's commitment to help and guide them.

Periodically, individuals recognized by the congregation as exhibiting both godly conduct and genuine hope of salvation stayed after the regular Sunday service to celebrate the Lord's Supper at a table in the front of the meeting house. This ritual reenacted the meal at which Christ gathered his disciples before his death, offering them bread and wine as representations of his body and blood. In its symbolism of body and blood, the Lord's Supper celebrated the redemption Christ purchased for his followers and the living manifestation of that redemption in the fellowship of the saints gathered around the table. As a meal unlike other meals, the Lord's Supper celebrated the participation in the body of Christ each member enjoyed on earth as well as their anticipated communion with God in heaven. It was an ideal representation of the fellowship of faith Puritans hoped would animate their ordinary tables, and their everyday relationships with one another.

Doing away with the altar customary in Catholic and Anglican churches, and replacing it with a communion table where visible saints gathered to reenact the Lord's Supper, Puritans registered their opposition to the Catholic belief that priests reproduced Christ's sacrifice over the altar during the Eucharistic mass. Puritans celebrated Christ's sacrifice in the Lord's Supper and its power to transform and guide their lives, but did not believe that priests had the power to recreate that sacrifice through the performance of certain gestures or by uttering certain words. In shifting the focal point of the sacrament to the hearts of believers as the place where the transformation produced by Christ's sacrifice occurred, Puritans emphasized their commitment to the internal nature of that transformation and to the experience of fellow feeling manifest around the communion table as saints shared the cup of the new covenant and the bread of God.

At the Council of Trent in 1537, Catholic churchmen confirmed their commitment to the living presence of Christ in the Eucharist through the doctrine of transubstantiation, which declared that the priest's consecration of bread and wine during the Eucharistic mass transformed these elements, in their essential substance, into the body and blood of Christ. In Calvin's theology, to which many Puritans subscribed, Christ was present in the Lord's Supper in the spiritual communion his believers enjoyed but not in a way, Calvin wrote, that seemed to "fasten him to the element of bread, nor enclose him in bread, nor circumscribe him in any way."[20] Puritans emphasized the change wrought in believers through grace, which they understood to be manifest in the Lord's Supper, conducted through the hearts of God's saints, but not lodged within the bread and wine themselves.

The Half-Way Covenant

The first generation of New England Puritans raised their children in the hope that these children, as they matured, would join other adult church members in celebration of the Lord's Supper. Both young and older people seeking participation in the full responsibilities and privileges of church membership conferred with their pastor about how their commitment to Christ had developed and under what circumstances their hope of salvation had occurred. With the pastor's approval, candidates appeared before the members of the church to present a personal relation, or narrative, of their conversion. In the congregational form of governance adopted by most New England churches in the seventeenth century, these members constituted the church, and the decision to admit new members rested with them. Of course, the pastor's preapproval carried great weight and, in many cases, the church members may simply have ratified his presentation of new members. In any event, candidates approved for membership joined other adult members in celebrating the Lord's Supper once the church approved their narratives of conversion.

The personal narratives that have survived are quite brief, conventional in format, and structured around references to hearing or reading specific biblical passages that promised hope of salvation.[21] While more than a few of the children born to the first generation experienced such hope, and duly presented themselves as candidates for admission to the Lord's Supper, not as many came forward as first generation members had anticipated. By 1660, the consequences of this failure to meet expectations had become clear. Children of first-generation saints were having children, and presenting their children for baptism, without having expressed a full commitment to Christ and hope of salvation of their own.

Faced with the dilemma of what to do with the grandchildren of professing saints whose parents had not been admitted to communion, most ministers were reluctant to cut the youngsters off from religious instruction or deny them the kind of active affiliation with church life their parents and grandparents wanted for them. In handling this problem, most ministers gradually implemented a "half-way covenant" of church membership that included anyone who had been baptized in the church, or in one of its recognized sister churches, but not yet fully converted or admitted to full church membership. Ministers encouraged these half-way members to present their children for baptism. This practice gradually expanded to permit unbaptized adults to present their children for baptism. The baptism of children was something the churches could offer parents, as well as something churches could do to increase membership.[22]

Extending the sacrament of baptism in this way gave the churches an evangelical mission they had not had before and broadened their role as centers of Christian life in an increasingly secular society in which the percentage of full church members steadily declined in relation to the larger population. This shift toward more emphasis on outreach expanded the mission and range of authority exercised by ministers. As proportionally smaller numbers of Puritans qualified for admission to the Lord's Supper as visible saints, candidates for admission grew more timid. In response to this growing reticence, a number of churches excused women from presenting their conversion narratives in person before the church and allowed pastors to present their narratives for them. Then in the 1670s and 1680s, these testimonial rituals disappeared altogether in some churches as pastors assumed full responsibility for judging whether individuals were converted or not. By this point, the reality of church life no longer expressed the earlier vision of a community of saints.

In the late 1670s, the pastor of the Northampton church in the Connecticut River valley of western Massachusetts, Solomon Stoddard (1643–1729), realized that the earlier vision of the church as a communion of saints had become anachronistic, and accordingly made changes that enabled his church to move forward with the times. Abolishing the distinctions between "full" and "half-way" membership, he admitted every baptized person of good standing to the Lord's Supper. He also used his sermons as means of drawing people into the church, and stimulated a series of "refreshings" that anticipated later revivals. Departing from earlier tendencies to think of the sacraments as celebrations of an implantation of grace that had already occurred, Stoddard invited his listeners to partake of baptism and the Lord's Supper as means of conversion. For this strategic use of the sacraments as means of grace and for the authority he wielded over his church and town, Stoddard acquired the nickname of Pope of the Connecticut River valley.

While Stoddard's revolution shook up Puritan ideas about the sacraments, it did not dislodge the idea that God had engaged the Christian people of New England in a special covenant relationship with him. Even as new church policies lowered the threshold of admission and made entrance into church life somewhat easier than before, extending baptism to the grandchildren of church members affirmed a sense of communal identity that set the founding generation of saints and their descendants on a plateau that later generations could admire. Praise of the founders of New England as icons of what Christians were supposed to be contributed to a sense of communal identity that continued to fuel analogies between New England and Israel. But the tone employed by the second and third generations to describe their identity and covenant relationship with God was markedly different from the robust confidence expressed by John Winthrop onboard the *Arbella* en route to New England. If lowering the threshold for participation in baptism thwarted the expectation that New England's churches would consist primarily of visible saints, it did little to remove the feeling, among many churchgoers, that the expectation *should* be met, and that the onus of failing to meet that expectation rested on the shoulders of the weaker descendants of New England's noble founders.

The sense of not measuring up caused considerable anxiety even as it reinforced the parallel between New England and ancient Israel. After all, God's covenant relation with Israel had involved numerous backslidings on Israel's part, each of which provided fresh occasion for chastisements from God that called Israel to repent and reaffirm her covenant with God. A number of ministers expanded on this theme in their sermons. Michael Wigglesworth used it as the basis of several long, popular poems. In "God's Controversy with New England," he explained the drought of 1662 as divine punishment for New England's decline in sanctity. Imitating the prophets of the Old Testament, he spoke with God's voice to chastise God's people:

> Is this the people blest with bounteous store,
> By land and sea full richly clad and fed,
> Whom plenty's self stands waiting still before,
> And powreth out their cups well tempered?
> For whose dear sake an howling wilderness
> I lately turned into a fruitful paradise?
>
> . . . .
>
> With whom I made a Covenant of peace,
> And unto whom I did most firmly plight
> My faithfulness, If whilst I live I cease
> To be their Guide, their God, their full delight;
> Since them with cords of love to me I drew,
> Enwrapping in my grace such as should them ensew.
>
> . . . .
>
> If these be they, how is it that I find
> In stead of holiness Carnality,
> In stead of heavenly frames an Earthly mind,
> For burning zeal luke-warm Indifferency,
> For flaming love, key-cold Dead-heartedness
> For temperance (in meat, and drinke, and cloaths) excess?
>
> . . . .
>
> For thinke not, O backsliders, in your heart,
> That I shall still your evill manners beare:
> Your sins me press as cheaves do load a cart,
> And therefore I will plague you for this gear
> Except you seriously, and soon, repent,
> Ille not delay your pain and heavy punishment.[23]

Relations with Indians

For all their visions of a New Jerusalem and fears of loosing their grip over New England society, seventeenth-century Puritans were a fairly insular group whose outreach extended mainly to people like themselves. This "tribalism" was nowhere more evident than in their attitudes toward Indians. While Puritans accepted few Indians into their own society, Indians figured prominently in how Puritans saw themselves in relation to their surrounding world. Along with Catholics (who rarely appeared in seventeenth-century New England) Indians were the quintessential outsiders against whom Puritans defined themselves.

Indian Wars

Before the first English settlers arrived in America, epidemics of diseases introduced by English and French explorers had already shrunk and weakened the Indian populations of New England. The Pilgrims settled near a place that had been a thriving Indian village only a few years before but had been abandoned after being decimated by disease. The Plymouth Separatists depended on Indian food and know-how for survival and on the friendship of the Wampanoag chief Masassoit (c. 1590–1661), who brought venison, fowl, and twenty men to the first English Thanksgiving feast in America. In a manner typical of New England's early Protestant settlers, the Separatists interpreted the behavior of the Indians in their region as providential acts in their own history—God cleared the way for their own English settlement, God sent Indian helpers to assist in the survival of this settlement, and so on.

With the immigration of hundreds of English settlers to the Massachusetts Bay Colony during the 1630s and the establishment of many new Puritan settlements and towns, conflicts with Indians in the region multiplied. In 1637, just as the controversy involving Anne Hutchinson was dividing Puritans in the Bay Colony against each other, they found a common enemy in the Pequots, a group of Native Americans living in southern and central New England. The Pequots resented incursions into their territories and the condescending way the Puritans treated them.

In May 1637, the Puritans of Massachusetts sent a militia led by John Underhill to join the Connecticut militia led by John Mason in a concerted effort to destroy the Pequot fort at Mystic. The Puritans justified this attack as retaliation for the murders of two English traders, John Stone and John Oldham. In fact, Niatics killed Stone and Narragansetts killed Oldham, but Puritans found it difficult telling one Indian group from another and did not take the trouble to sort things out. The men led by Underhill and Mason surrounded and set fire to the Pequot fort, which burst into flames and burned to the ground within half an hour, killing all of the men, women, and children inside. "Great and doleful was the bloody sight to the view of young soldiers that had never been in war," Underhill wrote, "to see so many souls lie gasping on the ground, so thick, in some places, that you could hardly pass along."[24]

Whatever doleful feelings it aroused in the young English soldiers, the leaders responsible for the slaughter clearly understood it in religious terms. As Mason recalled laying fire to the mats covering the wigwams with the cry, "WE MUST BURN THEM," he described his sense of God's hand at work through his own act of destruction: "such a dreadful Terror did the ALMIGHTY let fall upon their Spirits, that they would fly from us and run into the very Flames, where many of them perished." In representing his own actions and those of his men, Mason drew upon analogies between the Puritans of New England and the people of Israel so central to Puritan self-understanding. The destruction of Pequot Indians at Mystic recapitulated the destruction of Israel's enemies in Canaan, just as the Puritans' freedom from persecution in England, and freedom from harassment by Indians in America, recapitulated Israel's freedom from captivity in Egypt. With a sense of being swept along in a process beyond his control, Mason explained what it felt like to plunge into battle, "when the LORD turned the Captivity of his People, and turned the Wheel upon their Enemies; we were like Men in a Dream; then was our Mouth filled with Laughter, and our Tongues with Singing; thus we may say the LORD hath done great Things for us among the Heathen, whereof we are glad." As historian Ann Kibbey argued, Mason's description of his men's killing and rejoicing conveyed "a sense of having compulsively acted out a scriptural image while hypnotic power controlled them."[25]

Violence against Indians was an important part of Puritan religious experience in New England and not something the Puritans viewed simply in pragmatic, military, or secular terms. Nor was the justification for religious violence against Indians merely a product of the captains' lust for glory in war. Before the Connecticut militia marched off to Mystic, Thomas Hooker preached to the men from the Old Testament Book of Numbers about Israel's defeat of the Canaanites: "Only rebel ye not against the Lord, neither fear ye the people of the land; for they are bread for us: their defence is departed from them, and the Lord is with us: fear them not."

Hooker's Old Testament reference to the enemies of Israel as "bread for us" was loaded with symbolic meaning. Defeating the Pequots would be as easy and as fortifying as eating bread, much as defeating the Canaanites had been easy and fortifying for Israel, so long as they held steadfastly to their faith. "Bread for us" resonated with the Eucharistic imagery of the New Testament as well, evoking the linkage between blood sacrifice and the redemption of believers celebrated in the Lord's Supper. Given Hooker's masterful way with words, the rich ambiguity of these symbols and their interconnections would have encouraged the impression that the Puritans' own vitality would be nourished by a divinely ordained, even sacramental, violence against Indians.[26]

Over the course of the next few decades, Puritan belief in God's hand at work in their violence against Indians did not diminish. As English settlement expanded through the Connecticut River valley into western Massachusetts, the pressure on Indians in the region intensified. Hemmed in by the increasingly powerful Iroquois confederacy to the north and west, the remnants of several Algonquian groups in the region formed a confederacy to halt the expansion of English settlements in their midst. Under the leadership of Masassoit's son Metacom (c. 1638–1676), called Philip by the English, remnants of the Pequots, Wampanoags, and other groups joined forces with the still-powerful Narragansett Indians whose fathers had fought with the English in the Pequot War. With ties to the French and some of their Indian allies to the north, the confederacy led by King Philip posed a real threat to the survival of English settlements in western Massachusetts, Connecticut, and Rhode Island.

War broke out in 1675. Metacom and his men burned numerous English settlements, killed hundreds of English settlers, and took captives north into Canada. The Puritans interpreted these disasters in terms of the same covenant theology that had justified their victory over the Pequot Indians in 1637. Only this time, Puritans read the violence against them as God's punishment for their failure to live up to the pure faith of the founding generation and to abide by the covenant the founders had established with God. Ultimately, the Puritans won out over Metacom—hunting him down in a swamp, breaking the confederacy he had gathered against them, killing hundreds of his supporters, destroying whole villages, and driving to the west and north many Indians who survived. The war removed the Indian threat in southern New England, but it cost the settlers dearly. Colonists lost or expended an estimated £100,000 sterling in the conflict and every English family lost, on average, one immediate family member. Fifty-two Puritan towns were badly burned, and thirteen—Northfield, Deerfield, Brookfield, Worcester, Lancaster, Groton, Mendon, Wrenthen, Middleborough, Dartmouth, Warwick, Wickford, and Simsbury—were destroyed.[27]

King Philip's War also cost the Puritans in morale. Although the analogy between Israel and New England held, its implications became profoundly ambiguous. Along with the growing secularization of New England society—with Sabbath-breaking, swearing, whoring, swindling, and backbiting on the rise, and the ratio of visible saints in the general population on the decline—the disasters of King Philip's War raised serious questions about the direction religious life in New England was taking.

Puritan writers still relied on Old Testament parallels to explain King Philip's War, interpreting the devastating attacks on Puritan frontier settlements as punishments for Puritan iniquities. In this framework, the Indians played much the same role as Canaanites in the Old Testament who worshipped heathen gods, fought against the people of Israel, and resisted the settlement and divinely mandated establishment of God's kingdom. Building further on this scenario, Puritans imagined the Indians as devil worshippers and even devils themselves, bloodthirsty minions of Satan, the archenemy of Christ described in the book of Revelation and in medieval and Puritan literature.

But if the Indians' role as villains in a religious script was predictable, the Puritans' own role in relation to them had become unsettled. It was no longer so clear that the punishments enacted by these villains were means the Puritans could use to reestablish their covenant relation with God. Gone were the days when simple distinctions between visible saints and outsiders could be taken for granted. In an era when visible saints were proportionally much fewer and less sure of themselves and ministers regularly chastised people for their sinful behavior, pointing fingers at bad actors had become more self-referential than before. This move in the direction of fusing self and other was not a matter of eyeing Indians more charitably or objectively but rather of the Puritans' eyeing themselves and their neighbors in a more jaundiced light. An increasingly pervasive sense of malevolence destabilized Puritan identity. The people of New England might have sunk too deeply in sin and confusion to know if their own claims to be willing to repent and recommit themselves to God could be trusted as authentic.

Captivity Narratives

Narratives written by colonists after their release from Indian captivity reveal the heightened ambiguity in Puritan self-understanding that took place toward the end of the seventeenth century along with the older custom of applying Old Testament imagery to historical events. The most famous of these narratives, written by Mary White Rowlandson (c. 1636–1711), told of how Indians destroyed her home in Lancaster, Massachusetts, during King Philip's War, killed or captured several members of her family, forced her to walk northward, half-dead, to the Indian town of Wenimesset, where her captors delivered her to a cruel mistress. In her degrading march through the forests, Rowlandson carried a Bible in her apron and consulted it to find parallels to the situations she faced. Upon her arrival in Wenimesset, she identified with David in Psalm 27:13, who found strength and safety in the Lord in the midst of his enemies. Like David, she later wrote, "I had fainted, unless I had believed." On another occasion, thinking about her children—one dead, one missing, the third held captive apart from her—she identified with Jacob's grief over his children. At another time, Isaiah's words helped her pray for strength: "Oh, Lord, I am oppressed; undertake for me." Later, reading about Hezekiah gave her courage to plead her case before God: "Remember now O Lord, I beseech thee, how I have walked before thee in truth."[28]

The parallels that Rowlandson drew between her captivity and biblical events shaped her story. Israel's bondage in Egypt, wanderings in Canaan, and repeated defeats at the hands of powerful enemies helped her to define the spiritual and moral implications of the trials she underwent. Coincidentally, her vivid descriptions of Indian captivity contributed to the liveliness of the biblical events she recalled. Descriptions of the screams, wild dancing, filthiness, and cruelty of the "hell-hounds" who held her captive merged with biblical narratives, making them fresh, immediate, and compelling.

This fluidity between biblical events and Rowlandson's own experience contributed to the rich ambiguity of her narrative and to the profound uncertainty about her own spiritual state that her story conveyed. With the linkage between God's punishment of Israel and Israel's need for repentance as a point of departure, Rowlandson set her story in the context of covenant theology and its emphasis on suffering as an occasion for repentance and spiritual growth. Thus she affirmed with David that "It is good for me that I have been afflicted." Before her captivity, she had "lived in prosperity, having the comforts of the World," and had been "jealous" of others who "under many trials and afflictions, in sickness, weakness, poverty, losses, crosses, and cares of the World" had found God's love as a result of being chastised by suffering. "For whom the Lord loveth," Rowlandson reminded her readers, citing Hebrews 12, "he chasteneth, and scourgeth every Son whom he receiveth."[29]

However much she glamorized suffering before her captivity, the reality of it darkened Rowlandson's account of her ordeal. Her dreadful experience of Indian captivity took her places she would not have chosen to go. The longer she stayed with her Indian captors, the more her life merged with theirs and the more her indictment of their behavior merged with indictment of her own. Having attached herself to the economy of her captors by stitching clothes in exchange for food, she became as greedy and undisciplined as she perceived them to be. When she stole part of a boiled horse foot from a "slabbering" child, her Indian mistress threatened her for having "disgraced her master with begging." Despite the humiliation, Rowlandson could not control her desire for food, or even manage food, when she had it, with any reason. Citing Micah 6:14, "Thou shalt eat and not be satisfied," she lamented that "many times when they gave me that which was hot, I was so greedy, that I should burn my mouth, that it would trouble me hours after, and yet I should quickly do the same again."[30]

Although Rowlandson and her surviving children returned to Puritan society after colonists paid her captors a ransom, she seemed not to have experienced the spiritual relief of being ransomed from sin. Troubled by nightmares after her return, Rowlandson represented the uneasiness of Puritan culture at the end of the seventeenth century and the disturbing way that Puritan self-understanding had come to be haunted by fear and guilt. Her awareness of God's power, and his distance from her, produced an exquisite sense of her own vulnerability, causing her to say with Job, "Have pitty upon me, have pitty upon me, O ye my Frinds, for the Hand of the lord has touched me."[31]

In their preoccupation with problems of will, desire, pride, and guilt, the Puritans of Rowlandson's generation had begun to shape a distinctive kind of American literature, one that would come to dark flowering in the stories of Charles Brockden Brown, Nathaniel Hawthorne, and Herman Melville. In Hawthorne's most famous story, *The Scarlet Letter* (1850), the Puritan minister Arthur Dimsdale is consumed by self-recrimination and by the disparity between the sinner he knows himself to be and the saint he outwardly appears to be. As Hawthorne described the minister:

> He kept vigils, likewise, night after night, sometimes in utter darkness; sometimes with a glimmering lamp; and sometimes, viewing his own face in a looking-glass, by the most powerful light which he could throw upon it. He thus typified the constant introspection wherewith he tortured, but could not purify, himself. In these lengthened vigils, his brain often reeled, and visions seemed to flit before him; perhaps seen doubtfully, and by a faint light of their own, in the remote dimness of the chamber, or more vividly, and close beside him, within the looking-glass. Now it was a herd of diabolic shapes, that grinned and mocked at the pale minister, and beckoned him away with them; now a group of shining angels, who flew upward heavily, as sorrow-laden but grew more ethereal as they rose.[32]

As a meditation on the haunted inner world of Puritan life, Hawthorne's *Scarlet Letter* contributed to the shaping of American literary (and later, film) traditions of psychological thrill and horror.

Praying Indians

Although many Indians thought the English people, or their spirits, had evil powers, some renounced their native traditions and accepted Christianity. A small minority of Indians inhabiting New England underwent baptism at the hands of Puritan missionaries and lived in "Praying Towns" under the missionaries' close supervision. Puritans strongly encouraged these converts to accept the view that Indian religion was really a form of Satan worship. In his transcriptions of the examinations of Indians who applied for church membership in Roxbury in 1654, John Eliot indicated that at least one applicant identified the Indian deity Hobbomak as Satan. When asked, "Whether are not your sins, and the temptations of Hobbomak more strong since, then before you prayed to God?" the applicant replied, "Before I prayed to God, I knew not what Satan's temptations were."[33]

In 1671, Eliot published "Indian Dialogues," a series of reconstructed conversations, "partly Historical" and "partly Instructive," that he hoped would serve converts in the process of bringing more Indians to Christianity. In one conversation, the convert Piumbukhou identified traditional "prayers and Pawwuings" as "worship of the Devil" and told his unconverted relatives in Naumsheg what it meant to be a Christian: "I cannot serve two Masters: I have undertaken and promised to serve God, and I cannot go back again and serve *the Devil*."[34]

The Indians who embraced Protestant Christianity in seventeenth-century New England had few other options. As refugees from Indian communities ravaged by disease and violence, they joined "Praying Towns" established by Puritans in order to survive, even though it meant accepting virtual imprisonment and serfdom as well as renunciation of traditional forms of religious belief and practice. Reading between the lines of the writings of Puritan missionaries, the desperation of these converts can be discerned, along with the pressure they received to renounce their religious traditions as demonic. In a letter written in 1647, Thomas Mayhew (Matthew's father) lamented that the eldest son of the "great Sagamore Vakapenessue" had fallen back into witchcraft. The chief's son had expressed interest in Christianity during an illness but "sought againe unto Witches" after recovering. In the same letter, Thomas described the conversion of Icogiscat, a sixty-year-old Algonquian who turned to Christianity when Native shamans failed to heal him.

Thomas boasted that Icogiscat "speedily recovered" once the missionary "convinced him of the weaknesse and wickednesse of the Pawwawes power" and "commended [his] case unto the Lord."[35]

While Puritans taught their Indian converts to perceive other Native Americans as witches, hell hounds, and devil worshippers, most Native Americans thought differently. More than a few feared the Puritans as witches, and regarded themselves as victims of spells that Puritans cast. When the Algonquian shaman Papassaconnaway and his sons fled from the Puritan missionary John Eliot in 1647, the Algonquian men seem to have feared the missionary's preternatural evil power.[36] Another shaman attending a woman who "lay in great extremity and wholly impotent" caught the spirit possessing and tormenting her in a deerskin, and identified it as "the spirit of an English drowned." Warning he "could not long confine" the evil-doing English specter, he urged the woman to move to Martha's Vineyard where he could attend her.[37]

The conversion of Icogiscat and other "Praying Indians" to English Protestantism required an abdication of traditional ways that reflected the Puritan perception of those ways as diabolical. This English animosity toward Indian religion did not diminish in the course of the seventeenth century, but if anything, grew stronger, especially in the context of the violence and terror of King Philip's War in the 1670s. But while negative perceptions of Indian religion persisted, the dividing line between Indian witches and Puritan saints became less visible. Once clear cut and impregnable (except in the prophetic opinion of Roger Williams and his few fellow believers), this dividing line became broken and porous as second and third generation Puritans became increasingly anxious about New England's failure to live up to the covenant established by the founding generation. In the writings of this period, some of the most egregious sinners—the ones who allowed Satan to seduce them even though they had all the blessings and privileges of Christian teaching in their homes and churches—were Puritans themselves.

Witchcraft in New England

The anxiety associated with Puritan identity escalated. In the port towns of Boston, Salem, and New London, merchants vied with ministers as arbiters of New England culture. The rewards of merchant capitalism made the old Puritan commitment to "being knit together as one man" seem quaint. In an increasingly bustling economy, Puritan authorities lost some of their control over society but none of their ability to complain or chastise. A series of political and diplomatic disasters associated with the restoration of the British monarchy in 1660 helped to fuel their lamentations. In 1684, Charles II annulled the charter held by the Puritan government of the Massachusetts Bay Colony and the next year, the Catholic King James II installed Edmund Andross as royal governor of New England, New York, and New Jersey. In 1691, in the wake of James' flight, the accession of William of Orange, and the expulsion of Andross, Massachusetts received a new charter, but one less favorable to the Puritan establishment than the original. The new charter imposed religious toleration and stipulated that the Governor of Massachusetts be appointed by the Crown.

The outbreak of witchcraft accusations in Salem Village in 1692 is best understood against the backdrop of this destabilization of Puritan culture, as an expression of increasingly desperate attempts by religious believers to interpret their situation in terms of God's wrath and punishment of New England. Accusations of witchcraft were not a new phenomenon in seventeenth-century New England. People charged their neighbors with witchcraft when frustrations became intolerable and ties of communal solidarity frayed. As historian Carol F. Karlsen showed, widowed women who had inherited their husband's wealth and remarried were most vulnerable to accusation, along with single women who enjoyed some economic independence and often stood to inherit more, and thus represented a kind of female autonomy that could inspire jealousy, especially in other women.[38] Resentment of independent individuals, especially women, also played a role in the accusations of witchcraft coming out of Salem Village in 1692, along with the steady stream of religious rhetoric dwelling on the sinfulness of New England culture that encouraged people to sense the presence of the devil around them, threatening the Puritan way of life.

The accusing girls from Salem Village were an unhappy lot. Servants, farmers' daughters, and the daughter of the embittered Village minister who failed in commerce before turning to the church, the girls feared the future. With marriageable young men more able than they to leave Salem Village, the accusing group looked forward to lives as spinsters, servants, beggars, or at best, wives of poor farmers. The fortune-telling that preceded their frenzied accusations reflected their dismal prospects. While gazing into an egg and a crystal ball, the girls asked for some hint of "what trade their sweet harts should be of." In response, a frightening image of their future prospects had appeared— "a spectre in likeness of a Coffin."[39]

As historians Paul Boyer and Stephen Nissenbaum argued, the accusations the girls hurled at prominent townspeople in the prosperous seaport of Salem expressed the hostility many rural New Englanders felt toward people whose wealth seemed to grow at the expense of their

Witch riding to the Sabbath. From Ulrich Molitor's *Hexen Meysterey*, 1545.

own and whose affluent lifestyles suggested the devil's patronage. The accused included Mary Bradbury, the wife of a ship's captain, Rebecca Nurse, an upstanding member of the Salem Town church that for many years had denied Salem Villagers a church of their own, Philip English, one of the richest shipowners in New England and the merchant responsible for introducing trade between New England and France, Spain, and Portugal, and Bridget Bishop, who represented the antithesis of domestic morality in her "Red paragon Bodys," which she wore at her tavern on the road between the landlocked farmlands of Salem Village and the thriving commercial center of Salem Town. Villagers passed by her place of business when they traveled to Town to sell their produce to merchants who bought low and resold for a profit.[40] Those accused also included some ne'er-do-wells—the "Rampant Hag" Martha Carrier, the impoverished Susanna Martin, whose sharp tongue contributed to her reputation as "one of the most Impudent, Scurrilous, wicked creatures in the world," and Sarah Good, a quarrelsome woman past youth and reduced to begging. The accusers lashed out against these obvious candidates as well as against more respectable townspeople who seemed to be getting away with sin without paying any price.[41]

The accusations of witchcraft leveled by the Salem girls triggered a mass hysteria that led many to believe the girls' enactments of diabolical torture and also led the judiciary court to accept claims about spectral apparitions of accused persons as legal evidence against them. After the trial, Judge John Hale tried to explain how he had gotten caught up in the frenzy: "such was the darkness of that day, the tortures and lamentations of the afflicted, and the power of former presidents, that we walked in the clouds, and could not see our way." He described how the girls "were bitten and pinched by invisible agents; their arms, necks, and backs turned this way and that way, and returned back again, so as it was impossible for them to do of themselves, and beyond the power of any Epileptick Fits, or natural Disease to effect."[42] In desperate efforts to please the judges—and to stop the fits and screams of the afflicted girls in the courtroom—a number of accused women confessed to having attended a witches' Sabbath where, presumably, they entered into covenants with the devil. Sarah Bridges "owned She had been to the witch Meeting" at Andover with "@ 200 Witches" where they all "Eat bred & Drank wine." Abigail Hobbs confessed that "[s]he was at the great Meeting in Mr Parris's Pasture when they administered the Sacram'tt, and did Eat of the Red Bread and drink of the Red wine att the same Time." Her mother Deliverance testified she had seen George Burroughs, the former Salem minister, celebrating the unholy communion in the Parris pasture and that several women subsequently jailed on charges of witchcraft had "distributed the bread and . . . filled out the wine in Tankards." Elizabeth Johnson claimed that "20 or 30" witches had been at the meeting she attended and that the wine was bitter and had probably come from Boston. Mary Lacey confessed that, when she participated, "the bread was brownish & the wine Red they had also a table and Erthen Cups & there was so many that there was not bread Enough for them all."[43]

Nineteen people were hung and one man pressed to death before Governor William Phipps, representing the English crown, called a halt to the trials and executions. The jails were emptied and reliance on spectral evidence was condemned, or swept under the rug in embarrassment. Some of the judges expressed regret about the trials and, eventually, reparations were made to the victims' families. Belief in the devil became a favorite target of ridicule and lampooning among skeptics, and the Salem trials became a byword for fanaticism and the social dangers it unleashed. Still, belief in the devil hardly disappeared, but only grew more widespread and eclectic as Protestantism spread and flourished in

North America. Appeals to the devil as means of expressing fear and anxiety had sunk deep roots in American culture, as had the invitation such appeals extended to elide fear of outsiders with anxiety about one's own hidden sins.

Conclusion

Puritans were not the only Protestants in seventeenth-century North America, but they were the most significant group in terms of the number of permanent settlements they established and their influence on American culture, especially through the ideal of a holy commonwealth. The Puritan idea of planting a holy commonwealth in America never died out, but it did become enlarged over time as new waves of immigrants, pioneers, and utopians tried to realize their religious dreams. At the same time, efforts to construct a holy commonwealth also met with resistance. Roger Williams was only the first to challenge the arrogance and violence that often accompanied the idea.

In the context of disputes over religious visions for America, divisions opened between people critical of, and even repulsed by, the dangers of religious fanaticism on one hand, and those, on the other, whose enthusiasm for religious visions never lagged. The extraordinary capacity Americans have shown for entertaining religious scenarios tapped into dark fears as well as hopes for a brighter future, and these fears can be considered another legacy of the Puritans and their anxiety about themselves and their identity. Uneasiness about the presence of the Antichrist and his demonic minions helped to justify hostilities toward immigrant Catholics and Jews, as well as violence against Indians. The connections between these religious fears and Protestant concerns about spiritual purity only became more complicated and conflicted as whites enlisted Christianity in their efforts to dominate blacks. At the same time, the increasing diversity within Protestant Christianity served as a check against religious rule by one group over others, and helped to subvert ownership of religious symbols by any single group. It also fostered tendencies to view religion as a private matter, tendencies that had antecedents in Puritan introspection.

Notes

1. Euan Cameron, *The European Reformation* (New York: Oxford University Press, 1991), pp. 46–47.

2. See Herbert Grundmann, *Religious Movements in the Middle Ages: The Historical Links between Heresy, the Mendicant Orders, and the Women's Religious Movement in the Twelfth and Thirteenth Century, with the Historical Foundations of German Mysticism*, trans. Steven Rowan (Notre Dame: University of Notre Dame, 1995; orig. 1935 in German).

3. Quoted in Roland Bainton, *Here I Stand* (New York and Nashville: Abingdon-Cokesbury, 1950), pp. 354–355.

4. Peter Matheson, *The Imaginative World of the Reformation* (Minneapolis: Fortress Press, 2001), p. 18.

5. Quotation from Matheson, *Imaginative World*, p. 11.

6. William J. Bouwsma, *John Calvin: A Sixteenth Century Portrait* (New York: Oxford University Press, 1988), quotations from p. 19.

7. John Winthrop, *A Model of Christian Charity Written on Board the "Arbella" on the Atlantic Ocean*, reprinted in *The Puritans in America: A Narrative Anthology*, ed. Alan Heimert and Andrew Delbanco (Cambridge: Harvard University Press, 1985), quotations from pp. 90, 91.

8. See David G. Hackett, *The Rude Hand of Innovation: Religion and Social Order in Albany, New York 1652–1836* (New York: Oxford University Press, 1991).

9. See Arthur J. Worrall, *Quakers in the Colonial Northeast* (Hanover, NH: University Press of New England, 1980).

10. William Bradford, *Of Plymouth Plantation*, ed. Harvey Wish (New York: Capricorn Books, 1962), quotations from pp. 48, 40.

11. Winthrop, *Model of Christian Charity*, quotation from p. 91.

12. Roger Williams, *The Bloudy Tenent of Persecution for cause of Conscience, discussed, in A Conference betweene Truth and Peace* (London, 1644), reprinted in *Roger Williams: His Contribution to the American Tradition*, ed. Perry Miller (New York: Atheneum, 1970; orig. 1953), quotation from p. 150.

13. Williams, *Bloudy Tenent*, Miller, *Roger Williams*, quotation from p. 126.

14. Roger Williams, *A Key into the Language of America: Or, An help to the Language of the Natives in that part of America, Called New-England* (London: 1643), reprinted in Miller, *Roger Williams*, quotation from p. 64.

15. "The Examination of Mrs. Anne Hutchinson at the Court at Newtown," in *The Antinomian Controversy 1636–1638: A Documentary History*, ed. David D. Hall (Middletown: Wesleyan University Press, 1968), quotations from p. x. Also see Michael P. Winship, *Making Heretics: Militant Protestanism and Free Grace in Massachusetts, 1636–1641* (Princeton: Princeton University Press, 2002).

16. John Winthrop, *A Short Story of the Rise, reign, and ruin of the Antinomians, Familists, & Libertines, that infected the Churches of New England* (orig. 1644), reprinted in John Winthrop, *The History of New England, from 1630 to 1649*, 2 vols., ed. James Savage (Boston: Phelps and Farnahm, 1825; Boston: Little, Brown, 1853), p. x. Also see James G. Moseley, *John Winthrop's World: History as a Story; The Story as History* (Madison: University of Wisconsin Press, 1992).

17. Amanda Porterfield, *Female Piety in Puritan New England: The Emergence of Religious Humanism* (New York: Oxford University Press, 1992); Charles Lloyd Cohen, *God's Caress: The Psychology of Puritan Religious Experience* (New York: Oxford University Press, 1986).

18. Anne Bradstreet, "In my Solitary houres in my dear husband his Absence," *Poems of Anne Bradstreet*, ed. Robert Hutchinson (New York: Dover Publications, 1969; orig. 1867), quotation from p. 74.

19. Anne Bradstreet, "To my Dear and loving Husband," *Poems of Anne Bradstreet*, quotation from p. 41.

20. John Calvin, *Institutes of the Christian Religion*, ed. John T. McNeill, 2 vols. (Louisville: Westminster John Knox Press, 1960), quotation from vol. 2, p. 1381.

21. George Selement and Bruce C. Woolley, eds., *Thomas Shepard's "Confessions"* (Boston: Colonial Society of Massachusetts, 1981); Patricia Caldwell, *The Puritan Conversion Narrative: The Beginnings of American Expression* (Cambridge: Cambridge University Press, 1983).

22. Robert G. Pope, *The Half-Way Covenant: Church Membership in Puritan New England* (Princeton: Princeton University Press, 1969).

23. Michael Wigglesworth, "God's Controversy with New England Written in the Time of the Great Drought Anno 1662," reprinted in Heimert and Delbanco, *Puritans in America*, quotations from pp. 332–334.

24. John Underhill, *Newes from America, or, A New and Experimentall Discoverie of New England* (London, 1638), reprinted in *History of the Pequot War*, ed. Charles Orr (Cleveland: Helman-Taylor, 1897), quotation from p. 21.

25. John Mason, *A Brief History of the Pequot War: Especially Of the memorable Taking of their Fort at Mistick in Connecticut In 1637* (Boston, 1736), quotations from pp. 8, 22; Ann Kibbey, *The Interpretation of Material Shapes in Puritanism: A Study of Rhetoric, Prejudice, and Violence* (New York: Cambridge University Press, 1986), quotation from pp. 97–98.

26. Frank Shuffelton, *Thomas Hooker: 1586–1647* (Princeton: Princeton University Press, 1977), quotation from pp. 236–237. See Richard Slotkin, *Regeneration Through Violence: The Mythology of the American Frontier, 1600–1800* (Middletown: Wesleyan University Press, 1973).

27. Douglas Edward Leach, *Flintlock and Tomahawk: New England in King Philip's War* (New York: W. W. Norton, 1958), pp. 242–250.

28. *Narrative of the Captivity of Mrs. Mary Rowlandson* (Cambridge, 1682), reprinted in *Narratives of the Indian Wars 1675–1699*, ed. Charles H. Lincoln (New York: Barnes & Noble, 1913), quotations from pp. 124, 125, 145.

29. *Captivity of Mrs. Mary Rowlandson*, quotations from pp. 166–167.

30. *Captivity of Mrs. Mary Rowlandson*, quotations from pp. 121, 149, 146–147.

31. *Captivity of Mrs. Mary Rowlandson*, quotation from p. 166.

32. Nathaniel Hawthorne, *The Scarlet Letter* (New York: Holt, Rinehart and Winston, 1963; orig. 1850), quotation from p. 139.

33. John Eliot, "Letter of 1649," in *Glorious Progress of the Gospel amongst the Indians in New England*, ed. Edward Winslow (London, 1649), quotations from p. 123.

34. John Eliot, *Indian Dialogues for the Instruction in that great Service of Christ, in calling home their Country-men to the knowledge of God, And of Themselves, and of Jesus Christ* (Cambridge, 1671), quotations from pp. 3, 1, 20.

35. Thomas Mayhew, "Letter from Capawack November 18, 1647," in Winslow, *Glorious Progress*, quotations from pp. 115–116.

36. Eliot, "Letter of 1649," in Winslow, *Glorious Progress*, p. 121.

37. Matthew Mayhew, *A Brief Narrative of the Success which the gospel hath had, among the Indians of Martha's-Vineyard* (Boston, 1694), quotations from pp. 13–14.

38. Carol F. Karlsen, *The Devil in the Shape of a Woman: Witchcraft in Colonial New England* (New York: W. W. Norton, 1987). Also see Elizabeth Reis, *Damned Women: Sinners and Witches in Puritan New England* (Ithaca: Cornell University Press, 1997).

39. Karlsen, *Devil in the Shape of a Woman*, quotations from p. 101.

40. Paul Boyer and Stephen Nissenbaum, *Salem Possessed: The Social Origins of Witchcraft* (Cambridge: Harvard University Press, 1974); Paul Boyer and Stephen Nissenbaum, eds., *The Salem Witchcraft Papers: Verbatim Transcripts of the Legal Documents of the Salem Witchcraft Outbreak of 1692*, 2 vols. (New York: Da Capo Press, 1977), quotation from vol. 1, p. 102.

41. Boyer and Nissenbaum, *Witchcraft Papers*, quotations from vol. 2, pp. 368–369, 550.

42. John Hale, *A Modest Inquiry into the Nature of Witchcraft* (Boston, 1702), reprinted in *Narratives of the Witchraft Cases, 1648–1706*, ed. Burr (New York: Barnes & Noble, 1959), quotation from p. 427.

43. Boyer and Nissenbaum, *Witchcraft Papers*, quotations from vol. 1, p. 140; vol. 2, pp. 410, 423, 501, 504, 523–524.

Chapter 2

Evangelicalism and the Pursuit of Evidence

In his comprehensive history of American Christian thought before the Civil War, E. Brooks Holifield pointed to the emphasis Protestants placed on evidence of biblical revelation. While they disagreed with one another on many issues—free will, predestination, infant damnation, female preaching, and slavery, to name some of the most rancorous—the vast majority of Protestant theologians in the eighteenth and early nineteenth centuries presented Christianity in terms of evidence supporting the truth of some or all aspects of biblical revelation. What Holifield identified as "the evidential temper" of antebellum Protestant theology can also be discerned in a broad range of popular religious effort to produce evidence to support biblical revelation and supernatural reality.

As Holifield explained, the "evidentiary temper" among American theologians reflected a growing interest in natural philosophy and empirical investigations.[1] Along with their confidence that science and Christian faith were coextensive and mutually supporting, theologians in America, Scotland, and England celebrated the deductions of "natural reason" and "common sense" as complements to Christian faith. Against the Platonic notion of Reason as an eternal set of ideal forms contemplated by elitist philosophers, many American and British theologians in the eighteenth and early nineteenth centuries celebrated natural reason and common sense, which they associated with energetic men making their way in the world.

Ironically, the restraint on miraculous claims encouraged by early Protestant reformers diminished for many Americans in the context of empiricist tendencies in association with the rise of common sense philosophy, which emphasized the trustworthiness of sensory perception and the correspondence between empirical reality and sensory impressions in the human mind. Protestantism had emerged as a protest movement against the Catholic Church's venal exploitation of miracles, with Luther, Calvin, and other reform theologians claiming that the era of miracles associated with Christ's appearance on earth was long past. Preoccupation with supernatural events and signs hardly disappeared among Protestants, but it was restrained by the reformist emphasis on social order, patriarchal authority, and the efforts to discern God's will in ordinary events. One might suppose that the triumph of natural reason and common sense would dampen belief in the supernatural, but for many religious Americans, quite the opposite has been true. One of the great ironies of American religious history is the role that enthusiasm for empirical investigation played in stimulating experiences and reports of supernatural phenomena. In America, many evangelicals relied on common sense philosophy to validate their religious experiences and to objectify their religious feelings. To an important extent, the energetic presentation of evidence in support of biblical truth defined what it meant to be an evangelical.

This chapter focuses primarily on the history of American evangelicalism between 1700 and 1860 and on the stress on empirical evidence characteristic of American Protestant culture. A busy world of biblical revelation and supernatural presences flourished in the context of evangelical culture and its enthusiasm for natural reason and common sense. Not all Protestants participated in this widespread fascination with supernatural events and signs; some scoffed at the superstitions of their compatriots. But many others embraced supernatural events and signs as part of the fabric of natural reason and common sense.

Under the aegis of common sense philosophy, evangelicals used the word "empirical" in reference to experience. With notions of scientific validation and experimentation weaker and more fluid than they are today, many evangelicals in the eighteenth and nineteenth centuries stretched the meaning of empirical evidence to include experiences of supernatural manifestations. This elastic approach to evidence answered a need to validate religious principles and biblical authority. In a culture without encompassing or firmly established religious institutions, appeals to empirical evidence for religious belief were an important means of asserting religious authority.

The more confidence American evangelicals put in empirical evidence, the more evidence of supernatural phenomena they produced. Many evangelicals felt that the devil lurked nearby and interpreted their sensations of fear as evidence of his presence. Many also experienced the Holy Spirit as an active presence in their lives and as an agent of personal transformation, or "new birth." For God's elect, heaven was not far away in either space or time. Evangelicals envisioned tables set for them on high similar to the communion tables they gathered around on earth, and expected Christ's return to earth in the near future, when the saved would be exalted, and the reprobate cast down into hell. Orienting one's life in terms of such visions seemed to many evangelicals as commonsensical as settling the frontier, creating new communities, and building churches.

Enthusiasm for religious experience involved evangelical outreach to convince others of the need for "new birth" and the importance of vigilance against Satan. In this outreach, evangelicals often acted on the assumption that biblical events could and would be reproduced in real-time experience. While skeptics made fun of them, many evangelicals looked for evidence of the devil or the Holy Spirit in much the same way they looked for evidence of wooly mammoths or signs of an early frost.

The pressures and confusions of American society contributed to this rich and even congested dimension of American religious life. In a new society characterized by an ever-growing influx and increasingly complex mixture of new people, investment in an objective realm of supernatural reality helped satisfy the thirst for meaning that social change and confusion provoked. Evidence of supernatural realities also helped crystallize and objectify the fears of outsiders that people accustomed to tighter communities felt in a new, expanding, and, in many ways, open society. Religious beliefs and ritual practices created communal solidarity, and distinguished one group from another. They helped maintain divisions, hierarchies, and order within groups, while at the same time reflecting social tensions between rich and poor, male and female, white and black. In many cases, religious beliefs and rituals reinforced the dominance of some people and the submission of others. But in many other cases, they challenged and subverted social conventions, at least temporarily, and provided a medium through which people reimagined and renegotiated their relationships with one another.

Religion was (and continues to be) important in America at least partly because of the various social functions it served and the many social needs and desires it proved able to express. These social aspects of religion also begin to explain why manifestations of supernatural reality figured so prominently in American religious life. Many people held up these manifestations as empirical evidence of a cosmic order that made sense of the social confusion around them and offered guidance through it.

Leaving Medieval Aspects of Puritan Thought Behind

The Salem trials of 1692 represent the emergence of a modern kind of religious sensibility characterized by appeals to empirical evidence of supernatural forces and presences. Testimony based on "spectral evidence" was not unheard of before the Salem trials, but in earlier episodes in New England as well as in Europe, spectral evidence did not figure as centrally or decisively as it did in the Salem trials, where judges relied on testimony that the specters—spirits or souls—of witches were tormenting their accusers, even as the people accused sat quietly in the courtroom. This is not to say that earlier witchcraft trials were fairer or less cruel. But they rested primarily on consensus about the maleficarum, or evil doings, of the accused and on the imposition of consensus by recognized authorities (and their agents who extracted confessions through torture) rather than on the religious imaginations of otherwise powerless accusing girls.

In contrast to the frighteningly democratic form of religious expression let loose in Salem, Puritanism in its more traditional form carried a medieval respect for intellectual order and hierarchy, and for the patriarchal authorities representing them. In law and government, earlier Puritans adhered to the medieval view of two kingdoms, both ordained by God, one for the purpose of guiding the external affairs of civilized humanity, the other for guiding souls to heaven. Controversies, often violent, took place over questions of how these two spheres of human life ought to be related, but Puritans agreed with their medieval predecessors in presuming church and state to be rooted in the will of God and not simply derived from social contracts people made with each other.

Puritans looked to the Bible for ideal types of religious reality in light of which the meaning of earthly events might be discerned. As the inspired word of God, the Bible set forth God's will for humankind through great typological events that revealed his will and defined his relationship with his chosen people. Puritans disagreed with one another about how complicated and ingenious one might be in interpreting these typologies and about how far one could go in connecting them to contemporary events. They felt serious concern, and even terrible anxiety, about how to read the meaning of their own lives in the typologies laid out in God's relationship with Israel. But they could not foresee the extent to which belief in the existence of divine realities would come to depend on reports of their empirical manifestations. Nor could they have seen how the shift in emphasis toward empirical manifestations would dislodge the stability of biblical types, stimulating a profusion of new and unusual experiences of divine revelation, along with new opportunities for religious skepticism.

The use of spectral evidence in the Salem trials not only foreshadowed the growing authority of popular religion and its emphasis on empirical manifestations of supernatural realities, but also exposed a connection between cultural instability and openness to supernatural manifestations. The pervasive unease enveloping Puritan culture seems to have contributed to the judges' willingness to accept the accusers' appeals to spectral evidence; many New Englanders worried about the direction New England was taking and the ill omens besieging the country. The imposition of royal authority on local government was a serious concern. Inflation and mercantile greed, destructive caterpillars and drought, and expressions of disrespect, blasphemy, and sacrilege seemed to increase daily. But reaction against the judges' collaboration in the hysteria about the devil's activity was fairly swift, and the judges came to regret the executions they had authorized. Even at the time, some onlookers expressed astonishment at the judges' admission of spectral evidence. In a letter written in October 1692, the Boston merchant, mathematician, and astronomer Thomas Brattle registered dismay that the Salem judges whom he considered "to be well-meaning men, should so far give ear to the Devil, as merely upon his authority to issue out their warrants, and apprehend people." Lamenting the popular will to introduce claims about the devil's intentions into the proceedings of a court of law, Brattle closed his letter expressing sorrow "that ages will not wear off that reproach and those stains which these things will leave behind them upon our land."[2]

Brattle was not alone in his chagrin over what counted as evidence in the Salem trials or in being disturbed at how emotion had clouded the judgment of "well-meaning men." The attractions of supernatural experience were hard to resist in a culture where established forms of religious authority were weak and where ordinary people were becoming increasingly accustomed to voicing their complaints, claims, and religious feelings.

Revivalism

Half a century later, the religious revivals in New England and the middle colonies raised concerns about another epidemic of religious madness besetting the country. One critic writing under the name Theophilus Misodaemon identified a "wonderful WANDERING SPIRIT" as the cause of the disturbances. Mocking the religious enthusiasm of the revivals, the writer explained that this troublesome spirit was none other than "*Belial*, taking a tour in disguise." This spirit had "often haunted our Borders" in the form of Indian sorcery and other forms of witchcraft and was now "raised" again, even more powerfully, according to Theophilus, "but whether in the Conclave at Rome or where else, is not so certain." Whichever "Necromancers" called it to life this time, many people were succumbing to it, the writer warned, believing they were listening to gospel preaching. A wolf in sheep's clothing, "This Spirit," Theophilus explained, was "seen, felt and heard by Thousands in America."

With an ear for similarities between the language of conversion and the language used to describe demonic possession, the writer slyly fused the two, taking the rhetoric of the religious enthusiasts as evidence of their demonic possession. But if he made fun of people caught up in the extreme feelings and radical ideas of the revivals, the writer was serious about exposing the enthusiasts' abandonment of reason. The behavior prompted by the Spirit behind the revivals was unchristian and immoral: " 'Tis raging and proud; censorious and ill-natur'd; deals much by Feelings and Impulses, in violent bodily Convulsions, and pretends to uncommon Discernments. When it possesses the Mob, which it delights to torture, they swell and shake like ... those possess'd with the Devil." In sum, Theophilus wrote, " 'Tis remarkable for one Quality, that all that it bewitches generally bid farewell to Reason, and are carried by it to the Land of Clouds and Darkness."[3]

Appearing in the *General Magazine* published by Benjamin Franklin (1706–1790), this cunning essay may have been authored by the good doctor himself. Franklin certainly would have enjoyed the ironies of describing new birth as a form of possession and tracing the cause of the enthusiasts' religious experience to their own fevered brains. But if Franklin poked fun at his fellow colonists' religious excitement, he was not an enemy of Christianity or what he considered true religion. Franklin was a product of Puritan culture, and never lost the desire for the perfection of moral virtue that culture inspired. He admired the oratorical brilliance of the great English revivalist, George Whitefield (1714–1770), whose preaching tour through the colonies in the early 1740s stimulated positive change in many people's lives. Franklin published Whitefield's journal in his newspaper. He also admired Whitefield's skill in raising money and supported Whitefield's fund drive for a tabernacle in Philadelphia. Despite the fact that Whitefield's prayers for Franklin's conversion never met their desired end, the doctor and the minister enjoyed each other's company and prized their mutual friendship. In one letter to Whitefield, Franklin suggested that the two of them work together to establish a colony of "Religious and Industrious

People." Ever the pragmatist, Franklin promoted the plan by telling his friend that such a commonwealth would be "a Security to the other Colonies; and Advantage to Britain, by Increasing her People, Territory, Strength and Commerce."[4]

Whitefield's success as an itinerant preacher in America involved a genius for self-promotion, a booming, mellifluous voice that drew large crowds and enabled him to preach outdoors, and theatrical skills developed as an aspiring actor in London before his conversion. He paced and gestured, knelt and wept, sang and prayed as he preached, conveying feelings of remorse and joy with his whole body. He acted out conversion like a player on a stage. Of course, he believed that God directed the process of conversion, and that he was only an agent of God who helped guide the elect on their path to salvation. Always a Calvinist, Whitefield believed that God predestined saints for salvation and unrepentant sinners to hell and that, as a preacher of the new birth, he was simply a facilitator of God's will who lit the way along the path of salvation that others might follow. This sense of being a tool in the hands of God, a creature animated by God's will, only enhanced the emotional intensity of his performances. One frequent listener, Cornelius Winter, reported that, "I hardly ever knew him go through a sermon without weeping." Drawn to these painful performances, Winter went on to say, "I could hardly bear such unreserved use of tears, and the scope he gave to his feelings." At times, "he exceedingly wept, stamped loudly and passionately, and was frequently so overcome, that, for a few seconds, you would suspect he never could recover."[5]

Whitefield made good use of fledgling newspapers in the American colonies, inviting people in one place to read about his successes elsewhere, anticipate his arrival in their town, and feel connected to a widespread movement of religious revival. Through his media blitz and preaching tours in Georgia, Carolina, Virginia, the middle colonies, and New England, he became America's first real celebrity, a symbol of evangelical unity that American Protestants from a variety of denominational, cultural, and ethnic traditions could identify with. Some historians argue that Whitefield's celebrity in America laid the groundwork for the American Revolution by bringing people in different colonies together around a religious icon that everyone became familiar with, even if not everyone was persuaded by his preaching. Whitefield's success in dramatizing his religious feelings and proclaiming them outdoors to anyone who would listen, outside the conventional boundaries of formal worship, made him into a living embodiment of religious liberty. Although he was not a proponent of American independence until the furor over the Stamp Act drew his attention to politics and won him over to the

American cause, his popularity helped shape the culture of liberty out of which the American Revolution emerged.[6]

American enthusiasm for political independence developed within a cultural context in which religious enthusiasm was commonplace and often associated with expectations of the renewal of Christian society. Although thoughtful deliberation, focused debate, and strategic compromise figured centrally in the construction of the new American nation, the religious revivals of the eighteenth century made public displays of enthusiasm acceptable and helped to create a cultural ethos that encouraged the breaking of restraints. In its revolutionary spirit and celebrations of "new birth," this cultural ethos carried forward important vestiges of the Puritans' vision of America as a holy commonwealth and New Israel.

George Whitefield played an important role in promoting Puritan sensibilities, while recasting them in a new evangelical mode that moved empirical manifestations of biblical revelation to the center of attention, allowing the Platonic distinction between type and antitype to fade. His dramatic style of preaching revived and reconfirmed the Puritan sense of connection between ordinary time and biblical revelation, but in a way that made biblical revelation seem to burst forth into ordinary time. At the same time, he helped colonists break through anxieties about failure and sin. Whitefield had a real feel for the bottomless darkness of the human heart, but he also knew a way out. Through deliberate "methods" of dramatizing the subjective experience of new birth, he laid a path through the anxieties so many people felt, and he urged them to get along. He set many Americans emotionally free—or at least gave them an emotional experience of what freedom might be like.

Jonathan Edwards (1703–1758)

In 1740, Whitefield met face to face with the American theologian Jonathan Edwards, who invited Whitefield to preach in his Northampton church. Having published *A Faithful Narrative of the Surprising Work of God* (1737), describing the revival he supervised in Northampton in 1735, Edwards was already well known among evangelicals in Scotland, England, and New England as a defender of religious revivals. When Whitefield preached in the Northampton pulpit in October of 1740, Edwards responded openly; Whitefield reported that "Dear Mr. Edwards wept during the whole Time of Exercise."[7] Edwards built on the momentum Whitefield generated, and within six weeks, the people of Northampton were in the throes of another revival. By springtime, Edwards wrote, "an Engagedness of Spirit about Things of Religion was

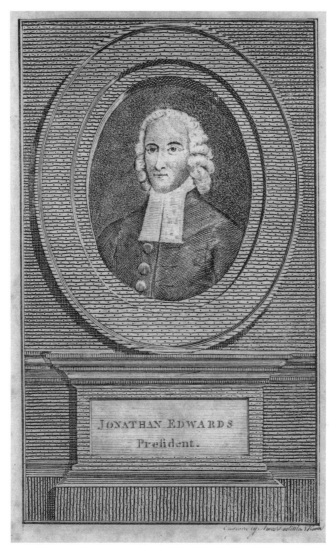

Jonathan Edwards. National Portrait Gallery, Smithsonian Institution, Washington, D.C./Art Resource, N.Y.

become very general amongst young People and Children, and religious Subjects almost wholly took up their Conversation when they were together." Unlike the earlier revival in Northampton in 1735, this one prompted exhibitions of feeling that included shouting, fainting, and bodily jerking: "Conversions were frequently wrought more sensibly and visibly," Edwards wrote, "the Impressions stronger, and more manifest by external Effects." And everyone seemed to grasp the "method" of moving through the conversion process: "the Progress of the Spirit of God in Conviction, from Step to Step, more apparent; and the Transition from one State to another more sensible and plain; so that it might in many instances, be as it were seen by By-standers."[8]

Edwards encouraged this overt delineation of the conversion process. In his famous sermon delivered in Enfield, Connecticut, in 1741, later published as "Sinners in the Hands of an Angry God," he raised the fears of his listeners to an excruciating degree, with the intention of defining and expediting the conversion process in those God elected to draw to himself. Not a pacer or arm waver like Whitefield (Edwards stood still and stared straight ahead as he preached) the sensational power of his words brought more than a few people to repentance. God had "many different unsearchable ways of taking wicked men out of the world and sending them to hell," Edwards preached; "the arrows of death fly unseen at noonday." With images of Indian attacks not far from mind, he warned that unconverted sinners were in imminent danger: "The bow of God's wrath is bent, and the arrow made ready on the string, and justice bends the arrow at your heart, and strains the bow, and it is nothing but the mere pleasure of God, and that of an angry God, without any promise or obligation at all, that keeps the arrow one moment from being made drunk with your blood."[9]

As the sheer force of this rhetoric suggests, Edwards had moved away from the formalist structure of earlier Puritan sermons toward a more expressive style, representing God less as an ideal above than as a gigantic force working through life on earth whose enormously powerful anger sinners with softened hearts could feel.[10] With Deuteronomy 32:35, "Their foot shall slide in due time," as his text for the Enfield sermon, Edwards warned sinners to be aware of the weight of sin dragging them down to hell, and the fire of divine wrath about to burst out to engulf them. Those who sat in the meetinghouse unconverted had a short and entirely undeserved moment of reprieve:

> The God that holds you over the pit of hell, much as one holds a spider, or some loathsome insect, over the fire, abhors you, and is dreadfully provoked; his wrath towards you burns like fire; he looks upon you as worthy of nothing else, but to be cast into the fire; he is of purer eyes than to bear to have you in his sight; you are ten thousand times so abominable in his eyes, as the most hateful and venomous serpent is in ours. You have offended him infinitely more than ever a stubborn rebel did his prince: and yet it is nothing but his hand that holds you from falling into the fire every moment: it is ascribed to

nothing else, that you did not go to hell the last night; that you was suffered to awake again in this world, after you closed your eyes to sleep; and there is no other reason to be given, why you have not dropped into hell since you arose in the morning, but that God's hand has held you up: there is no other reason to be given why you have not gone to hell, since you have sat here in the house of God, provoking his pure eyes by your sinful wicked manner of attending his solemn worship: yea, there is nothing else that is to be given as a reason why you do not this very moment drop down into hell.[11]

Edwards' contributions to American Protestant experience were multidimensional. At one level, he altered Calvinist theology by recasting it in an eighteenth-century idiom characterized by fascination with the sensations of emotional feeling. At another level, he enhanced the staying power of Calvinist theology, and its emphasis, not only on predestination, but also on the power of grace to enable moral virtue. At still another level, he developed the correlation between virtue and pleasure in a peculiar way, arguing that the fixation on self-interest characteristic of sin made human beings miserable, and kept them from true enjoyment of the beauty of creation. While he insisted on the absolute dichotomy between supernatural grace and natural self-interest and rejected every argument that human beings were naturally inclined to salvation, he simultaneously shifted the terms of theological debate toward the great American preoccupations with pleasure and happiness.

Perhaps most important, Edwards contributed to the evidentiary focus of Protestant experience and to the inclusion of supernatural activity as a crucial part of the empirical signage of Christian life. He resisted the tendency to incorporate grace within nature and did not want to confuse all of the emotional intensity associated with the revivals with saving grace; the reorientation of the Christian's will toward complete love of God might or might not be accompanied by weeping, trembling, falling, or shouting. Such manifestations might even be caused by Satan. Nevertheless, he believed that the revivals of the early 1740s were part of a Great Awakening of the Holy Spirit. He also believed there was empirical evidence of that happy transformation, such as humility, sweetness, and benevolence, along with delight in everything associated with God. That evidence could and should be used, Edwards believed, to determine who got to participate in the Lord's Supper, and who did not. Thus divine things could be openly manifest without being determined or limited by natural law.

Edwards' *Treatise on the Religious Affections* (1746) identified twelve things that might accompany religious conversion but should not be considered evidence of it, as well as twelve signs of true piety that always appeared in cases of genuine conversion. Edwards laid out these two sets of signs as criteria hopeful Christians might use in assembling evidence for or against the likelihood of their salvation. For example, eloquence and fluency in talking about religion were not an essential sign of conversion, although some converts were indeed eloquent and fluent. On the other hand, love toward God and all divine things derived from God was evidence of true holiness, and always present in true Christians.[12]

Method-ism

Edwards' understanding of sin as an underlying tendency to self-interest made him more cautious about raising passions than some of the other preachers who participated in the revivals of the eighteenth century. Whitefield, for example, was much less concerned than Edwards about the difference between saving grace and simulations of grace motivated by self-interest, and much more willing to dramatize the feelings associated with conversion as a model for others to follow. Edwards' wife Sarah registered her sensitivity to this difference between Whitefield and her husband, even as she affirmed the importance of firsthand experience in judging whether Whitefield's humility and inspiration were genuine or not. In a letter to her brother shortly after Whitefield's visit to Northampton, she endorsed the evangelist's preaching this way: "A prejudiced person, I know, might say that this is all theatrical artifice and display; but not so will anyone think who has seen and known him."[13]

As a student (and servant) at Oxford, Whitefield became involved in "method-ism" when he joined other young men of common birth in prayer and Bible-study sessions led by John and Charles Wesley. The term derived from the deliberate, methodical efforts these "Bible Moths" employed to infuse every aspect of their lives with piety. Beginning in the 1760s, Methodist "societies" sprang up in Baltimore, New York, and Philadelphia for the purpose of inculcating piety in everyday life. In 1769, John Wesley (1703–1791) began sending men he had trained as preachers and religious organizers to America. Beginning in the 1770s, his emissary Francis Asbury rode more than 200,000 miles on horseback in efforts to reach people in frontier areas to preach and encourage the development of Methodist societies.[14] Asbury's athletic efforts became the model for the American practice of "circuit riding," which involved sending out young preachers to make the rounds of a number of frontier settlements on a periodic basis.

In England, Methodism developed as the evangelical wing of the established (Anglican) Church of England; the Methodist Church was not founded as a separate entity until 1795, four years after John Wesley's death. Many of the Anglicans remaining in America after the Revolution became Episcopalians disconnected from the authority of the English crown, although still tied ecclesiastically to the Archbishop of Canterbury. Methodist piety and organization were more free ranging in the early republic of the United States than in England, where it was more closely tied to the English church, and Methodist preachers in America appealed as much to Congregationalist, Presbyterian, Baptist, and unchurched people, as they did to Anglicans and Episcopalians. The Methodist approach to religion was an enormous success in the new territories acquired by the new government of the United States, as well as in the growing cities and towns within many of the thirteen original colonies. In the early nineteenth century, the Methodist church became the biggest and fastest growing denomination in America, and contributed significantly to the authority of Protestant culture as a shaping force in American society.[15]

One of Methodism's great attractions was its emphasis on evidence of Christian life. Cultivating religious emotion and nurturing piety in everyday life, Methodism challenged tendencies to associate Christian virtue with wealth, intellectual attainment, or social class. At the same time, as an organizing force in the lives of individuals, Methodism was a source of social and emotional order for many, and an attraction to people seeking some control over the anarchy and brutality associated with both frontier and urban life. For this reason, historians of late-eighteenth- and early-nineteenth-century America have sometimes understood Methodism as an important agent in the formation of American middle-class culture.[16]

In their encouragement of religious experience as a natural and necessary part of human life, John Wesley and his followers moved much further away from Edwards than Whitefield did. Both Edwards and Whitefield were Calvinists who emphasized the omnipotent and uncompelled initiative of God's will and the helplessness of sinners in bringing about their own conversion. In contrast, Wesley affirmed the importance of free will and the sinner's ability to seek and find God. In this rejection of Calvinist determinism, Wesley encouraged people to take initiative for their own salvation and to pursue Christian virtue methodically. He also emphasized Christianity's compatibility with human nature and fulfillment of it. While Edwards stressed the conflict between human nature and divine grace and the need for grace to completely transform a person's human nature in order for that person to be saved, Wesley and his followers viewed religion and nature as being on more of a continuum than a crash course.

Fear of the Devil

Wesley was cautious about dreams, visions, and the terrors of hell, and encouraged a moderate and balanced approach to the emotions associated with conversion and piety. But his writing and preaching about the importance of palpable experiences of supernatural power helped to justify enthusiasm for extreme forms of religious feeling and concrete manifestations of supernatural power. Among such manifestations, the activities of Satan often commanded attention. Sometimes amorphous, and at other times a distinct personage, the devil functioned as a lightning rod for all kinds of fears and anxieties troubling Americans.

In an essay on popular religious life in eighteenth-century New England, historian Douglas Winiarski called attention to the fear of being possessed by the devil that one young woman described in her diary, arguing that her fear was not perceived as odd or eccentric but rather typical of evangelical life. Lydia Prout and her friends were upstanding young matrons who attended church regularly and reflected dutifully on sermons and scripture. Fears of vulnerability to Satan's dark, seductive forces tormented many people in their culture, including those who embodied respectability and normality. If Prout's diary is any indication, the preoccupations with sin so widespread in eighteenth-century New England cannot simply be explained as expressions of humility and desire to better glorify God. They often involved terrible anxieties about sinister forces and intrusive, anthropomorphized forms of supernatural power.[17]

Fear of the devil was not confined to New England. As historian Christine Leigh Heyrman found, the earliest forms of southern evangelicalism showed similar obsessions with the devil, who was known all too familiarly as "Old Horney," "Old Harry," and "Old Clooty." By 1755, travelers in the Blue Ridge Mountains knew of one steep and narrow place called "Devil's Three Jumps," named after sightings of the evil spirit. In the Carolina mountains, a ritual practice developed called "treeing the devil," which involved chasing the evil spirit up a tree and then pelting and taunting it, and trying to make it fall down. In the context of this sort of fascination with the devil as a sinister, almost physical person, Jesus acquired a kind of matching reality. As she readied herself for yet another "ingagement" with the devil and his life-threatening "assaults," one Methodist woman claimed that the dark lord would have to "tear me from the feet of Christ," where she would "die reather than yeald." In 1781, the Methodist layman George Lewis warned his twelve-year-old daughter that the "black man would catch her" if she lied. When the black man visited her in a dream early the next morning, Lewis heard the girl say in her sleep, "so you are come again you need not come, for I have got your Master. O Lord Jesus keep me from him."[18]

In the South, this devil-obsessed form of evangelicalism developed alongside the orderly devotions of Anglican worship. The Anglican establishment was deeply invested in social hierarchies defined by race, class, and property; participation in church reinforced those hierarchies. Wealthy families rented pews at the front of eighteenth-century Anglican churches, and took the occasion of Sunday worship to display clothes, horses, and manners appropriate to their station. African Americans, when permitted to attend, sat or stood at the back of the church or in the balcony. Sermons often extolled the rational order and hierarchies of civilized society, and the Christian duties and virtues involved in upholding social order. As the slaveholding planter culture grew in power, Anglican churches grew in number and size, enjoying the support of British and colonial governments at least until the American Revolution, as well as the support of the slaveholding elite.

During the eighteenth century, evangelical culture in the South stood out in contrast to Anglican formality—much less restrained or bound by respect for social order, gentility, and hierarchy, and much more flamboyant in expressing fear of the devil, the terrors of hell, and the need for "new birth." The planter culture supported by the Anglican church was hardly passive; the violence associated with its honor code and investment in slavery was pervasive. But the Anglican religion supporting this culture was orderly, formal, and elegant. Visions of the devil, and the religious dreaming, weeping, falling, and convulsing characteristic of southern evangelical culture were disruptive threats to the rational order of planter society and its claims to moral virtue.

The emotional effusiveness of evangelical culture was, in some respects, a leveling and democratizing influence. The commitment to "new birth" so characteristic of evangelical culture disrupted social hierarchies based on lineage, race, gender, and wealth. The meek were exalted and the mighty fallen not only in the prospect of the hereafter, but also in the here and now of collective religious worship. At the same time, however, the fears and frenzies associated with evangelical worship hardly provided a solid or stable basis for social reform. Indeed, the fear of the devil characteristic of evangelical culture worked against rational deliberation and strategic planning for social change. Emotional impulses might lead to visions of heaven and hopes of salvation, but just as likely to anxieties about demonic forces infesting the environment and lurking within one's own thoughts and desires. If evangelical culture encouraged individualism in religious experience, it also undermined self-confidence by encouraging people to experience the instability of their virtue and their vulnerability to hostile, unpredictable, and invisible forces.

Moderating Expressions of Natural Reason

American Protestants also constructed governments designed to mediate legal disputes between competing factions and interest groups. Most of the men who served as political representatives in the Continental Congress and early republic strove for compromise between factions and for arm's length distance from religious controversy. They represented a highly educated elite, and most of them belonged to established (primarily Anglican) churches. Along with their relatively composed demeanor and moderate approach to Christian belief and practice, they shared some of the same Protestant beliefs and sensibilities as their more evangelical compatriots.

The Virginian Thomas Jefferson (1743–1826) was one of the most liberal religious thinkers of his day in America, and yet he shared with even the most strident evangelicals of his time elements of political philosophy derived from Protestant thought. The opening sentences of his draft of the Declaration of Independence reflected characteristically Protestant themes of commitment to the importance of freedom of individual conscience, respect for the intentions and moral virtues of ordinary men, and resentment of arbitrary authority. Although the ideas expressed in the Declaration have subsequently come to be affirmed by people representing a variety of different religious traditions, to many living in the American colonies in 1776, the outgrowth of these ideas from Protestant principles would have been obvious:

> When, in the course of human events, it becomes necessary for one people to dissolve the political bands which have connected them with another, and to assume among the powers of the earth the separate and equal station to which the laws of nature and of nature's God entitle them, a decent respect to the opinions of mankind requires that they should declare the causes which impel them to the separation.
>
> We hold these truths to be self evident: that all men are created equal; that they are endowed by their Creator with inherent and inalienable rights; that among these are life, liberty, and the pursuit of happiness; that to secure these rights, governments are instituted among men, deriving their just powers from the consent of the governed; that

whenever any form of government becomes destructive of these ends, it is the right of the people to alter or abolish it, and to institute new government, laying its foundation on such principles, and organizing its powers in such form, as to them shall seem most likely to effect their safety and happiness.[19]

Theological doctrines regarding salvation through Christ make no appearance here. Nor are there any jabs against priestly authority that might make the declaration appear anti-Catholic. The tolerance for differing opinions and belief implicit in this foundational document make it accessible to people from many different traditions and backgrounds. At the same time, the sentiments expressed in the Declaration reflect the "self-evident" commitment to natural reason that developed among Protestant thinkers on both sides of the Atlantic during the eighteenth century, a commitment to self-government that developed in the context of American Protestant religious and political life, and an investment in the common man that derived, at least in part, from Protestant ideas about the priesthood of all believers. Last but not least, the "decent respect to the opinions of mankind," honored in the opening sentence of the Declaration, reflected an emphasis on reading and reasoned public discourse characteristic of the Reformed Protestant tradition associated with John Calvin and especially with the liberal development of that tradition through John Milton and John Locke.

Natural Reason's Discernment of Natural Order

While the irenic Protestant outlook of the founding fathers shaped the political and legal systems of the new republic, evangelicalism acquired new strength in the decades after the American Revolution when hostility to religious authority expressed during the French Revolution caused a reaction in America against any suggestion that the revelations of the Bible might not be empirically true. When Thomas Jefferson ran for president in 1800 and 1804, evangelicals railed against him, depicting his diplomatic relations with the French as evidence of his immorality and misrepresenting his disbelief in miracles as atheism.[20]

Jefferson emphasized the rational integrity of God's work as Creator and regarded belief in God's ongoing intervention in the world as unnecessary, even petty and superstitious. Along with Thomas Paine (1737–1809), the author of the revolutionary pamphlet "Common Sense," Jefferson denied the trinity, the divinity of Jesus, and the whole panoply of biblical miracles—except the original work of creation, which neither Jefferson nor Paine would have denigrated by calling a miracle. God was not a disrupter of nature, these deists felt sure, but the author of all its manifestations and laws. They revered Jesus not for his resurrection from the dead or sacramental atonement for human sin (neither of which they accepted), but for his ethical teachings and the moral perfection of his life, which they took as a model of how human beings should conduct themselves.

In important respects, deists and evangelical theologians shared the respect for natural reason and preoccupation with empirical evidence characteristic of Protestant culture on both sides of the Atlantic. In this regard, deists can be considered Protestant thinkers, too, even if their emphasis on the humanity of Jesus and rejection of his divinity disqualified them as theologians as eighteenth- and early-nineteenth-century Americans understood that term. Jefferson approached the Bible with a critical spirit and departed from evangelical thinkers in declining to take biblical depictions of God and his work at face value, believing that many biblical stories contained more fancy than fact. But his disdain for Catholic priestcraft and sacramental mysteriousness was just as strong as that of his orthodox opponents, and his underlying commitment to God as Creator, and to nature as God's design, just as clear.

Jefferson's reverence for God as the Creator of all life and matter developed into a lifelong fascination with the rational organization of nature and with the divisions and hierarchies he found manifest in the specimens and descriptions of natural phenomena he collected. His *Notes on the State of Virginia*, a compilation of observations and theories of geology, plant, and animal life, reveal an evidentiary temper grounded in religious belief not dissimilar from that of contemporary evangelicals. Thus Jefferson defended the categorical distinction between the elephant and the giant mammoth by observing that "nature seems to have drawn a belt of separation between these two tremendous animals," with the elephant assigned to hotter, southern climates and wooly mammoth to northern ones. "When the Creator has therefore separated their nature as far as the extent of the scale of animal life allowed to this planet would permit," Jefferson reasoned, "it seems perverse to declare it the same, from a partial resemblance of their tusks and bones." As to the question of the mammoth's possible extinction, Jefferson argued that the mammoth could not be extinct because the original design of creation was unalterable. The fact that no evidence of living mammoths had been found did not deter him from putting them on the list of North America animals: "It may be asked, why I insert the Mammoth, as if it still existed? I ask in return, why I should omit it, as if it did not exist? Such is the economy of nature," Jefferson reasoned, "that no instance can be produced of her having permitted any one race of her animals to become extinct; of her having formed any link in her great work so weak as to be broken." Primitive lore about the mammoth might be counted as support for this principle, but was hardly necessary to make the case: "To add to this, the traditional testimony of the Indians, that this animal still exists in the northern and western parts of America, would be adding the light of a taper to that of the meridian sun."[21]

Many evangelicals in Jefferson's day also believed in the rational order of nature and maintained lively interest in the evidences of God's creative hand in nature. While deists like Jefferson challenged the miraculous claims of the Bible as irrational fantasies that invited dishonesty and tainted Christianity with superstition, more orthodox religious thinkers defended the miracles described in the Bible as entirely reasonable, given the power and oversight of an almighty God. The miracles recounted in the Bible transcended the laws of nature, they believed, but not in a way that denigrated those laws, which, after all, God had created.

Among the writings on nature frequently cited by American evangelicals was Joseph Butler's *Analogy of Religion...to the Constitution and Course of Nature*, first published in London and New York in 1736 and remaining in print through the nineteenth century. Viewing Protestant doctrine through the prism of empirical reason and assumptions about the rational organization of God's work in nature, Butler argued that spiritual questions could be answered by finding analogies for spiritual life in nature. In his best-known example of this principle, Butler claimed that the evidences of life's continuity through natural stages of transformation—worms changing into flies and birds bursting out of their shells—constituted a good case for personal immortality. While admitting that no conclusive evidence for personal immortality existed, he nevertheless maintained that analogies in nature made disbelief in immortality irrational.

American evangelicals affirmed the importance of empirical investigation and common sense, but also held the line against their sufficiency. Unaided by biblical revelation, natural reason and human curiosity fell short of the full truth, and all too easily into sin and rebellion against God. Nineteenth-century evangelicals tended to view deists like Jefferson and Paine as religious enemies who slighted revelation, despite the fact that they shared the evidentiary temper and respect for gospel teaching characteristic of Protestant culture.

The Eclecticism of Evangelical Culture

Evangelical culture drew its vitality from several sources and from the interplay of a variety of different forms of religious thought and practice. Puritan and Methodist influences mixed with Scotch-Irish Presbyterianism and with various forms of Dutch and German pietism. Native American and African elements played important roles in the development of evangelical culture, with African Americans contributing especially to the vibrancy of evangelical worship and to the expansion of Protestant religious practice to incorporate elements derived from Africa and African American experience. In the middle colonies, where burgeoning cities hosted immigrants from many places, the multi-ethnic hybridity of evangelicalism was especially robust. In the southern colonies, the effusive, devil-haunted eclecticism of evangelical culture vied with, and eventually blended with, the religion of honor, race consciousness, and gender differentiation derived from planter culture.

Some immigrants to the middle and southern colonies came from New England, where rocky, overworked soil, divided with each generation into smaller parcels, frustrated many young farmers. Missionaries from New England's Separatist Baptist churches moved through Pennsylvania into the Shenandoah Valley in the 1740s, into the Carolinas and Georgia in the next decades, and from there into Kentucky and Tennessee. Baptist populations grew steadily in both the settled and frontier areas of Anglo-America, as did Methodists. English Methodists immigrated in significant numbers to the middle and southern colonies, along with lesser numbers of Moravian, Mennonite, and other German Protestants whose emphasis on the emotional aspects of religion derived from both Lutheran and Reformed traditions. But the largest and most influential group of evangelical Protestants in the middle and southern colonies during the eighteenth and early nineteenth centuries was Scotch-Irish.

Scottish Evangelicalism

Most of the Scots who immigrated to North America from Ireland and Scotland in the eighteenth century were Presbyterian. Religious descendants of the Scottish Reformer John Knox (1513?–1572), Presbyterians held ideas about the sovereignty of God and the nature and importance of Christian government similar to those of John Calvin and his religious descendants in England and New England. Presbyterians developed a distinctive system of church governance that enabled religious uniformity through committee oversight rather than through recourse to bishops, resented by reformers in both England and Scotland as arbitrary over-lords unsanctioned by biblical authority. In the 1740s, Scottish Presbyterians, some of whom had been living in and around Ulster in Ireland, began moving to America in large numbers, first to New York and New Jersey and then to Virginia.

By the time of the American Revolution, Presbyterians were the second largest group of Protestants in North America, outnumbered only by Congregationalists centered in New England. Bitter disputes over the necessity of "new birth" and its relationship to Presbyterian doctrine divided them. The evangelical wing of Scotch Presbyterians played a major role in promoting religious revivals, while those who identified with less exuberant and more traditional forms of Presbyterian practice were skeptical of revivals and other forms of religious enthusiasm.

In the middle colonies, the Presbyterian Tennent family, especially William (1673?–1746) and his son Gilbert (1703–1764) figured importantly in the revivals of the 1730s and 1740s, gathering considerable attention through their insistence on "new birth" as a qualification for ministry. Gilbert's sermon, "The Danger of an Unconverted Ministry," delivered in Pennsylvania in 1740, had a polarizing effect on Congregationalists as well as Presbyterians, setting "New Light" Congregationalists and "New Side" Presbyterians against their "Old Light" and "Old Side" rivals. Gilbert Tennent condemned preachers who did not take the experience of new birth as the point of departure for their sermons, claiming that "Pharisee-Teachers, having no Experience of a special Work of the Holy Ghost, upon their own Souls, are therefore neither inclined to, nor fitted for, Discoursing, frequently, clearly, and pathetically, upon such important Subjects." With "the Craft of Foxes" and "the Cruelty of Wolves," Tennent exclaimed, unconverted ministers "do but strengthen Men's carnal Security, by their soft, selfish cowardly Discourses." Hypocrites in the face of sin, unable to awaken listeners to the prospect of hell before them, "[t]hey have not the Courage, or Honesty, to thrust the Nail of Terror into Sleeping Souls."[22]

While "Old Side" Presbyterians criticized him for creating religious dissension, and even some proponents of evangelical Christianity were taken aback by his combative style, Tennent's appeal to the necessity of "new birth" fell on fertile ground and contributed to the momentum of what supporters of the revivals of the early 1740s called "The Great Awakening." In many cases, their evangelical clamor for "new birth" involved a radical, antiestablishment impulse that challenged Christianity's captivity by men of wealth, formal education, and political power. This radical religious impulse contributed to the revolutionary ethos of the late eighteenth century. It also represented utopian tendencies that had appeared periodically in the history of Christianity, and still continue to appear—tendencies that can be traced to the radical ethic expressed in gospel accounts of the sayings of Jesus and to the later reform movements that surfaced periodically in Christian history. Moral indignation against established religious institutions and their complicity in manipulating the poor to shore up the wealth and status of ruling elites fueled enthusiasm for "new birth" in the eighteenth century as it had fueled reformation movements and animosity to Catholic prelates in the sixteenth. Religious enthusiasm for justice not only spilled into political demands for independence in the 1760s and 1770s, but also carried within it visions of an ideal society ruled by the pure of heart.

Intense personal experiences of the immediacy of divine reality, often nurtured and directed through revivalism, made this radical, utopian aspect of Christianity compelling. Experiences of the power and presence of God, Christ, and the Holy Spirit contributed to many conversions, and to Christianity's appeal to people with less access than others to ordinary forms of social power. Enthusiasm for empirical evidence helped fuel the demand for immediate experiences of divine things, contributing to the construction of a popular religious culture that celebrated immediate personal experience of supernatural realities as an empirical and expected part of life.

Sacraments celebrating the vitality of God and his presence in the lives of believers encouraged these kinds of immediate experience, as did sermons on the dangers of sin and need for "new birth." As historian Leigh Eric Schmidt showed, Scottish Presbyterians introduced the tradition of celebrating communion outdoors during the "sacramental season" of summer and early fall, a tradition popular in Scotland and among Scots settled in Ireland. In America, these outdoor gatherings lasted days and even weeks, and participants often traveled some distance to set up camp on the edge of the groves cleared for religious work. Preaching, Bible study, and catechetical teaching prepared participants for the Lord's Supper, warning them of the dangers of coming to the Lord's Table in bad faith or without being fully prepared through prior experience of new birth. At the culminating hour, the faithful gathered at long tables set out in the grove. In these inviting situations, many people heard, saw, felt, and tasted divine realities, realities made all the more real and objective by being shared with others hearing the same sermon, envisioning the same image of heaven, and partaking in the same sacramental meal.

The famous Kentucky revivalist James McGready (1758?–1817) was ambivalent about how far participants might go in actually seeing angels, saints in heaven, or Jesus Christ himself. In one sermon delivered in the early years of the nineteenth century, he warned listeners against "a deception of the Devil" that led people to imagine they could actually see "something in the form of a man bleeding and dying on a cross," and he rejected some testimonies in which people claimed to "have seen his bloody robe—the wound in his side—and the blood running in streams." But in the same sermon, McGready assured his listeners that they might experience what he seemed to have just condemned. They might encounter Christ "in the lonely wood" or "at his table," or even encounter him appearing before them as he "shows them his pierced hands and feet, and permits them to look into his bleeding side."[23]

In a sermon on the similarities between communion and the "heavenly meeting" in New Jerusalem, McGready explained that

> when our Lord's Table is spread in the wilderness, and he holds communion with his saints, I think it is rational and scriptural to suppose that the angels are hovering over the table and the assembly, rejoicing with Christ over the dear bought purchase of his blood, and waiting to bear joyful tidings to the heavenly mansions. And while they are sitting at this table, and communing with their Lord, it is more than probable, that some of their christian friends and brethren, who once sat with them at the same table, and under the same sermons—with whom they spent many happy days and nights before, but now have left the world and gone home to the church triumphant above; I say it is more than probable, that some of these will be mingling with the angelic band around the *"heirs of salvation."*[24]

African American Influences

In some ways similar to Native Americans, African Americans entered evangelical culture both as images in the minds of Euro-Americans and as real participants. Images of African Americans haunted Euro-American dreams and visions, contributing to Euro-American uneasiness about the evil lurking around, much as images of Native Americans also represented Euro-American ideas about evil. But while fears of Native Americans fueled images of hell as a place of surprise attacks, fiery tortures, and flesh-tearing, limb-ripping, bloodthirsty demons, fears of African Americans fed more directly into Euro-American feelings of guilt. Of course, Euro-American colonists also had reason to feel guilty about their treatment of Indians—indeed, their images of hell as a savage camp where people were tortured with fire may reflect the brutality of their attacks on Indians as much as the brutality of Indian attacks on them. Still, in the short run, Euro-American fear of being overpowered by Indians was well founded. By contrast, Africans had been delivered to America in chains, and Euro-Americans were the captors, never the captives of Africans. As objects of fear in the minds of Euro-Americans who condoned and participated in their captivity, Africans were kept subdued and subordinate, not only to prevent their taking revenge, but also to keep the injustice of the system hidden. The mental effort to justify slavery was considerable, especially after 1776, given the investment in liberty and natural rights that Americans expressed so forcefully in their Declaration of Independence.

The religious behavior of African Americans only added to Anglo uneasiness about the religious implications of African American presences. Torn from societies organized around ancestral traditions, Africans brought beliefs, practices, and memories associated with indigenous tribal religions and with West African Islam to America, recasting these traditions in new cultural contexts often dominated by slavery and Protestant Christianity. Although Africans came to North America from a variety of different tribal backgrounds, each with specific rites and beliefs, they also shared common religious characteristics that came to new expression as they forged new religious bonds with one another, often in response to evangelicalism. Belief in a high God, respect for the dead, spirit possession, circle dances, and call-and-response prayer and song were some of the common features of African religious tradition that helped unite Africans in America, empower their experiences of Christianity, and enable their contributions to it.

These African forms of worship enhanced the sensationalism of evangelical experience in America. Thanks in part to the inspiration of African American music, singing became increasingly important within evangelicalism as a means of praising God and making his presence felt. Part of Protestant worship in America since the Puritans, singing increased in importance as a facilitator of religious experience as a result of at least two important influences, Wesleyan hymnody and African American song. Hymns by Charles Wesley and other evangelical writers guided people through the emotional turns of repentance, new birth, and sanctification. African American gospel singing expressed, even more directly, the liberating power of grace.

African practices of spirit possession also added to the realism and emotional intensity of gospel singing, conversion, and sanctification. Practices of spirit possession derived from Africa and African American experience dovetailed with Methodist affirmations of the body as the natural site of grace, much as the richness of African American gospel singing complemented the profusion of new Methodist hymns. In both singing and religious experience, African, Anglo, and European behaviors came together in America, contributing to the emotional power and richness of evangelical experience.[25]

The presence of African Americans as virtuosos of evangelical worship and experience caused white evangelicals concern. As Christine Heyrman pointed out, the possibility that "new birth" had different meaning for blacks troubled whites: "Could it be that when black worshippers wept and screamed, collapsed and sank into trancelike states, that such behavior meant something other to them than what it did to white evangelicals?" In other words, "Did those African Americans who seemed so fluent in the language of Canaan colonize its cadences to express spiritual truths of their own devising?"[26] In at least two ways, African Americans did express evangelical Christianity differently—by fusing it with aspects of African religious tradition and by interpreting it as a means to liberation from slavery and racial discrimination.

Conflict over slavery permeated Protestant life in nineteenth-century America. In the decades leading to Civil War, advocates and opponents of slavery both claimed that the Bible justified their views. Advocates pointed to numerous passages that mentioned slavery without condemning it, while opponents held up passages that linked salvation to freedom. Both advocates and opponents of slavery used the Bible to argue that God was on their side. As historian Mark Noll showed, religious dispute over God's will with respect to slavery played a determining role in the bloody conflict between North and South.[27]

The ambiguous relationship between skin color and spiritual purity played into debates about the relationship between slavery and biblical rule. Many Euro-Americans, especially in the South, enlisted biblical passages to support a racial identity that was morally superior to that of Africans. In addition, by separating themselves from African Americans for the purposes of Christian worship, whites imputed a divine sanction to racial categories that justified African American subjugation. Such discrimination led African American Baptists and Methodists to form their own churches, and to a thoroughgoing separation of white and black religious institutions that persists in some religious communities in the United States to this day. On the other hand, the association of whiteness with sanctity and moral purity could cut the other way to undermine racial division and hierarchy. References to whiteness in descriptions of the cleansing purity of divine grace or the shining brightness of saints in heaven suggested that the real division between people was not racial but rather moral and spiritual and that, with respect to salvation, blacks had better prospects than many whites.

New Religious Movements

Evangelical religion became extremely concrete during the early nineteenth century, with millennial imagery crossing back and forth among various groups, amplifying expectations of the end times in new, startling ways. These expectations reached a peak in the early 1840s, when men and women representing a variety of different evangelical groups found themselves swayed by predictions made by the Baptist preacher William Miller (1782–1849) that the end of the world was at hand. Although ridiculed by many, these fervent evangelicals and their apocalyptic predictions inspired thousands of Americans to prepare to meet their maker in the most literal way. As the final date for the end arrived in 1844, at least a few white-robed believers stood ready and waiting atop hills or close to church steeples.[28]

A profusion of new religious movements came to expression through American evangelicalism in the nineteenth century as the result of interactions with other religious traditions. While not all participants in these new movements considered themselves to be Christian, they borrowed from evangelical beliefs and practices, and often had firsthand experience of Methodist, Baptist, or Presbyterian practices. In addition to appropriating evangelical ideas about history and absorbing evangelical fascination with empirical evidence of supernatural powers revealing themselves through history, Native religious traditions stamped some of these new religious movements in the most foundational way.

Native American Prophet Movements

In the 1760s, the Delaware Indian prophet Neolin sold religious maps drawn on deerskin that depicted long and short routes Indians could take to heaven. As a Native alternative to the Bibles printed and studied by Congregationalists, Baptists, Anglicans, Quakers, and Presbyterians, Neolin's maps reflected the influence of evangelical preaching and missionary outreach, including a strict code of moral behavior and emphasis on the importance of getting to heaven, with instructions how to get there. Neolin's claim to be a prophet derived in part from Protestant preaching about biblical prophets, and his travels from place to place, reaching out to people with a fresh, compelling, and helpful religious message emulated the behavior of Protestant missionaries, offering Native Americans an alternative to Protestant conversion. Merging biblical stories with Native American beliefs about spiritual life and practice, Neolin described climbing a mountain into the spirit world where he had received, like Moses, instructions from the Creator. He also described his tour of the spirit world where, at a fork in the road, the narrow path to heaven split off from the wider one to hell.

In the early 1800s, the Seneca prophet Handsome Lake founded a new religious movement among the Iroquois of upstate New York that drew from Neolin's gospel and from the teachings of Quaker missionaries residing in the area, as well as from his own tribal traditions. In his visions, Handsome Lake received detailed instructions from the Creator about ritual practices that should be revived and rules for moral behavior that should be followed. In a vision indicative of Catholic influence among the Iroquois and teachings about purgatory, Handsome Lake's tour of the spirit world took him to the house of punishment where Indians who had succumbed to drink and other European vices underwent tortures appropriate to their sins—drunkards were forced to drink molten lead, gamblers were forced to play with red hot cards, and so on. Another path took him to a realm of abundance, with fresh springs and happy people. On his way to this paradise, Handsome Lake met Jesus, who encouraged him on his way as an equal whose role as the Creator's spokesman to Native people was analogous to Jesus' role as the Creator's spokesman to people of European descent.[29]

While both these new religious movements reflect the influence of biblical stories and preaching about morality and salvation, participants did not identify themselves as Christian. In a world intruded upon by Euro-American Christians, Native prophets led movements of resistance to the hell-fearing, salvation-thirsting people swarming over traditional Indian homelands and hunting territories. If the presence of biblical symbols in the visions of Native prophets reflected the growing dominance of evangelical culture in the minds of Native peoples as well as the eclipse of traditional lifeways, their new religious movements often involved economic, military, and religious opposition to Euro-American expansion. Neolin's preaching against dependence on Euro-American trade helped galvanize support for the Indian rebellion against British forces led by the Ottawa Chief Pontiac in 1763. After the Iroquois had been crushed economically and militarily, Handsome Lake warned against the dangers of Westernization and called for the preservation of Iroquois culture in a world increasingly dominated by Americans.

The significance of Native religious movements as vehicles of resistance against American power is even more evident in the pan-Indian confederacy led by the Shawnee warrior Tecumseh and his brother, the prophet Tenskwatawa, prior to the War of 1812. Identifying the dangerous underwater serpent in the Shawnee creation story with white men coming onto Indian land from the ocean bringing chaos and destruction, Tecumseh traveled through Native communities in the eastern woodlands, urging a united effort to push the monster back into the sea. In conceptualizing Indian resistance against white predators as a cosmic battle between good and evil, Tecumseh appropriated some of the apocalyptic thinking current among evangelical Protestants who imagined that each new crisis in their own history brought them closer to the cosmic battle between Satan and Christ that would usher in a new age. Anticipation mounted when reports went out that Tenskwatawa had accurately predicted and perhaps had caused a solar eclipse. When a series of earthquakes rattled across the country in 1811 and 1812, rumors circulated that Tecumseh started at least one of the quakes by stamping his foot.

Tenskwatawa and Tecumseh reversed the roles of Indians and whites with respect to God and the devil and turned apocalyptic expectations against the whites who introduced them. The Muskogee people in Georgia and what later became Alabama acted similarly, partly through the influence of the Shawnee brothers. In the Redstick Rebellion of 1812–1814, Muskogee warriors set out to destroy the whole world associated with white culture, including their own cattle, which they had acquired as a part of a process of assimilating to white culture. Historian Joel Martin estimated that, at its peak, the number of believers in the Redstick movement ran as high as 9,000.

Martin pointed out the resemblance between the Redstick Rebellion and the Muskogee rite of initiation into manhood, arguing that the Rebellion can be understood as an expression of traditional Native ritual.[30] But Muskogee leaders also recast older tribal practices of purification and expulsion of evil, ritual destruction of childhood security, and attainment of virile power in the context of new traumas of colonization, and through exposure to biblical stories disseminated by evangelicals. The Redsticks understood themselves to be engaged in a cosmic battle between good and evil that they hoped would usher in a new age and restore their people to the paradise they had once enjoyed. The end-of-time behavior manifest in the Redstick Rebellion reflected the enormous frustration resulting from the erosion of traditional lifeways; it also reflected acquaintance with biblical narratives and the influence of evangelical demands for real-time, empirical manifestations of biblical revelation.

At the same time that prophet movements swept through Iroquois, Shawnee, Muskogee, and other Native American groups in the early decades of the nineteenth century, other new religious movements sprang up from within Anglo-Protestant culture. While participants in the new Indian religions resisted American evangelical culture even as they absorbed some of its characteristics, Shakers, Mormons, and other religious perfectionists pushed the envelope from the inside. Drawing most of their members from the ranks of Anglo-American immigrants and their descendants, Shakers and Mormons developed beliefs and practices that more mainstream evangelicals found extreme, bizarre, and sometimes dangerous.

Shakers

Families of the United Society of Believers, commonly known as Shakers, traced their origin to Ann Lee (1742–1784), a Christian visionary from Manchester, England, who immigrated with a few followers to upstate New York in the late 1770s. Shaker communities grew in New York, Massachusetts, Connecticut, New Hampshire, Maine, Ohio, Kentucky, and Indiana in the early decades of the nineteenth century, with populations ranging from 100 to 600 in each of sixteen villages by the 1820s. Shakers revered Ann Lee as the female incarnation of Christ and structured their communal life around her belief that sexual intercourse should be given up as the epitome of original sin. Shaker commitment to the "gospel of Christ's second appearance" came to expression in a highly regulated form of communal family life. Believers ceded all their worldly possessions to the Society and endeavored to live as participants in a new world order. The Society's Millennial Laws, first codified in 1821, prohibited "all private union between the two sexes" and required Shaker families to make arrangements preventing contact between males and females, including separate staircases, separate seating, separate confession, and separate work. Shakers brought order to every aspect of daily life, treating labor as a form of worship, and worship as a form of labor that brought spiritual things to immediate reality. Industry, thrift, and invention were spiritual virtues; songs, dances, marches, prophecies, healings, and visions were labors that manifest the spiritual realm through the Shaker community.[31]

In the late 1830s and early 1840s, preoccupation with messages and signs from the spirit world increased in all the Shaker villages and even disrupted the order of regular work in some communities. In this so-called Era of Manifestations, ecstatic trances and spiritual audiences with Mother Ann were common. Believers marched up hills to "mountain feasts" where they gathered around spiritual fountains (invisible to the natural eye) to sing, dance, eat manna, get drunk with heavenly wine, and commune with spirits representing a variety of ethnic groups and historic periods.[32] Numerous accounts circulated of spirits possessing Believers and using Believers as "Instruments." In 1842, spirits identified as Native Americans took over Believers in a number of villages. In one song "translated" into English, the spirit of Chief Contoocook proclaimed

Shakers near Lebanon. Courtesy of the Library of Congress.

through his Instrument, "Me love to ramble round as me feel as me choose." The loud, barbaric behavior of Believers possessed by Indian spirits alarmed older Shakers used to more orderly expressions of millennial harmony.

Strange as these practices seemed to other Americans, some of whom attended Shaker performances as curious tourists, the United Society of Believers was part of the continuum of Protestant evangelicalism. In fact, the visions, trances, jerking, and love feasting that evangelical Presbyterians, Methodists, Baptists, Disciples, and Christians engaged in during camp meetings at the end of the eighteenth and beginning of the nineteenth centuries were similar to the spiritual labors of Shaker practice, and Shakers often recruited new members during camp meetings from these more mainstream groups. Shakers stood out from other evangelical groups because of their tight communal order, which brought all aspects of domestic life into a utopian plan, and because of their equation of sex with sin and effort to live without both. But in their commitment to biblical principles and desire to make the divine empirically manifest, the Shakers had much in common with other evangelicals.

Like other evangelicals, the Shakers combined avid enthusiasm for supernatural things with practical science, ingenuity, and close attention to the mechanics of how things operated. As inventors of packaged spices, capsule pills, and the horse-powered washing machine (among other things), Shakers had a flair for practical engineering and economic organization that exemplified the Protestant work ethic. In their heyday in the mid-nineteenth century, the Shakers were as creative in business and industry as they were in religion. And like many of their more conventional fellow citizens, Shakers approached supernatural things with much the same attentiveness to evidence with which they approached material forms of reality.

Mormons

Much the same can be said about the Church of Jesus Christ, later named Church of Jesus Christ of Latter-day Saints, and commonly known as the Mormons. This important new religious group emerged during the 1820s in upstate New York, a region so susceptible to the fires of revivalism in the 1820s and 1830s that it was nicknamed the "Burned Over District." Like the Shakers, the Mormons pushed the envelope of Protestant evangelicalism from the inside to create new and total forms of religious community designed to establish a New Jerusalem.

The founder of the new religion, Joseph Smith Jr. (1805–1844), dabbled in occult practices as a teenager and found occasional employment as a treasure hunter who claimed spiritual powers that enabled him to see underground. He was well versed in the beliefs and practices of Free Masonry, a popular fraternal organization that traced its roots to the builders of ancient pyramids and to lore about ancient Near Eastern beliefs concerning the all-seeing eye of God and the inspired eyes of craftsmen throughout history who perceived nature's design. Smith was also familiar with the array of different evangelical groups competing for converts in New York and with their various theological opinions and special practices. In an early vision in 1820 when he was only fourteen, God and Christ appeared to Smith to warn him not to join any of these denominations. Three years later, Moroni (son of Mormon) visited Smith in angelic form with the news that the ultimate empirical evidence of the authority of his utterances—golden tablets inscribed with the history of Moroni's people—were buried nearby in Cumorah Hill. Moroni explained that these tablets revealed the relationship between Moroni's people, the Nephites, and ancient Hebrews who sailed to America around the time of the destruction of the first temple in Jerusalem in 597 BCE. In America these people had divided into two rival groups, the Lamanites, whose descendants were the Native Americans of Smith's day, and the Nephites, whose last survivor was Moroni.

Four years later in 1827, Smith found the tablets through a vision and proceeded to translate the "Reformed Egyptian" writing on them with the help of two seeing stones, the Urim and Thummim, similar to stones, mentioned in the Bible, used by ancient Hebrew priests in casting lots to determine God's will. In 1830, Smith published his translation of the tablets as *The Book of Mormon*, explaining that the tablets themselves had disappeared from the earth after his translation. The same year, he founded a new church, established a priesthood of male believers whose titles and practices derived from Masonic rites and biblical accounts of Hebrew priesthood, and a new form of baptism that initiated believers into a covenant of eternal life.

In some respects similar to Shakers and new religions among Native Americans, the new Church of Jesus Christ involved communal practices designed to support the transformation of the world as it was emerging through a prophet's revelations. Members in all these groups believed that the millennial age was coming about through their communities and that the successful establishment of their communities carried enormous importance for the future of the world. The Mormons differed from other groups in their understanding of sex and marriage as the means by which pre-existent souls acquired bodies, families, and opportunities to win great kingdoms in heaven.

Mormons also differed in attempting to restore the Hebrew religion as it was practiced by Jesus and his followers. Smith and his followers built temples modeled on the ancient temple of Israel in Jerusalem and attempted to restore rituals they believed had been practiced by ancient Hebrew followers of Jesus prior to the destruction of the Temple in 70 CE. Like other evangelicals in the early nineteenth century, Mormons believed that, after the apostolic age passed, the redemption promised by Jesus had been obscured and postponed due to the corrupt influence of the Catholic Church. Like other evangelicals, they believed in new manifestations of divine revelation in their own day and in the compatibility between these manifestations and natural reason, common sense, and practical science. The Mormons simply went further and differently than others in their efforts to restore the practices of early Christianity, forge connections between the era of Christ's first appearance and their own time, and resume history's progress toward the millennium.

Although Mormons were enormously successful in promoting and institutionalizing their beliefs and practices, their efforts to establish a

New Israel in America also met with great hostility, especially in the early decades of the religion's growth. Smith and his followers relocated in Kirtland, Ohio, in the early 1830s, where they attracted followers of Thomas Campbell and his son Alexander (1788–1866), Scotch-Irish leaders of the Disciples of Christ who broke off from the Presbyterian Church in their efforts to restore primitive Christianity. Following an unsuccessful attempt to institute a church-controlled form of communism in Kirtland, to the relief of Kirtland's non-Mormon population, Smith and his followers headed further west to Missouri, where they thought the original spot of the Garden of Eden might have existed. When things did not work out in Missouri, where they thoroughly alienated the local population by attempting to establish a theocracy, the Saints traveled back to Illinois where they obtained a state charter allowing them to rename the small city of Commerce as Nauvoo, meaning "beautiful plantation" in the special version of Hebrew known only to Mormons. Fears of Mormon dictatorship inspired considerable resentment among nonbelievers living in Nauvoo. Awaiting trial in jail after destroying the presses of a rival newspaper, Smith was seized by a mob and killed.

The charismatic organizer Brigham Young (1801–1877) took over the main body of the church, whose size was increasing as a result of Mormon missionaries in Britain and Scandinavia sending converts to America. Beginning in 1846, Young led his followers across the prairies to the territory of Utah, where they established a government based on religious principle and leadership. They also established an extensive system of irrigation and economic cooperation that literally made the desert bloom. In this success, the Mormons brought aspects of the Protestant work ethic shared by many Americans to fruition, even as they harbored beliefs about sex, marriage, heaven, and ancient history that set them apart as a peculiar group. In Utah, they went considerable distance in realizing the long-standing Protestant dream of a holy commonwealth, a New Jerusalem with a new covenant as God's chosen people. The close connection between their practical ingenuity and economic success on one hand and their commitment to the establishment of a millennial kingdom on the other exemplified the investment in empirical manifestations of divine things that inspired many evangelicals in eighteenth- and nineteenth-century America.[33]

Voluntarism

While nineteenth-century Mormons combined belief in the importance of freedom of the will with belief in the union of church and state, most evangelicals endorsed the separation of church and state as a means of promoting voluntary religious activism. Many evangelicals believed that Christianity was better off having to depend on willing volunteers than on religious institutions established by the state. Arguments to this effect had figured importantly in the establishment of religious freedom and separation of church and state in the new American republic. The principal author of the First Amendment to the U.S. Constitution, James Madison, referred to the benefits of religious voluntarism in his brief for religious freedom in Virginia, writing that "During almost fifteen centuries has the legal establishment of Christianity been on trial." The verdict of this trial was clear: "More or less in all places, pride and indolence in the Clergy, ignorance and servility in the laity, and in both, superstition, bigotry and persecution." Like many other Protestants of his day, Madison advocated the "restoration" of Christianity to its "primitive state in which its Teachers depended on the voluntary rewards of their flocks."[34]

Some Protestants took longer than others to get with the voluntarist program. In Massachusetts, the Congregational Church did not loose its privileged government support until 1833, after a bitter battle over church properties left a good deal of Congregational wealth in the hands of liberal Unitarians. Fifteen years earlier, when the Congregationalist Church became disestablished in Connecticut, its leader, Lyman Beecher (1775–1863), was initially disconsolate. "The injury done to the cause of Christ, as we then supposed, was irreparable." Before long, however, he realized he had misread the situation: "For several days I suffered what no tongue can tell *for the best thing that ever happened to the State of Connecticut*." Although "they say ministers have lost their influence; the fact is," Beecher asserted, "they have gained. By voluntary efforts, societies, missions, and revivals, they exert a deeper influence than ever they could by queues, and shoe-buckles, and cocked hats, and gold-headed canes," symbols of an elite clergy who held themselves over and above the people.[35]

Beecher's embrace of voluntarism reflected his endorsement of a process of democratization that defined Christianity, to a considerable extent, in terms of lay activism. This endorsement of lay activism as an effective organizing principle and stimulus for the development of religious societies and the promotion of religious revivals coincided with increasing enthusiasm for voluntarism as a theological principle that explained the nature of conversion. "All obedience to God is voluntary," wrote Jonathan Edwards' grandson Timothy Dwight (1752–1817), "Nothing is, or can be, demanded by him, which is not in its nature voluntary."[36] Dwight's emphasis on the Christian's voluntary obedience to God struck a different chord than his grandfather's rejection of free

SINGING UP A CROWD AT THE OLD ADOBE ON THE PLAZA.

Singing up a Crowd, Seven Years Street Preaching. From Reverend William Taylor, *Making of America* (page 92A), University of Michigan.

will and corresponding emphasis on the absolute dependence of each individual's fate on the will of God. Of course, Jonathan Edwards would have agreed that converted saints loved God with their whole will and that their ability to obey God depended on their will to do so. Dwight, in his turn, acknowledged his grandfather's point that God knew who obeyed him and who would not, as well as Edwards' point that grace was necessary in order for anyone to truly love God or truly desire to follow his will. Nevertheless, in their descriptions of the voluntary nature of religious virtue, Dwight and his student Lyman Beecher shifted their emphasis away from the Christian's compulsion to obey God, and toward the Christian's voluntary efforts.

Growing investment in religious voluntarism coincided with Methodism's rising popularity. The famous Methodist circuit rider Francis Asbury and those who emulated him covered the new territories of the United States on horseback, preaching salvation as a free gift to the willing, establishing societies and churches, and encouraging people to live virtuous and holy lives. Methodists gained many adherents through religious camp meetings in frontier areas and through revival meetings conducted in America's growing towns and cities. By 1850, Methodists claimed more churches than in any other denomination in twenty states, reflecting a broader geographic reach than any other religious group could boast. (Baptists came in second with more churches than any other denomination in seven states.)[37]

In their enthusiasm for religious activism sweeping the country prior to the Civil War, even the Congregationalists, Presbyterians, and Baptists who stood within the Reformed tradition associated with John Calvin tended to minimize the problem of reliance on works that had caused such concern among previous generations. A leading proponent of new methods within the Reformed tradition was Charles Grandison Finney (1792–1875), a lawyer who left his practice to accept "a retainer from the Lord Jesus Christ to plead his cause" as a Presbyterian minister and effective revivalist preacher. Finney advocated "new measures" for promoting revivals, such as prolonging religious meetings, especially at night, permitting women to pray aloud, and incorporating the "anxious bench," a seat up front where the preacher asked individuals who were visibly struggling to sit. As examples of repentance and conversion in action, sinners on the anxious bench served as live models of the struggle preachers believed everyone should go through.

"A revival is the result of the *right* use of the appropriate means," Finney explained in 1834. A revivalist was like a farmer who diligently planted and tended his crop while not forgetting the necessity of God's blessing. Refusing to rely on human effort to create a revival would be just as inappropriate, Finney maintained, as telling farmers that "to plow and plant and labor as if they expected to raise a crop is very wrong, and taking the work out of the hands of God, that it interferes with his sovereignty, and is going on in their own strength; and that there is not connection of the means with the result on which they can depend."[38] While more conservative Protestants were sometimes disturbed by his willingness to manipulate the means of conversion, resistance to Finney softened over time. Lyman Beecher dropped his initial resistance to the "new measures" in the face of Finney's success, and invited the charismatic revivalist to preach in Boston.

In 1857, a so-called Businessman's Revival swept through Boston and other American cities, revealing the success and development of Finney-like strategies of religious catharsis. As historian John Corrigan showed, leaders of the Businessman's Revival adjusted evangelical practices of preaching, prayer, and conversion to the busy schedules and economic outlooks of urban workers, scheduling religious meetings for the lunch hour and presenting investment in Christ as a contractual enterprise from which the investor received a clean conscience and a leg ahead in the race to prosperity. As Corrigan showed, leaders of the Businessman's Revival enlisted Christianity in the service of capitalism as much as they enlisted businessmen in the cause of Christ.[39]

Missionary Benevolence

Evangelicalism succeeded not only because of the benefits it offered individuals, but also because of the opportunities it offered them to exercise benevolence and lead the way in the reconstruction of society. Practical emphasis on cultivating means of conversion complemented the idea that benevolence was an essential expression of Christian life, and a sign that the conversions associated with revivals had really taken place. Enthusiasm for benevolence also complemented optimistic hopes about America as a place where reforms of various sort could take hold, where society could be reconstructed if not perfected, and where the Puritan dream of a holy commonwealth might be realized, even if that meant revising certain aspects of Puritan thought. As a transitional figure between Puritanism and evangelicalism, Jonathan Edwards used the term benevolence to describe "true virtue," the capacity for active and loving dedication to the well-being of others that represented love and conformity to the will of God.[40] Edwards' understanding of benevolence reflected eighteenth-century ideas about moral virtue as a higher sensibility or taste as well as earlier Puritan ideas about Christian love as a bond that joined people of different rank together, enabling the kind of mutual respect and responsibility that social order in a holy commonwealth required.

In addition to having roots within Puritanism, the evangelical concept of benevolence drew from new enthusiasm for voluntarism as both a theological principle and a stimulus to religious organization and social reform. As a crucial step in this evolution of the term, Edwards' disciple, Samuel Hopkins (1721–1803), made benevolence synonymous with unselfishness. While Edwards had used the phrase "disinterested benevolence" to describe the transcendence of self-love that characterized genuine love toward God and others, and thereby enabled true happiness, Hopkins used it to express a kind of heroic selflessness that came across as more arduous than joyful. For Hopkins and his followers, benevolence demanded voluntary and strenuous efforts of self-sacrifice. These efforts facilitated the development of spiritual life in aspiring Christians. They also served as empirical evidence of conversion.[41]

The concept of disinterested benevolence figured importantly in American Protestant missionary thought and in the growth of missionary expressions of evangelicalism. In his promotion of disinterested benevolence, Hopkins worked, as a young man, as a missionary to Housatanic and Mahican Indians. Later, as a pastor in Newport, Rhode Island, he vigorously supported missionary outreach to Africans in America and in Africa. In affluent Newport, where the slave trade contributed to the wealth of prominent families, Hopkins attacked that trade as the epitome of self-interest and synonymous with sin. He made rejection of slavery an essential indicator of conversion, preaching that no one involved in slaveholding could be a Christian. A believer in the nearness of Christ's Second Coming, Hopkins described slavery as an ingredient in the sixth vial of tribulation described in the book of Revelation, and predicted that the abolition of slavery would lead to the outpouring of the seventh vial that would precede the dawning of God's kingdom on earth.

Hopkins' theology appealed especially to women. His strongest supporters in Newport were women whose prayers, tears, and lobbying helped secure his ordination in 1770. But Hopkins' influence was not limited to Newport. Throughout New England, and long after his death, Hopkins' celebration of disinterested benevolence inspired many people, especially women, to donate money to missionary societies, pray over the desperate plight of heathens in remote corners of the world, and, in some cases, embark on missionary careers themselves. First in New England, and then in other parts of the country where the influence of New England culture was felt, engagement in missionary causes enabled women to feel they could contribute to the betterment of women's lives in other cultures. It also enabled them to affirm their own importance as full participants in building God's kingdom on earth and stretch the boundaries of gender-appropriate behavior within evangelical culture. Celebration of self-sacrifice and eagerness to suffer all hardship in the service of Christ legitimated these efforts.

Most of the early women who performed missionary service in India, Persia, China, Africa, or among Native tribes in the western territories of North America did so as wives of missionaries. Before the Civil War, the few single women sent abroad by missionary societies, like Fidelia Fiske, who started a girls' school in Persia, were listed as "assistant missionaries" in missionary society records. Since female preaching was frowned upon by many Congregationalists, Presbyterians, and Baptists, and since preaching the gospel was often viewed as a missionary's main job, women took up work as teachers and, later, as medical workers. In the minds of most of the men who ran American

The Transplanted Shamrock. Courtesy of Shaping the Values of Youth digital collection, Michigan State University.

missionary societies, teaching was clearly secondary to preaching the gospel. But it acquired profound importance for American women at home and abroad, as it did for men in the field who believed that people should be educated as part of the process of conversion to Protestant Christianity.

Teaching offered unprecedented career opportunities for women, whether or not they left home, and women who went into teaching in nineteenth-century America often embraced their work as a form of religious vocation. In the early decades of the nineteenth century, schools for girls multiplied and public instruction that included girls expanded at a fast rate. Teaching was the one really respectable line of work, outside the home, that evangelicals agreed women could pursue. Evangelical women who went into teaching did so in a spirit of benevolence and self-sacrifice, even as teaching gave them new opportunities for advanced education, independence, and professional work. Indeed, the burgeoning industry of American education developed in harmony and cooperation with evangelical expressions of missionary enterprise, each contributing to the need for, and justification of, the other.[42]

The Globalization of American Evangelical Culture

Evangelicals played formative roles in shaping American attitudes toward the larger world during the nineteenth and twentieth centuries and in creating impressions about Americans in other parts of the world that continue to exist today. The combination of admiration and resentment that characterizes present perceptions about America in other parts of the world derives not only from the ascendance of American power after World War II and from the ubiquity of American media and corporate economic clout, but also from a longer history of American evangelical outreach. For 200 years, American evangelicals have worked hard to transmit their energetic spirit, concepts of moral virtue, idealism about the kingdom of God, and sense of responsibility for helping bring the kingdom to earth and to people in other parts of the world.

The roots of resistance to American culture, and to the brashness of American policies, go way back before current complaints about American unilateralism to much earlier efforts by Protestant missionaries to stamp out pagan superstition and bring light to heathen cultures. At the same time, respect for American ideals of democracy and human rights have some antecedents in the respect generated by missionary idealism, and by missionary emphasis on the urgent needs for education, social reform, and health care that would enable people in nonwestern cultures to live better lives. For example, nineteenth-century British and American missionaries in India had little success in converting upper-caste Hindus to Christianity, but their arguments for female education and for various kinds of social reform, including the abolition of caste, had real influence, and played a significant role in Indian history.[43]

Of course, Americans were not the only Christian missionaries in the early-nineteenth-century world. German, Dutch, and Scandinavian Protestants sent out missionaries, and British missionaries outnumbered Americans, especially in India. But however much they relied on the support of colonial governments, and however condescending they were toward people of other cultures, Americans had a degree of independence from colonial power that missionaries from other countries lacked. They also tended to view Christianity as coextensive with American self-government, entrepreneurship, and practical science. The distinctive combination of evangelical Christianity, American political theory, and practical culture promoted by American missionaries caught the attention of young leaders in many parts of the world, even as those leaders recast the message in their own terms and created new forms of religious and political expression that left missionaries behind. In southern Africa, for example, American missionary ideas and institutions figured importantly in the emergence of modern black African leadership, even as the establishment of independent black churches and the dismantling of white control was essential in the further development of that leadership.[44]

Conclusion

Early-nineteenth-century America was flooded with religious salespeople promoting a variety of methods of salvation, passageways to heaven, means of drawing down the sacred, and blueprints for constructing the New Jerusalem. Interchange and competition between representatives of different sects stimulated this profusion of religious schemes, as did the widespread view that religion ought to be promoted in order for individuals and society to be improved and perfected. This enthusiasm for religion overlapped in part with the optimistic, entrepreneurial spirit that took hold of many Americans after Independence, especially those with means and inclination to go after the abundant resources of a big new land. The defeat of the French and Indians in the northeast in 1763, the overthrow of British rule in 1783, and the takeover of the Mississippi River and opening of the territory beyond with the Louisiana Purchase of 1803 generated tremendous self-confidence among Americans and stimulated this optimistic, entrepreneurial spirit and the ambitious religious agendas associated with it.

There was a darker side to this spirit as well. Hatred of Mormons led to vigilante efforts to kill and drive them away. Hatred of Catholics led to the burning of the Ursuline convent in Charleston, Massachusetts, in 1834, to riots, bloodshed, vandalism, and the burning of a Catholic Church in Philadelphia in 1844, to considerable support within the American Party for anti-Catholic platforms and legislation, and to the fast-spreading influence of a No-Popery movement that emerged from the secret Order of the Star Spangled Banner. In the 1850s, the No-Popery movement rose to national prominence and participants acquired the name Know-Nothings because of their mysterious origins and agnostic stance on slavery and other issues in order to concentrate on resistance to Catholic immigration.[45] Along with anti-Catholicism, hatred of Native Americans accompanied the massive displacement of Indian tribes and seizures of Indian land. Despisal of African Americans was commonplace, especially among participants in the violent cult of honor that flourished among Anglicans in the South.

In the common parlance of the new republic, the word "American" was largely synonymous with Anglo-Protestant, and did not include Indians, slaves, or French and Spanish Catholics in Florida, Louisiana, or Mexico. At the time of the American Revolution, all but 15 percent of colonists were English Protestants. By 1860, the population of the United States had multiplied eightfold, and was spread out over a much larger terrain. This population was also more religiously, ethnically, and linguistically diverse. But it was still heavily dominated by Anglo-Protestants, especially in the region east of the Mississippi, where the old stock Anglo-American population was centered. Irish Catholic immigrants in Boston and other eastern cities had to make their way in an often hostile Protestant culture. Germans representing various churches had an easier time of it, first in Pennsylvania, where religious and ethnic diversity was better tolerated than in most of the other twelve colonies, and then in the territories of Ohio and Illinois. Scandinavians passed through the Anglo-dominated East on their way to Utah and other western territories. The tiny population of Asian immigrants and their descendants did not make much of a dent in the "American" mind until 1850, when California, where most of them lived, became a state.[46]

Protestant experience in eighteenth- and early-nineteenth-century America was often combative, conflicted, and far from homogenous. Yet running through much of this boisterous history were a number of common threads, among the most salient of which were insistence on visible evidence and practical, world-building enthusiasm. In American foreign missions in the early nineteenth century, this evidential temper came to expression in an urgent commitment to participate in the dawning of the millennium, in the gathering of heathen souls to Christ, and in the construction of a new social order of global extension. If missionaries failed to bring their visions to reality, it was not because they did not expect a practical outcome. In fact, American Protestant missionaries were criticized for being too pragmatic and this-worldly—for losing sight of the transcendence of spiritual life in the effort to generate concrete manifestations. Commenting on this American tendency to bring divine things down to earth, one Japanese Christian described Americans "as the least religious among all civilized peoples." If "mankind goes down to America to learn how to live the earthly life," Kanzo Uchimura wrote in 1926, "to live the heavenly life, they go to some other people."[47]

The evidentiary temper of American Protestant thought came to the fore in the eighteenth and nineteenth centuries, when demands for "new birth" caught up many Americans and, especially in the decades before the Civil

War, when new sects and new religious movements seemed to spring up everywhere. The common man's "natural reason" was also widely touted, despite the apparent irrationality of so much American behavior, and often understood to include respect for all kinds of spiritual manifestations. Enthusiasm for religious experience contributed to a strong cultural investment in the evidentiary signs of religious life that has persisted ever since.

In seventeenth-century Puritanism, signs of divine reality were terribly important, but they were often counted as shadows of the real thing. Thus John Winthrop laid out a "model of Christian charity" for the governance of everyday life in Puritan New England that represented, on an earthly plane, God's will in heaven. Anne Bradstreet wrote about her love for her husband being *like* her love for Christ. Both these Christians hoped that what they experienced on earth would approximate what existed in heaven. For eighteenth- and early-nineteenth-century American Protestants, on the other hand, manifestations of spiritual reality came to be seen as divine things in and of themselves. Descriptions, investigations, and promotions of religious experience consequently became more popular and more detailed than before and American Protestant leaders who could manage and facilitate such experience rose to prominence. Revival preachers developed new strategic methods to bring about conversion. Shakers and Mormons built millennial communities and developed elaborate rituals and stories that made participation in God's kingdom a real-time event that could be planned out and methodically reenacted.

After the Civil War, the method-istic, evidentiary temper of evangelical religious experience did not disappear. But a competing, romantic approach to religious experience grew in strength and popularity. New scientific discoveries about the natural world emerged to challenge the validity of popular religious claims about spiritual manifestations and caused many American Protestants to rethink the relationship between Christianity and evidences in nature.

Notes

1. E. Brooks Holifield, *Theology in America: Christian Thought from the Age of the Puritans to the Civil War* (New Haven: Yale University Press, 2003), pp. 5–8.

2. "Letter of Thomas Brattle," in *What Happened in Salem: Documents Pertaining to the Seventeenth-Century Witchcraft Trials*, ed. David Levin, 2nd ed. (New York: Harcourt, Brace & World, 1960), quotations from pp. 132, 135.

3. "The Wandering Spirit" (1741), reprinted in *The Great Awakening, Documents Illustrating the Crisis and Its Consequences*, ed. Alan Heimert and Perry Miller (Indianapolis: Bobbs-Merrill, 1967), quotations from pp. 147–151.

4. Ralph Ketcham, *Benjamin Franklin* (New York: Washington Square Press, 1965), pp. 168–169, 102–103, quotations from p. 102. Also see Harry S. Stout, *The Divine Dramatist: George Whitefield and the Rise of Modern Evangelicalism* (Grand Rapids: William B. Eerdmans, 1991), pp. 220–233.

5. Stout, *Divine Dramatist*, quotation from p. 41. Whitefield dramatized biblical scenes by recasting them in the idioms of his own time and place. In one sermon he gave in many American towns, "Abraham Offering His Son," he began by asking his audience to imagine "the good old man walking with dear child." Scene two took place at the altar, with Whitefield enacting Abraham's willingness to sacrifice his son if God required, and God's last-minute reprieve. "Methinks I see the tears trickle down the patriarch Abraham's cheeks," Whitefield preached, "adieu, my Isaac, my only son, whom I love as my own soul; adieu, adieu." In the final scene, Whitefield made the feelings generated in his listeners the point of connection to the sufferings of Christ. "Did you weep just now when I bid you fancy that you saw the altar?" he asked. "Look up by faith, behold the blessed Jesus, our all-glorious Immanuel, not bound, but nailed on an accursed tree." His audience should weep even more, Whitefield insisted, as he drew them into the biblical drama: "let me exhort you to look to him whom you have pierced, and mourn, as a woman mourneth for her first born." (pp. 93–94, quotations from p. 94.)

6. For arguments supporting the thesis that Whitefield, and the Great Awakening more generally, laid important groundwork for American Revolution, see Alan Heimert, *Religion and the American Mind: From the Great Awakening to the Revolution* (Cambridge: Harvard University Press, 1966); and Harry S. Stout, "Religion, Communications, and the Ideological Origins of the American Revolution," *William and Mary Quarterly* 34 (1977): 519–541.

7. George Whitefield, *A Continuation of the Reverend Mr. Whitefield's Journal . . . Seventh Journal* (1741), quoted in Edwin Scott Gaustad, *The Great Awakening in New England* (New York: Harper & Brothers, 1957), p. 48.

8. *Christian History*, vol. 1, pp. 367–381, 372, quoted in Gaustad, *Great Awakening in New England*, p. 49.

9. Jonathan Edwards, "Sinners in the Hands of an Angry God," reprinted in *Selected Writings of Jonathan Edwards*, ed. Harold P. Simonson (Prospect Heights, IL: Waveland Press, 1992; orig. 1970), quotations from pp. 101, 106.

10. See Perry Miller, "The Rhetoric of Sensation" (orig. 1950), in *Errand into the Wilderness* (New York: Harper Torchbooks, 1956), pp. 167–183.

11. Edwards, "Sinners," quotations from pp. 104, 106–107.

12. Jonathan Edwards, *Religious Affections* (orig. 1746), ed. John E. Smith (New Haven: Yale University Press, 1959), pp. 135–142, 253–266.

13. Stout, *Divine Dramatist*, quotation from p. 127.

14. Peter W. Williams, *America's Religions: From Their Origins to the Twenty-first Century* (Urbana: University of Illinois Press, 2002), p. 138.

15. Stout, *Divine Dramatist*, quotations from pp. 19–20. For a nice overview of the early development of Methodism, see Williams, *America's Religions*, pp. 135–139.

16. For example, see Paul E. Johnson, *Shopkeeper's Millennium: Society and Revivals in Rochester, New York, 1815–1837* (New York: Hill and Wang, 1978).

17. Douglas Winiarski, "Lydia Prout's 'Dreadfullest Thought': Satan, Sinners, & the Perils of Parenthood in Provincial Boston," unpublished manuscript.

18. Christine Leigh Heyrman, *Southern Cross: The Beginnings of the Bible Belt* (Chapel Hill: University of North Carolina Press, 1997), quotations from pp. 55, 53, 55.

19. In the second sentence quoted here, Congress replaced "inherent and" with "certain." See Thomas Jefferson, *Autobiography* (1821), reprinted in Thomas Jefferson, *Writings* (New York: Library of America, 1984), quotation from p. 19.

20. Edwin S. Gaustad, *Sworn on the Altar of God: A Religious Biography of Thomas Jefferson* (Grand Rapids: William B. Eerdmans, 1996).

21. Thomas Jefferson, *Notes on the State of Virginia* (orig. 1785), ed. William Peden (New York: W. W. Norton, 1972), quotations from pp. 47, 53–54. Also see Daniel Boorstin, *The Lost World of Thomas Jefferson* (Boston: Beacon Press, 1960; orig. 1948).

22. Gilbert Tennent, "The Danger of an Unconverted Ministry," reprinted in *American Christianity: An Historical Interpretation with Representative Documents*, 2 vols., ed. H. Shelton Smith, Robert T. Handy, and Lefferts A. Loetscher (New York: Charles Scribner's Sons, 1960), vol. 1, pp. 322–328, quotations from pp. 323–325.

23. James McGready, *The Posthumous Works of the Reverend and Pious James M'Gready* (1837) quoted in Leigh Eric Schmidt, *Holy Fairs: Scottish Communions and American Revivals in the Early Modern Period* (Princeton: Princeton University Press, 1989), p. 149.

24. McGready, *Posthumous Works,* quoted in Schmidt, *Holy Fairs*, pp. 102–103.

25. Ann Taves, *Fits, Trances, & Visions: Experiencing Religion and Explaining Experience from Wesley to James* (Princeton: Princeton University Press, 1999), pp. 79–111; John H. Wigger, *Taking Heaven by Storm: Methodism and the Popularization of American Christianity* (New York: Oxford University Press, 1998).

26. Heyrman, *Southern Cross*, quotations from p. 50.

27. Mark A. Noll, *America's God: From Jonathan Edwards to Abraham Lincoln* (New York: Oxford University Press, 2002), pp. 367–446.

28. William R. Hutchison, *Religious Pluralism in America: The Contentious History of a Founding Ideal* (New Haven: Yale University Press, 2003), pp. 35–38.

29. Anthony F. C. Wallace, *The Death and Rebirth of the Seneca* (New York: Random House, 1972; orig. 1969).

30. R. David Edmunds, *The Shawnee Prophet* (Lincoln: University of Nebraska Press, 1983); Joel W. Martin, *Sacred Revolt: The Muskogees' Struggle for a New World* (Boston: Beacon Press, 1991).

31. Stephen J. Stein, *The Shaker Experience in America: A History of the United Society of Believers* (New Haven: Yale University Press, 1992), quotations from p. 96.

32. Stein, *Shaker Experience*, pp. 165–184, quotation from p. 176.

33. See Jan Shipps, *Mormonism: The Story of a New Religious Tradition* (Urbana: University of Illinois Press, 1985); Michael D. Quinn, *Early Mormonism and the Magic World View* (Salt Lake City: Signature Press, 1987); Williams, *America's Religions*, pp. 235–245.

34. James Madison, "To the Honorable General Assembly of the Commonwealth of Virginia, A Memorial and Remonstrance" (1785), reprinted in *James Madison on Religious Liberty*, ed. Robert S. Alley (Buffalo: Prometheus Books, 1985), quotations from p. 58.

35. Lyman Beecher, *The Autobiography of Lyman Beecher*, ed. Barbara M. Cross, 2 vols. (Cambridge: Harvard University Press, 1961), quotations from vol. 1, pp. 252–253.

36. Timothy Dwight, *Theology Explained and Defended*, 5 vols. (Middletown: 1818), quotation from vol. 2, p. 532.

37. Edwin Scott Gaustad, Philip L. Barlow, and Richard W. Dishno, *New Historical Atlas of Religion in America* (New York: Oxford University Press, 2001), p. 221.

38. *Memoirs of Rev. Charles G. Finney, Written by Himself* (New York, 1876), quotation from p. 24; Charles Grandison Finney, "What a Revival of Religion Is" (1834), reprinted in *Lectures on Revivals of Religion* (1835), ed. William G. McLoughlin (Cambridge: Harvard University Press, 1960), quotations from pp. 12–13.

39. John Corrigan, *Business of the Heart: Religion and Emotion in the Nineteenth Century* (Berkeley: University of California Press, 2002).

40. Jonathan Edwards, *The Nature of True Virtue* (1765), ed. William Frankena (Ann Arbor: University of Michigan Press, 1960).

41. For fuller discussion of these developments, see Joseph A. Conforti, *Samuel Hopkins and the New Divinity Movement: Calvinism, the Congregational Ministry, and Reform in New England between the Great Awakenings* (Grand Rapids: William B. Eerdmans, 1981); and Joseph Haroutunian, *Piety versus Moralism: The Passing of the New England Theology* (New York: Henry Holt, 1932).

42. Amanda Porterfield, *Mary Lyon and the Mount Holyoke Missionaries* (New York: Oxford University Press, 1997). Also see Clifton Jackson Phillips, *Protestant America and the Pagan World: The First Half Century of the American Board of Commissioners for Foreign Missions, 1810–1860* (Cambridge: Harvard University Press, 1969); Kathryn Kish Sklar, "The Founding of Mount Holyoke College," in *Women of America: A History*, ed. Carol Ruth Berkin and Mary Beth Norton (Boston: Houghton Mifflin, 1979).

43. Porterfield, *Mary Lyon*, pp. 87–111. Also see Keshari N. Sahay, "The Christian Movement in India: A Historical Perspective," in *Christianity and Social Change in India* (New Dehli: Inter-India Publications, 1986), pp. 15–52; and Sushil Madhava Pathak, *American Missionaries and Hinduism: A Study of Their Contacts from 1813 to 1910* (Dehli: Munshiram Monoharlal, 1967).

44. Porterfield, *Mary Lyon*, pp. 112–138. Also see Norman Etherington, *Preachers, Peasants, and Politics in Southeast Africa, 1835–1880: African Christian Communities in Natal, Pondoland, and Zululand* (London: Royal Historical Society, 1978); and Jean Comaroff and John Comaroff, *Of Revelation and Revolution: Christianity, Colonialism, and Consciousness in South Africa* (Chicago: University of Chicago Press, 1991).

45. Ray Allen Billington, *The Protestant Crusade, 1800–1860: A Study of the Origins of American Nativism* (Chicago: Quadrangle Books, 1964; orig. 1938).

46. Hutchison, *Religious Pluralism*, pp. 19–27, esp. 21, 24.

47. Quotation from Andrew F. Walls, "The American Dimension in the History of the Missionary Movement," in *Earthen Vessels: American Evangelicals and Foreign Missions, 1880–1980*, ed. Joel Carpenter and Wilbert R. Shenk (Grand Rapids: William B. Eerdmans, 1990), p. 2.

Chapter 3

Romantic Responses to Modernity and Religious Loss

E ven as common sense empiricism helped shape American Protestant experience in the antebellum years, romantic interpretations of Christianity offered alternatives to its literalistic interpretations of biblical events and supernatural revelation. Romantic interpretations of Christianity appealed to Americans disaffected by evangelical preachers and their manipulative approach to conversion and salvation. Romantic Protestants did not lack for religious feeling or reverence for God. But rather than conceptualizing God as another person who demanded repentance in return for assurance of salvation, as many evangelicals did, romantics thought of religious experience as an intuitive sense of divine consciousness within and beyond the self, often stimulated by meditation on nature.

While evangelicals took feelings about God as responses to external reality, romantics shifted the ground of divine inspiration to the mind, raising the status of subjective experience and enlarging its latitude. This exaltation of subjective reality offered a way out of the crises of belief stimulated, in part, by evangelicals who described God as a man in the sky, and heaven and hell as if they were pieces of real estate. At the same time, however, evangelicals and romantics often shared common religious interests that enabled them to interact and even join with one another. Both evangelicals and romantics considered personal religious experience central to Christian life and both emphasized the emotional components of religious experience. Both looked to Christianity to support their ideas about how society should be organized. In the North, romantics and evangelicals shared an enthusiasm for social reform that sometimes made it hard for southerners to tell northern romantics apart from northern evangelicals. In the South, romantics and evangelicals eventually got together around shared commitments to social conservatism and a Christian nation.

Romanticism can be described either as a philosophy or as a religious mood. Both figured importantly in the historical development of American Protestant experience. As a philosophy, romanticism can be traced to the writings of the German philosopher Immanuel Kant (1724–1804), who questioned the idea that the mind simply received and processed sensory data from the outside world. In his *Critique of Pure Reason* (1781), Kant argued that the mind conditions all of the information passing through it and that we can never know, in any direct, immediate, and straightforward sense, what lies outside the mind. Beliefs about God and other metaphysical realities could never be proven, according to Kant, but he emphasized their importance for human conduct nonetheless. Romantic philosophers accepted Kant's critique of empiricism; they also went further than Kant to equate religious experience of God with the mind's intuitive grasp of its own power to shape reality.

Romantic philosophy reached America primarily through English and Scottish writers. During the 1830s, the interpretation of romantic philosophy advanced by the English philosopher-poet Samuel Taylor Coleridge (1772–1834) influenced Protestant intellectuals both North and South. The first American edition of Coleridge's *Aids to Reflection* caused a considerable stir in the decade after the Vermont clergyman James Marsh published an American edition in 1829. In the North, some romantics used Coleridge to reformulate Christian thought in terms of democratic individualism. Others drew on his ideas to develop connections between Christian feeling and the natural harmonies of middle-class family life. In the South, defenders of a Christian social order based on slave labor also found Coleridge congenial. Perhaps amused by the multiple ways Americans embraced his work, Coleridge remarked in the 1830s, "I am a poor poet in England, but I am a great philosopher in America."[1]

As Coleridge defined the terms, Reason was the intuitive faculty of mind that penetrated through facts and events to grasp the truths they symbolized. Understanding was an inferior but necessary faculty responsible for organizing sensory perceptions. Coleridge and his American followers criticized evangelical Protestantism for its obsession with empirical manifestations and the strategic calculations associated with Understanding, which for them fell far short of Reason. Coleridge associated Reason with divine inspiration, and with God. Reason enabled people to apprehend the spiritual truths symbolized in nature and history. It was also the creative faculty that enabled poets and other inspired people to represent spiritual truths to others.

In romantic theory, modern industrialization separated man from his innocent, aboriginal relationship with nature. The damage was not irreparable, however, but a lesson to be learned; the fall from innocence opened the way for construction of a new world. Mind would rescue nature by consciously reuniting with her in a new spirit of love— what the English poet William Worsdworth (1770–1850) called "reason in her most exalted mood." This "higher love" made sense of evil— "rashly named by those / Who know not what they say." As Wordsworth explained, "All truth and beauty" returned from lost innocence through this "pervading love," traditionally symbolized by Christ, now realized in nature, and in romantic interpretations of human history.[2]

In his classic study of romantic literature, M. H. Abrams emphasized the importance for romantic writers of *Paradise Lost* (1667), the epic written by English Puritan John Milton (1608–1674). As Abrams explained, romantic writers reworked Milton's interpretation of the biblical story of God's creation and humanity's fall into sin and struggle for redemption "at a time of profound cultural crisis" characterized by the emergence of industrial economies within modern nation-states, the transformation of the social and natural landscape through industrialization, and widespread fear of losing belief in God. Perceiving "themselves as elected spokesmen for the Western tradition," romantics responded to these crises with post-Kantian reformulations of Milton's thought. Reading human history written on the face of nature and seeing the human fall into sin mirrored in the landscape's degradation by urban industrialization, romantics hoped for "a rebirth in which a renewed mankind will inhabit a renovated earth where he will find himself thoroughly at home." In their reformulation of Milton's Puritan theology, romantics perceived the creative human mind as coextensive with God and represented mind and nature coexisting as subject and object, creator and creation.[3]

While the philosophy of romanticism derived from Britain and Europe, the romantic mood Americans developed in the 1830s derived as much from homegrown sensibilities as from anything imported from abroad. American society was fertile context for the feelings of loss that seeped into people's consciousness to create the sense of longing and wrecked nobility that characterized romantic mood; many Americans longed for return to God, natural innocence, and communal belonging as a result of their own situations, histories, and native expectations. For example, in remembering her New England childhood in the 1830s, the poet Emily Dickinson (1831–1886) identified "[a] loss of something" as "[t]he first that I could recollect." From the beginning of

The Pilgrim of the Cross at the End of His Journey, by Thomas Cole (1801–1848). Smithsonian American Art Museum, Washington, D.C./Art Resource, N.Y.

her own conscious development, she wrote, "[a] Mourner walked among the children." And this sense of lost inheritance persisted for decades. Even after becoming older and "wiser," Dickinson confessed in 1864, "I find myself still softly searching / For my Delinquent Palaces," still "looking" for "the Kingdom of Heaven."[4]

Like other romantics in New England, Dickinson grew up in a Protestant culture divided between evangelicals who demanded complete emotional and intellectual assent to the conversion process of new birth and Unitarians who emphasized the rationality of Protestant faith and its support of moral propriety and a merchant class. Similarly in the South, the intense emotionalism of evangelical Christianity coexisted with the formalism of Anglican culture and its concern for social propriety and class. In both regions, romanticism appealed to people uncomfortable with evangelicalism, who yearned for a recovery of spiritual life. In both regions, romantics turned to poetry and fiction as means of religious expression that invited expansive, emotionally charged depictions of human society in relation to nature.

Romantic sentiments about nature, society, and self developed amidst grim realities and clouds of disappointment, frustration, and conflict gathering over America in increasingly ominous ways. Buoyant optimism about the new republic declined after the 1820s; Americans stopped thinking about their leaders, as they once had about George Washington, in lavishly heroic and reverential terms. Visions of a shining Republic and holy commonwealth did not disappear, but for many Americans, especially the moody, poetic ones, those visions seemed fainter, further removed from possibility, and sadly lost in the past. The vast territory of North America seemed less of a pristine expanse than it had when Thomas Jefferson acquired the Louisiana Purchase in 1803 and more of a killing ground run wild with fanaticism, greed, and hatred. The popular romances of Walter Scott—including the *Waverley Novels* celebrating brave Scottish clansmen and *Ivanhoe* featuring knights of valor, elegant ladies, and castles of old—fed this nostalgia for the past. A sense of paradise lost was, for moody Protestants, hard to avoid, even as they searched for redemptive meaning in their self-knowledge and struggle for self-conscious maturity.

It is no coincidence that romanticism began to impact American religious thinking in a major way during the 1830s, at the same time industrialization was transforming society and the natural environment, and creating a national market economy. Romantic feelings became popular through an outpouring of novels and poetry made possible by a rapidly expanding publishing industry and print culture. Those Americans who embraced romantic conceptions of Christianity felt unease about changes occurring in America. Some of them hoped America would become more open, egalitarian, and pluralistic. Others cherished more hierarchical and conservative visions of social order.

In New England, proponents of self-reliance wanted to restore the natural and communal harmony they believed had existed prior to industrialization, while leaving behind the harsh discipline, rigid thinking, and authoritarian social order associated with their Puritan predecessors. These egalitarian romantics hoped to correct the abuses of industrialization, especially its connection to slavery, without relinquishing modern investment in human progress and material improvement.

Alongside these egalitarian expressions of self-reliance, more conservative forms of Protestant romanticism developed that promoted social agendas grounded in natural hierarchies of race and gender. And in the South, conservative expressions of romantic ideas about nature and society were even more prevalent. As the production of cotton and reliance on slave labor increasingly dominated the economies of southern states in the 1830s, Protestant clergymen rose up in defense of slavery, white female purity, and the southern way of life, expressing nostalgia for Christian civilizations in the past and the need to preserve deference to authority and Christian feeling against infidelity, social leveling, and moral anarchy. Southern ministers, politicians, and writers advanced romantic sentiments about society and family life based on natural differences in race and gender and bolstered those sentiments with citations of numerous biblical passages in support of slavery and patriarchal authority.

Romantic religious thinking contributed to the conflicts involved in the American Civil War and to efforts to try to explain the war after the South surrendered. In trying to make sense of enormous suffering and loss of life in the Civil War, Americans in both the North and South embraced mystical notions of the nation they died for as an altar of blood sacrifice. As historian Harry S. Stout argued, romantic expressions of patriotism and civil religion forged in response to Civil War went beyond earlier idealism about America as a place where holy commonwealths might be established.[5] Romantic religious thinking continues to influence Protestant experience in America today, fueling conflicting interpretations of Christianity that differentiate liberals and conservatives, and constructing shared moods and symbols through which disputes between them continue to be expressed.

Egalitarian Romanticism

In New England, belief in the mind's intuitive power to penetrate and interpret ordinary reality led to a flowering of literary expression and religious thought. Ralph Waldo Emerson, Henry David Thoreau, Theodore Parker, Bronson Alcott, Margaret Fuller, Nathaniel Hawthorne, Emily Dickinson, and others with ties to New England produced a substantial body of religious literature that fused romantic philosophy with ideas about individual conscience derived from New England Puritan thought.[6] Called Transcendentalists for their belief in the universality of consciousness, these romantic Protestants took the Puritan hope for America in a direction that was both more romantic and more egalitarian than anything New England Puritans had imagined, calling for a society that nurtured self-expression and a democratic fellowship of mutual self-respect.

Ralph Waldo Emerson (1803–1882)

The leading formulator of American Transcendentalism, Ralph Waldo Emerson, recast the iconoclastic spirit of Protestant thought and the foundational moral values of New England Puritanism in terms of romantic theories about consciousness and intuition. In time-honored Protestant fashion, Emerson condemned superstition, cowardly adherence to clerical authority, and befuddling rituals that encouraged superstition and passivity. At the same time, he moved beyond earlier Protestant reformers in reconceptualizing the individual's relationship to God in terms of the mind's awakening to the transcendental realm of consciousness. In Emerson's romantic revision of Protestant thought, self-reliant individuals were the redeemers of the world because they saw the world through Reason, recognizing that their own truest thoughts emerged from the mind of God.

Like his Puritan predecessors who condemned churchgoers for posturing Christian piety in conformity to social expectation, Emerson contrasted genuine moral virtue with superficial conventions of good behavior. Like Puritans who distinguished grace from reliance on works, he believed that obedience to God required an active, honest conscience and openness to divine truth, and ought never be confused with simply following rules and ritual procedures. Like Jonathan Edwards, Emerson thought that efforts to gain status and glory for oneself ultimately resulted in failure and dissatisfaction and that in the end, only an immediate and honest relationship with God generated holiness, social harmony, personal happiness, and genuine moral virtue. A right relation to God, Emerson believed, made even the most mundane activity morally sufficient. As he wrote in his famous essay "Self-Reliance," first published in 1841, "In this pleasing contrite wood-life which God allows me, let me record day by day my honest thought without prospect or retrospect, and I cannot doubt, it will be found symmetrical, though I mean it not and see it not."[7]

Emerson first became acquainted with Coleridge in 1826 as a student at Harvard Divinity School. In 1830, after reading *Aids to Reflection*, he embraced Coleridge's effort to reformulate Christian theology, criticizing Protestants for representing Christianity in terms of the lower faculty of Understanding and urging reliance on the higher faculty of Reason. Emerson was particularly critical of preachers who reduced the sublime truths about the individual's relation to God to a catalogue of empirical facts and to threats and promises about the future. He set himself to the task of proclaiming the individual's capacity to experience God in the present, voicing his own experience in ways that he hoped would generate moral and social reform.[8]

The reckless greed and divisiveness of American society troubled Emerson, as did the apparent inability of the Protestant churchmen to provide an inclusive vision of society that would repair and inspire friendship and community. Impatient with the self-serving platitudes of

Ralph Waldo Emerson. Courtesy of the Library of Congress.

Boston's elite theologians as well as with the literal interpretations of heaven and hell promulgated by evangelicals, he criticized the failure of Americans to meet God face to face, and called attention to the social consequences of that failure.

Emerson's vision of democratic individualism drew from several sources—romantic ideas about the power of individual genius to shape the surrounding world, Puritan ideas about a holy commonwealth composed of individuals whose capacities for mutual affection and cooperation derived from their personal relationships with God, and enlightenment ideas about the interdependence of religious and political liberty associated with the English philosopher John Locke.[9] Emerson developed the equation between religious and political liberty as force-fully as anyone of his time, arguing that democratic individualism, rightly perceived, led not to social fragmentation and divisiveness as conservatives feared, but to true social harmony and to the construction of an enlightened social order based on "the mutual reverence that is due from man to man." Many of America's leaders, preachers, and young men failed to grasp these truths, Emerson believed, and as a result, he complained, "now we are a mob."[10]

Americans were not too individualistic; they were not individualistic enough. "Trust thyself" was Emerson's motto; "every heart vibrates to that iron string." But if "[e]very *true* man is a cause, a country, and an age," he lamented that so many men found it hard to stay true. In the 1841 essay "Self-Reliance," he wrote that man was "a sort of sot, but now and then wakes up, exercises his reason and finds himself a true prince." People would get along better and respect each other, he thought, if they acted honestly and respected themselves. "If you are noble, I will love you; if you are not, I will not hurt you and myself by hypocritical attentions. If you are true, but not in the same truth with me, cleave to your companions; I will seek my own." With that inde-pendent spirit, people could respect each other as citizens, and coexist without fear and animosity. "It is alike your interest, and mine, and all men's," he explained, "to live in truth."[11]

Just as American democracy extended romantic idealism about indi-vidual genius to every citizen and common man, so the enormous open land of the North American continent seemed poised to host the ro-mantic recovery of nature. Emerson wanted his countrymen to see na-ture as a mirror of the self, and to find insight into nature a source of their own moral advancement. While other preachers encouraged Americans to "grope" for God "among the dry bones of the past," Emerson preached that opportunities for "an original relation to the universe" were boundless and close at hand. In a small book simply titled *Nature*, first published anonymously in 1836, he described his own experience of rediscovering God in nature. "Crossing a bare common, in snow puddles, at twilight, under a clouded sky, without having in my thoughts any occurrence of special good fortune," he wrote, "I have enjoyed a perfect exhilaration." Feeling "glad to the brink of fear," and "uplifted into infinite space," he discovered that nature was a see-through to God, a tissue of material symbols through which the mind of man and the mind of God met as one. "I become a transparent eyeball," he wrote, "I am nothing; I see all; the currents of the Universal Being circulate through me; I am part or parcel of God."[12]

Emerson turned to nature as a way to come to terms with personal grief as well as to symbolize the more general feeling of loss that pervaded his culture. As was true for many romantics, personal and public expression coincided for Emerson, with each representing and abetting the other. He published *Nature* five years after his frail wife, Ellen Louisa Tucker, died of consumption in 1831, before their second anniversary. After Ellen's death, he gave up his pastorate as a Unitarian minister at the Second Church in Boston and used his inheritance from Ellen to travel in Europe, where he met Coleridge, Wordsworth, and the Scottish philosopher Thomas Carlyle. He returned home with a religious appreciation of nature that enabled him to make some sense of Ellen's loss and instilled him with a new sense of being at home in the world. He remarried, settled in Concord in the rural outskirts of Boston, and wrote *Nature*, in which he confessed, "In the presence of nature a wild delight runs through the man, in spite of real sorrows." As he explained, "this delight does not reside in nature, but in man, or in a harmony of both." Happy or sad, "Nature always wears the colors of the spirit. To a man laboring under calamity, the heat of his own fire hath sadness in it." As he knew firsthand: "there is a kind of contempt of the landscape felt by him who has just lost by death a dear friend. The sky is less grand as it shuts down over less worth in the population."[13]

If nature's apparent receptivity to his grief over Ellen's death consoled Emerson, the tenor of his thought became more melancholy after his five-year-old son Waldo succumbed to scarlet fever in 1842. While Ellen's death propelled him toward an idealistic view of nature and life's events, Waldo's death forced him to confront the stubborn facts of reality with deeper sadness. As he wrote in his lamentation for Waldo, "vainly do these eyes recall / The school-march" where his "hyacinthine boy" commanded everyone's eye. "With children forward and behind / Like Cupids studiously inclined," Waldo was "the chieftain paced beside, / The center of the troop allied." Emerson's grief over Waldo's death coalesced with disappointment in his countrymen and sadness about America's lost childhood. "The little captain innocent / Took the eye with him when he went," Emerson wrote shortly after Waldo's death, "I am too much bereft."[14]

Although critics sometimes simplify Emerson as a sunny idealist, closer inspection of his religious point of view reveals a more somber and even chilly aspect to his thought. In an essay published in 1844 titled "Experience," he listed "Illusion, Temperament, Succession, Surface, Surprise, Reality, Subjectiveness" as "the lords of life." Not presuming to know their "order" or "completeness," he admitted, "I name them as I find them in my way." He continued to express profound respect for God, but after Waldo's death, Emerson's God was more like fate and less like himself. Even nature was no longer the solace it once had been. If her consolations after Ellen's death sent "wild delight" running through him, he was not so restored after Waldo's death. Thus in "Experience" he wrote, "There are always sunsets, and there is always genius; but only a few hours so serene that we can relish nature and criticism."[15]

Social Context

American Transcendentalism was not only a religious and literary movement, but also a social reform movement that emerged in reaction against the new forms of economic and cultural stratification caused by industrialization and the emergence of a national economy. As social reformers, Transcendentalists were staunch opponents of slavery involved in a wide range of social causes and practical efforts aimed at remedying the ills of American society. Incorporating their enthusiasm for moral progress with a longing for the self-sufficient, face-to-face communities they associated with life in the past, Transcendentalists wanted to call a halt to the corrupting effects of the breakdown of

Uncle Sam's Thanksgiving by Thomas Nast, *Harper's Weekly*, November 2, 1869. Courtesy of Florida State University.

community life that attended the development of a national market economy and the moral spoilage of the merchant class.

The wealth of New England merchants increased dramatically after the War of 1812, when trade embargos with Britain led them to invest heavily in domestic manufacture. In Massachusetts, textile mills and industrial cities grew up around Boston, first in Waltham and then in Lowell, where workers, many of them immigrants, spent long hours over power looms for small wages in poor conditions. Lowell went from a village of twelve houses in 1822 to a city of more than 20,000 in 1840 and it was in this era of dramatic social change that Transcendentalism developed. As an offshoot of Unitarianism, Transcendentalism emerged as a way of extending the cultural values of liberal Protestantism to the larger society, a mission that Unitarian churches failed to execute, critics believed, because of their elitism and commitments to insulating and upholding the merchant class.[16]

In addition to its encouragement of greed, the development of commerce also drew the economy of New England into increasing dependence on slave labor. Textile mills used cotton as raw material and the cheapest cotton in the Atlantic world was picked by slaves in the South. After the slaves picked and baled the cotton, slave owners sold and shipped it to port cities in the northern states and across the Atlantic. In both Old and New England, poor workers toiled under grueling conditions in textile factories, described by the English poet William Blake in his poem "Milton" as "dark Satanic Mills."[17]

Transcendentalists were keenly aware of the role that slavery played in the manufacturing system on which a good deal of Northern wealth depended. They all opposed slavery, and some of them, like Theodore Parker, figured prominently in the abolitionist movement. Transcendentalists were as much concerned about the moral corruption infecting their own culture as they were about the injustice suffered by slaves. In a similar way, Transcendentalists were concerned about the plight of factory workers and reached out to them with educational programs of various kinds. The failure of self-reliance involved in the exploitation of other people's labor, and the implications of that failure for the moral fiber of American culture, disturbed them more than anything.

Romantic Attraction to Other Religions

In contrast to the hatred of Catholicism among conservative evangelicals, Transcendentalists often appreciated the richness of Catholic art, the beauty of some Catholic devotions, and the organic sense of community that Catholic worship encouraged. If Transcendentalists perceived Catholicism through romantic eyes, downplaying the authoritarian dimensions of the Roman Church and overlooking the supernatural devotions of Irish immigrants pouring into mill towns like Waltham and Lowell, they nevertheless perceived contributions that Catholic sensibilities made to American culture.

To Orestes A. Brownson (1803–1876), who converted from Transcendentalism to Catholicism, the sacraments of the Catholic Church offered Christ in his "concrete existence," while Protestant churches relied merely on preaching *about* Christ. The immediate experience of Christ in Catholic sacraments would help Americans overcome their alienation and isolation from one another, Brownson believed. Furthermore, even as the Catholic Church had much to offer America, America had much to offer the church. In countries where Catholicism was established, authoritarian rules and procedures encouraged passivity in believers and undermined the morally energizing effects of the sacraments. In America, however, where religious liberty was guaranteed, the Catholic Church, Brownson wrote, was "thrown back on its naked rights and resources, as the spiritual kingdom of God on earth."[18]

Romantic belief in the universality of Reason led Transcendentalists to downplay the need for adherence to doctrinal formulations that separated one church from another, and enabled them to entertain the possibility that many different religious traditions contained variants of truth. Henry David Thoreau translated a Buddhist text from the French in 1844, and many Transcendentalists read the Hindu Bhagavad-Gita in English. Hindu ideas about the one god behind all gods and Buddhist ideas about the impersonality of consciousness complemented Transcendentalist ideas about Reason. And Transcendentalist respect for other religions did not stop with Hinduism and Buddhism. Emerson quoted from "the Koran" in his essay "Love," and from "Mahomet" in his essay on heroism—"Paradise is under the shadow of swords."[19] To be sure, Transcendentalists took out less from these scriptures than they read into them, and had only slight knowledge of how Hindus, Buddhists, and Muslims actually practiced their devotions. Nevertheless, they were among the boldest of their day in affirming religious pluralism as a natural expression of religious freedom and respect for individual conscience.[20]

In this affirmation, Transcendentalists extended the Protestant ideal of the priesthood of all believers to new dimensions. They also retained certain principles from the Puritan past. Like Puritans before them, Transcendentalists believed that virtuous individuals were the key to a good society, and that individual virtue sprung from the internal and invisible relationship between the individual and God, made visible in the virtuous actions of individuals and in their mutual regard for one another. In imagining the good society that would result from such individual attunement to God, Transcendentalists inherited the Reformed Protestant vision of a holy commonwealth and the New England Puritan hope that this Christian vision of society might be realized in the new world.

Connections to Evangelical Protestantism

Transcendentalists also inherited the concern for practical results and manifestations of grace that characterized the evangelical culture around them. In some respects, Transcendentalists were evangelicals, too, even if they did not interpret the Bible as a record of events that had occurred in the past, or would occur in the future, as conservative evangelicals did. For all their infatuation with the sublimities of Reason and heady readings of nature and history, Transcendentalists committed themselves to what they perceived as practical, socially useful action. Indeed, American romanticism might be distinguished from its European counterparts by its entrepreneurial zest and insistence on practicality, even if some of its "practical" schemes were a little hare-brained. Like Fruitlands, the short-lived commune created by Bronson Alcott in 1843, where simply "to be" was sufficient principle and members were expected to abstain from all commerce, hired labor, ownership, and selfishness.[21] If the Transcendentalists promoted a more egalitarian vision of social harmony than conservative evangelicals, they were no less interested in moral virtue and its social effects.

Transcendentalists shared with more conservative evangelicals a commitment to classifying subjective experience and directing it toward moral ends. This commitment derived, at least in part, from the exposure to common sense philosophy that Transcendentalists and conservative evangelicals shared. Transcendentalists rejected the mechanistic epistemology of common sense philosophy and the empiricist approach to the Bible associated with it. But they retained a similar interest in emotional feelings and their relation to moral virtue.

Emerson's early development as a religious thinker exemplifies the bridge from common sense philosophy to Transcendentalism. While a student at Harvard in 1820, he read the Scottish common sense philosopher Dugald Stewart and incorporated Stewart's concept of "moral sense" into his own thinking. Revising John Locke and other British philosophers who stressed the need for education in morality, Stewart argued that the human mind contained an innate moral sense implanted by God. In 1821, at the urging of his aunt Mary Moody Emerson,

Emerson read the overview of moral philosophy written by the dissenting English minister Richard Price, where he found Stewart's natural principle of moral sense equated with intuition. More than a decade later, after studying Coleridge seriously, Emerson linked the intuitive moral sense described by Price and Stewart to Coleridge's concept of Reason.[22]

By the time he published *Nature* in 1836, Emerson had repudiated the mechanistic aspects of Scottish common sense philosophy, especially the assumption that objects and events in nature existed independent of the mind. But he retained the strong emphasis on moral virtue of both Puritanism and common sense philosophy, along with an understanding of religious experience as an engagement of the moral sense, which he shared with many conservative evangelicals. Emerson disagreed with them about the relationship between God and the self. But he was no less committed to a reform of American society grounded in the moral virtue of individuals.

Emily Dickinson

Another proponent of individual religious experience, the Amherst poet Emily Dickinson lived in relative obscurity, but left a body of literature to exert considerable influence on American poetry and on religious attitudes toward self and nature that grew in popularity over time. She exemplifies the spirituality of nature that developed in nineteenth-century American culture and its roots in romantic Christianity. Many Americans inspired by her poetry found religion in their gardens as she did. "Some keep the Sabbath going to Church," she wrote around 1860, "I keep it, staying at Home— / With a Bobolink for a Chorister— / And an Orchard, for a Dome."[23]

Although Dickinson's investment in Christianity was considerable, she preferred the church of nature to the coercions of evangelical preaching. As a student for one year at Mount Holyoke Female Seminary, where all students were expected to undergo conversion and many of them were schooled to be missionaries, Dickinson was classified as "impenitent" and subjected to a series of religious lectures and special meetings.[24] She did not give in to this pressure at school or back at home, and announced, at age nineteen, "I haven't changed my mind yet—either, I love to be surly—and muggy—and cross." Wearing her noncompliance as a badge of integrity, she made fun of the idea that her resistance to conversion made her immoral. In one letter to a friend, she referred to herself as "one of the lingering *bad* ones," and in another, signed off as "Your very sincere, and *wicked* friend, Emily E. Dickinson."[25]

Emily Dickinson. Courtesy of the Library of Congress.

Dickinson had a way of seeing grandeur in small things, her own coy acknowledgement of sublimity in nature. "Two Butterflies went out at Noon," she wrote around 1862, "and waltzed upon a Farm— / Then stepped straight through the firmament / And rested, on a Beam."[26] Like Emerson, she anthropomorphized nature, but in a way that reflected her self-consciousness as a woman. "The Butterfly's Numidian Gown / With spots of Burnish roasted on / Is proof against the Sun," she wrote around 1876, "Yet prone to shut its spotted Fan / And panting on a Clover lean / As if it were undone."[27]

In Dickinson's version of self-reliance, "[t]he Soul selects her own Society / Then—shuts the Door."[28] She took pride and refuge in "a Columnar Self" that gave protection "In Tumult—or Extremity—." While

Emerson emphasized the friendship and respect for others that resulted from self-reliance, Dickinson celebrated a more isolated self, a defensive structure "That Lever cannot pry— / And Wedge cannot divide." Yet like Emerson, she identified self-reliance with moral integrity. "Suffice Us—for a Crowd," she wrote around 1863, "Ourself—and Rectitude." And just as Emerson sought solitude as a way of meeting God, Dickinson believed that the "Assembly" of the self was "not far off / From furthest Spirit—God."[29] Although her funny juxtaposition of terms carried a sense of humor Emerson might have envied, they shared the romantic conviction that, as she put it, "[t]he Brain—is wider than the Sky." Indeed, she proclaimed, "[t]he Brain is just the weight of God," and invited readers to "[H]eft them—Pound for Pound." If her proclamation mocked materialist conceptions of God, she was nevertheless serious that, in the end, brain and God "will differ—if they do— / As Syllable from Sound."[30]

Herman Melville (1819–1891)

Although he was less popular in his own day than Emerson, the writings of Herman Melville, like those of Emily Dickinson, exerted considerable influence on later American writers. Like both Dickinson and Emerson, Melville saw God in nature and, like them, he prized self-reliance. Yet his response to romantic philosophy, especially with regard to its implications for Christianity, was distinctive and in some respects more radical than that of the New England Transcendentalists. He parodied Christian claims to virtue and superiority, called attention to human evil and hypocrisy, and described the tragic as well as laughable implications of religious behavior. Melville exemplifies the quest for honest realism in some forms of American romanticism and the connections of that quest back to the New England Puritans on one side, and forward to existential theologians in the twentieth century on the other.

Melville's first book, *Typee* (1846), was a sea story based on his own travels in the South Pacific. It caused a sensation because of the contrast it drew between the robust pagans of the Marquesas and the degeneracy of the Hawaiian natives converted to Christianity by American missionaries. The book distressed many evangelicals. In certain respects, his criticism of Protestant missions was comparable to that of strict antimission Baptists who opposed missionary work because they believed Christians were few in number and not to be confused with proponents of conventional morality or with self-righteous people who attempted to convert other people to their way of living. Melville's estimate of the number of true Christians was similarly bleak.

The narrator of *Typee* proclaimed his respect for the Christian gospel and contrasted the honest and egalitarian virtue described there with the "missionary undertaking," which "is in itself but human; and subject, like everything else, to errors and abuses." In Hawaii at least, errors and abuses had overtaken the missionary enterprise. As Melville informed his readers, "There is something decidedly wrong in the practical operations of the Sandwich Island Missions." Hoping to enlighten supporters of missionary causes who had never seen where their dollars went, the narrator indicated his moral obligation to expose the difference between what missionaries said and conditions on the ground. "To read pathetic accounts of missionary hardships, and glowing descriptions of conversions, and baptisms taking place beneath palm-trees, is one thing," the narrator explained, but "to go to the Sandwich Islands and see the missionaries dwelling in picturesque and prettily furnished coral-rock villas, whilst the miserable natives are committing all sorts of immoralities around them, is quite another."[31]

In his most ambitious work, *Moby-Dick* (1851), Melville wrote another sea story to express his understanding of human society and the distance between humanity and God. As the literary critic Leslie Sheldon argued, Melville systematically reworked the imagery, themes, and plot of Milton's *Paradise Lost* in *Moby-Dick*. Much as Satan in *Paradise Lost* seeks vengeance against "the Son" for casting him out of heaven, Melville's Captain Ahab takes his ship and its crew on a mission against the great White Whale Moby-Dick, who humiliated and crippled Ahab in a previous hunt. Like Satan, who ensnares others in a world of lies centered on him, Ahab leads his men to death for the sake of his own revenge. Ultimately, Ahab is not victorious any more than Satan in *Paradise Lost*, nor is there any diminishment in the beauty or power of the vast ocean that swallows the malevolent captain and most of the crew. Ishmael, the narrator and only sailor to survive, recognizes the majesty of the White Whale, "the glistening white shadow from his broad, milky forehead," and the whale's close relationship to the godlike sea: "behind, the blue waters interchangeably flowed over into the moving valley of his steady wake; and on either hand bright bubbles arose and danced by his side."[32]

In Milton's *Paradise Lost*, the "Son" is not as vividly delineated as Satan; the Son is a haunting presence not clearly discerned. His wrathful judgment against Satan is clear, but his judgment against the whole of humanity is not definitive; there is an element of redemption and a promise—as well as dire warning—for the future. Melville's story is no less complex or ambiguous with respect to the future. The sole survivor of Ahab's battle with the whale is the narrator Ishmael, floating on a coffin. Thus Melville advanced a view of religious and moral life different from the salvation in heaven that evangelicals preached. While evangelicals often portrayed Christ as an idealized version of themselves, Melville's Messiah was less anthropomorphic, more intimidating, and reminiscent of the "Being in general" that Jonathan Edwards associated with the sheer presence of God and the "divine and supernatural light" that awakened sinners.

As Melville drew on Puritan theology to construct *Moby-Dick*, he cast some of the underlying principles of that theology through the prism of romantic interpretations of nature and society current in nineteenth-century America. Melville's understanding of sin and redemption, while drawn from the Bible and Puritan theology, is couched in more secular terms. While Milton wrote a poem about the motivations of individual characters represented in the Bible, Melville wrote a whaling adventure in which a captain takes his crew across the oceans in a quest for personal revenge. In *Moby-Dick*, biblical themes are more implicit and embedded within Melville's depiction of nature and human history.

Moby-Dick can also be read as a commentary on democracy. The book explores a demagogue's power to exploit the minds and bodies of less powerful men and the men's inability to assert their own individuality against him. The crew aboard the *Pequod* cannot withstand the force of their captain and they all finally submit to his egoistical drive. Yet, the one who survives has a tale to tell that sets Ahab's rage in perspective—against the tremendous beauty of the sea, and the humanity and brotherhood of the crew.

Romantic literature and philosophy influenced Melville, but he expressed the romantic sense of religious alienation more straightforwardly than Emerson and other American Transcendentalists. His vision of God and Christ was as terrifying as that of Jonathan Edwards. But unlike Edwards, Melville was a lover of democracy who viewed the egalitarian fellowship of self-reliant individuals as the epitome of moral virtue. At the same time, the dangers and limits of democracy concerned him more than they did many of the New England Transcendentalists, and he was more circumspect about democracy's prospects. Yet he did not fear anarchy and was never happy about the social conservatism characteristic of much of Protestant society. In many respects, as Melville scholar Clare Sparks suggested, he was a radical Puritan who resisted dreams of a holy commonwealth along with mysticism about American civil religion.[33]

Melville carried forward something like the vision of the seventeenth-century Puritan radical Roger Williams, who rejected any notion of America as a New Israel, and advocated religious tolerance and commitment to secular government as consequences of the belief that true

Christians were hidden in society and scattered throughout the world. Much as Williams warmed to the natural humanity and open-hearted generosity of Native Americans and warned that God might open heaven to wild Indians, and shut out many English people who called themselves Christian, Melville created a noble savage in the character of Queequeg, a native of the South Seas and, for all his idols, a man of honest self-reliance. Ishmael describes Queequeg as the epitome of Emersonian virtue: "Savage though he was, and hideously marred about the face—at least to my taste—his countenance yet had a something in it which was by no means disagreeable. You cannot hide the soul." His strong face bore a remarkable resemblance to that of the first President of the United States, Ishmael thought, leading him to conclude that "Queequeg was George Washington cannibalistically developed." In a comment worthy of Emerson, Ishmael noted, "He looked like a man who had never cringed and never had had a creditor." As a result of his "self-collectedness"—"content with his own companionship; always equal to himself"—Queequeg was an ideal companion. For melancholy Ishmael, the brotherly comfort provided by this "pagan friend" was an even greater boon "since Christian kindness has proved but hollow courtesy."[34]

Walt Whitman (1819–1892)

A New Yorker, as was Melville, the poet and essayist Walt Whitman took the egalitarian romanticism to the streets of Brooklyn and Manhattan and onto the battlefields of the Civil War. Inspired by Emerson's idea of self-reliance, Whitman extolled the heroism of young men wounded during the war. In addition to his celebration of human nature in *Leaves of Grass* (1855), which Emerson called "the most extraordinary piece of wit & wisdom that America has yet contributed," Whitman spent several years as a nurse in Union hospitals outside of Washington, distributing small gifts, penning letters for soldiers, and writing about their bravery in suffering. In notebooks written during the war, he wrote about the heroism he witnessed in the hospitals, as well as the heroism of the thousands of "our hardy darlings," as he called them, who died in the field. "Unnamed, unknown, remain, and still remain, the bravest soldiers," he wrote in 1863. The typical one "crawls aside to some brush-clump, or ferny tuft, on receiving his death-shot—there sheltering a little while, soaking roots, grass and soil, with red blood" until he finally "crumbles in mother earth, unburied and unknown."[35]

Whitman left a memorable description of President Abraham Lincoln, whom he regularly passed in the streets of Washington during the war. Complaining that no portrait of Lincoln did his justice to his presence, Whitman described the President's "dark brown face, with the deep-cut lines, the eyes, always to me with a deep latent sadness in the expression." Suggesting parallels between Lincoln and Christ, Whitman called Lincoln "the greatest, best, most characteristic, artistic, moral personality." Lincoln stood for "UNIONISM in its truest and amplest sense," Whitman wrote, noting that "The tragic splendor of his death, purging, illuminating all, throws round his form, his head, an aureole that will remain and will grow brighter through time."[36]

In a recent discussion of the importance of Emerson and Whitman in the cultural tradition of American democracy, religious ethicist Jeffrey Stout pointed to Whitman's emphasis on the humanity of ordinary people and the supreme value of the individual. These elements of democratic tradition in America, Stout argued, are as important for the future of the United States as any of the numerous religious traditions that American democracy supports. As the chief poet of this democracy, Whitman saw individual freedom and citizenship, based "on one broad, primary, universal, common platform," as a political faith derived from Protestant Christianity. "What Christ appear'd for in the moral-spiritual field for human-kind," citizenship in a democracy carries out at a political level, "namely, that in respect to the absolute soul, there is in the possession of such by each single individual, something so transcendent" that "it places all beings on a common level, utterly regardless of the distinctions of intellect, virtue, station, or any height or lowliness whatever."[37]

Sentimental Christianity

Egalitarian romantics perceived moral truths in the individual's relationship with God, nature, and other people in terms of the credo of self-reliance. Others influenced by romantic philosophy interpreted Christianity more conservatively and concluded that God sanctioned natural differences between people and intended human society to be constructed hierarchically. For romantic conservatives, reverence for nature often meant that men were morally obligated to defend and protect the weaker sex and that Anglo-Saxons were a superior race, destined to dominate other races and obliged to control and teach them.

Belief in the divine ordination of social hierarchies was hardly new or limited to Protestants affected by romantic philosophy or mood. But the romantic emphasis on intuition enabled conservative Protestants to justify their conceptions of social order by appeals to a "natural" order of society that elevated their desire for social dominance above rational analysis and moral challenge. Thus both democratic individualists and social conservatives used romantic philosophy to salvage Christian faith and negotiate social change. The divergent interpretations of romantic philosophy and mood expressed in nineteenth-century America derived from differences in how the emerging national economy affected people in different regions with different social interests and ways of handling social change.

With a boldness derived, perhaps, from a sense of belonging to an educated class of post-Puritan religious thinkers, Emerson, Dickinson, Melville, and Whitman all grieved over lost innocence. To a considerable extent, their creativity sprang from efforts to express their own religious insight and sense of moral justice against conventional piety. More conservative Protestants relied on an emotional sentimentality these bolder, self-reliant types often eschewed, and this sentimentality contributed to their conservatism. Emerson, Dickinson, Melville, and Whitman were not immune to sentimentality, but they were also concerned to describe the dissonance between what they felt and what they knew, and were more able to resist the recourse to nostalgia to avoid facing unpleasant realities. Willing to risk desolation rather than succumb to dishonesty and hypocrisy, Emerson, Dickinson, Melville, and Whitman were similar, in at least one respect, to Jonathan Edwards' wife Sarah, whose well-known declaration of willingness to be damned "for the glory of God" expressed a heroic form of Calvinism.[38]

For many reasons—upbringing, education, temperament, fear, disappointment, or unrepentant desire for dominance and power—sentimental Protestants chose to see the dissonance between what they felt and what they knew more as a problem to be overcome (or overlooked) than an opportunity for self-reliance. Sentimental Christians expected reality to conform to their idealistic expectations, and took the strength of their feelings about how things should be as evidence of how they would be. In using emotion to hold onto idealism about the past, their approach to religion was emotionally conservative. As an aid to self-protection and cultural defense, sentimental religion was a natural ally and contributor to social conservatism.

Attitudes toward death illustrate the difference between the self-reliance of egalitarian romanticism and the sentimental romanticism of conservatives. For Emerson and Dickinson, death was a torment. Although both sought ways of minimizing, justifying, and coping with it, Emerson never recovered from Waldo's death and Dickinson called death "the supple suitor / That wins at last."[39] For all romantics, death was a test of how far human feeling could go in controlling reality.

While more self-reliant types explored the limits of feeling in the face of death, many sentimentalists took their emotional intolerance for death as evidence of its unreality and portrayed heaven as a materially improved extension of life on earth.

The popular novel *Gates Ajar* (1868), by the theologically trained writer Elizabeth Stuart Phelps (1844–1911), captured the sentimental attitude toward death. As the novel opens, Mary's grief over the death of her brother Roy in the Civil War causes her to question God's goodness. Benevolent Aunt Winifred, who communicates with her deceased husband John and looks forward to recovering her "pretty brown hair" in heaven, arrives to comfort Mary and bring her back from doubt. An expert in overcoming grief, Winifred explains that, like all "organized society," heaven includes "homes, not unlike the homes of this world." And she lays out the sentimental strategy of taking feeling as evidence of reality: since "a happy home is the happiest thing in the world," Winifred cannot "see why it should not be in any world." Familiar with the latest trends in romantic philosophy without succumbing to its underlying melancholy, Winifred wrestles troubled souls back from the brink of existential awareness. She refers to her version of Christian theology as "spiritual materialism" and expresses full confidence in its logic and moral virtue.[40]

Gates Ajar came to print amidst widespread anguish about loss of life in the American Civil War, and the novel's popularity is an indicator of how difficult it must have been for Americans to develop a clear-eyed assessment of that blood bath. While sentimental Christianity emerged prior to the war as a way of coping with crises of faith, salvaging idealism, and controlling social change, the slaughter of so many brothers, sons, fathers, husbands, and friends in the war exacerbated these crises of faith and longings for the past. The Civil War gave people new reason to want to live in imaginary worlds. If nineteenth-century American Protestants were awash in sentimentality, the war invited that inundation.

The embalming business sprung up during the Civil War as one especially concrete form of sentimental Christianity and its "spiritual materialism." Embalmers slowed the deterioration of corpses and shipped them back home ready for open-casket viewing. A new cadre of professional corpse handlers strove to recreate a life-like appearance in dead bodies by coloring the skin and pumping chemical fluids into veins. As a religious rite, embalming disguised the ugly reality of death and provided a material symbol of the deceased person's life after death and bodily resurrection in heaven.[41]

In a theological equivalent of embalming and its spiritual materialism, many Protestants wanted to preserve the sanctity of blood shed in the Civil War as a guarantee of future redemption. Sentimentalists not only linked the blood of the Civil War dead to the sacrifical blood of Christ; they also turned the horror of war into a mystical transport to cultural glory.

In his oration in honor of fallen alumni at Yale College in 1865, the Hartford Congregationalist Horace Bushnell (1802–1876) offered the Union version of the idea that the Civil War was part of America's providential destiny. One of the most influential American readers of Coleridge aside from Emerson, Bushnell construed the philosophic distinction between Reason and Understanding outlined by Coleridge to mean that ideals that alleviated grief and guilt could be presented as insights into the true nature of reality. Speaking to an audience that had seen the broken bodies of many young men return home, Bushnell took the grief they experienced as a force destined to move history forward. Instead of regretting such tremendous loss, or suggesting that it might have been wasteful, he celebrated the blood shed by soldiers on both sides as a sacrifice insuring a brighter, grander future for America.

Bushnell represented the dead as embodiments of Christ whose bloodshed carried out a divine plan for America and the world. "And here it is that the dead of our war have done for us a work so precious, which is all their own—they have bled for us; and by this simple sacrifice of blood they have opened for us a new great chapter of life," Bushnell proclaimed, "a really stupendous chapter of history." Before the war, "we had a little very beautiful history, which we were beginning to cherish and fondly cultivate. But we had not enough of it to beget a full historic consciousness." America had been a callow nation, divided immaturely against itself: "We had not bled enough, as yet, to merge our colonial distinctions and make us a proper nation." But now that "this war-deluge is over," America is like the earth "when the flood of Noah receded." The nation would be stronger, more closely attuned to the will of God, and the union now coming forth "will be that bond of common life that God has touched with blood; a sacredly heroic, Providentially tragic unity" in which "the sense of nationality becomes even a kind of religion."[42]

Bushnell emphasized the tragic dimensions of the war to underscore the nobility of character that developed through the terrible ordeal and to anthropomorphize America as a noble character akin to Christ himself. Using a classical definition of tragedy, he linked the Civil War to a cathartic and ennobling outcome distinct from accidental or mean-ingless catastrophe. As a Christian tragedy, the Civil War marked an important turning point in an unfolding, providential history that re-quired suffering and blood sacrifice as part of a larger process of redemption. Just as Christ died to set believers free of sin, and enable them to rise to "true manhood," Bushnell explained, so "the Christian son, and brother, and friend" laid down his life in "the cause of Christ" and "in the testimony of a common martyrdom." The blood of the Civil War dead purchased a sanctified future in which America itself had become a sacred entity worth dying for, a national embodiment of Christ himself.[43]

The contrast between Bushnell's vision of the war and that of Abraham Lincoln (1809–1865) shows that American Protestants had resources within their own religious experience to resist such patriotic sentimentality. While Bushnell linked the blood of the Civil War dead with the sacrifice of Christ, Lincoln worked against the tendency to define God's will in terms of human partiality. In the Gettysburg Address (1863), he used some of the symbols of religious sacrifice and American destiny that Bushnell later expanded upon, but his emphasis on the commitment Americans owed to God never crossed into self-assurance about God's relationship to America. Lincoln declared that "the brave men, living and dead, who struggled" at Gettysburg had "consecrated" the battlefield, and "the living" should "be dedicated here to the unfinished work which they who fought here have thus far so nobly advanced." But he never equated the blood of the men who died at Gettysburg to the redemptive blood of Christ, as Bushnell would. And while he linked their "devotion" to the resolve the living should have, that "that this nation, under God, shall have a new birth of freedom," he never conflated American resolve to live under God with any divine plan for American greatness.[44]

In his Second Inaugural Address (1865), Lincoln moved further away from the idea that America had a special relationship to God, observing that Americans on both sides had expected the conflict to be resolved in their favor and enlisted God in their opposing causes. "Both read the same bible, and pray to the same God; and each invokes His aid against the other." However "strange" it seemed that defenders of slavery "should dare to ask a just God's assistance in wringing their bread from the sweat of other men's faces," Lincoln warned against self-righteousness: "let us judge not that we be not judged." With a sense of both the obscurity and omnipotence of God, Lincoln declared, "The Almighty has His own purposes."[45]

Like Herman Melville, Lincoln resisted the idea that America had a special relationship with God that privileged her history and people above others. Like Melville, he had a lively sense of human depravity and of the justice implicit in God's destruction of men. In a vision of God's punishment of America not unlike Melville's vision of the White

Whale's wrath in destroying almost the entire crew of humanity aboard the *Pequod*, Lincoln declared in his Second Inaugural Address that "if God wills" the war to "continue, until all the wealth piled by the bondman's two hundred and fifty years of unrequited toil shall be sunk, and until every drop of blood drawn with the lash shall be paid by another drawn with the sword, as was said three thousand years ago, so still it must be said: 'the judgments of the Lord, are true and righteous altogether.'"

While resisting sentimentality, Lincoln sought inspiration and guidance from the Bible through a reformulation of Christian thought influenced by romanticism. As Lincoln historian Stewart Winger argued, Lincoln lost the belief in miracles of supernatural revelation that were part of his upbringing as a strict Baptist, but retained the moral outlook of that tradition. He never lost sight of the Calvinist vision of humanity as inherently sinful, prideful, and rebellious against God, or of the necessity of having an honest relationship with God. But he recast this vision in terms of a romantic sense of the deity present in the depths of the human mind. As he explained in 1846, in a defense against the charge of religious infidelity, he believed the mind of each individual "was impelled to action, or held in rest by some power, over which the mind has no control."[46] Like Melville, Lincoln thought God acted within the minds of individuals as an underlying intelligence too deep for the human mind to grasp fully. As Melville did in *Moby-Dick*, Lincoln expressed a romantic version of Calvinism in the Second Inaugural that focused on awareness of human depravity and on the moral sense, however dimly perceived, connecting the human mind to that of God.

If Bushnell's interpretation of the Civil War as a blood sacrifice was sentimental in comparison with that of Lincoln, southern interpretations were even more so. Many southern writers identified the sacrifice of Christ with that of their own brave men and interpreted the defeat of the Confederacy with the death of Christ and promise of resurrection. As one minister assured war veterans in Louisville, "the memories of your Gethsemane" and "the agonies of your Golgotha" would not go unredeemed. Similarly, Henry Wharton's novel *White Blood* (1906) described an upstanding clergyman who likened the plight of the South toward the end of the war to "the blessed Saviour who passed from gloomy Gethsemane to the judgment hall, through the fearful ordeal of being forsaken by His friends, and then on to the bloody Cross." Thus, "the South shall rise again" was not a secular boast; it was religious battle cry that linked the reappearance of the Christian nation of southern culture to the resurrection that followed the death of Christ. As historian Charles Reagan Wilson argued in his influential book, *Baptized in Blood: The Religion of the Lost Cause*, southern ministers and politicians created a cultural religion out of defeat, and based this religion on the fusion of Christian symbols with nostalgia for antebellum southern culture.[47]

Sentimental Christianity in the South

Protestant defenders of southern culture interpreted the Bible as sanctioning a patriarchal society based on land, agriculture, slavery, and the glorification and protection of white female virtue. In their reading, the Bible endorsed a stable and conservative social order. By contrast, northern efforts to reform society along egalitarian lines struck against the divine order of society ordained by God. South Carolina's leading men embraced such conservative views with special fervor and hauteur. An English visitor attending a dinner in 1835 with South Carolina College President Thomas Cooper and several members of his faculty was "particularly struck" by "the total want of caution and reserve in the ultra opinions they expressed about religion and politics." As some of the first and foremost spokesmen for secession from the United States, Cooper and his men resented any infringement on their own dominance: "imbibing from their infancy the notion that they are born to command," the Englishman observed, "it will be intolerable to them to submit to be, in their own estimation, the drudges of the Northern manufacturers, whom they despise as an inferior race of men."[48]

Perceiving Christianity among slave owners as a means of their securing dominance, the former Maryland slave Frederick Douglass (1818–1895) observed that "of all slaveholders with whom I have ever met, religious slaveholders are the worst. I have ever found them the meanest and basest, the most cruel and cowardly, of all the others." Citing the Reformed Methodist minister Reverend Daniel Weeden as an example of a "merciless, *religious* wrench" who beat slaves to show who was master, Douglass recalled that Weeden's "maxim was, Behave well or behave ill, it is the duty of a master to occasionally whip a slave, to remind him of his master's authority."[49]

South Carolinians led the way in developing a political and religious justification for secession that involved taking a stand against the perceived moral perversions and aggressions of the North. They also led the way in infusing evangelicalism with romantic rhetoric and in infusing romantic rhetoric with evangelical zeal. Thus in 1861, writing in the *Keowee Courier*, a periodical for South Carolina intellectuals, Reverend T. L. McBryde preached that the North had launched "an unrighteous and unchristian war" against the harmonious Christian culture of the South, a culture that included the practice of slavery sanctioned by

J. P. Moore   Miss Lydia Lawrence
RECITATION ROOM

The Recitation Room, Joanna P. Moore. Courtesy of *Documenting the American South* (http://docsouth.unc.edu), The University of North Carolina at Chapel Hill Libraries, Rare Book Collection.

biblical texts. All of the disharmony, self-righteousness, and corruption that threatened Christian civilization were on display in the North. "Abolition," he claimed, was a sin against God, and "but one of the fruits of the evil tree that grows so luxuriantly in the North." With a similarly disdainful view of northern reforms, another writer for the *Keowee Courier* argued in 1861 that Satan could be called "the first abolitionist" since he was the first to falsely invoke a "higher law" aimed at undermining the divine order of society. In 1863, South Carolina's *Confederate Baptist* chimed in, proclaiming that the North had "chosen Lucifer for their patron divinity, and are seeking to reinstate him to his lost dignity and honor."[50]

To paint an idealistic picture of Christian culture in the South, writers in Charleston, Richmond, and New Orleans drew on conservative romantic writers on the other side of the Atlantic, especially the romantic Scottish philosopher and literary critic Thomas Carlyle (1795–1881) who championed the virtues of organic and authoritarian societies that could resist modern infidelity and anarchy. An influential British interpreter of German romanticism, Carlyle translated Goethe's *Wilhelm Meister* in 1824 and, in 1825, published a biography of the

German philosopher Friedrich Schiller, who turned away from common sense philosophy to celebrate mankind's esthetic impulse. Emerson read Carlyle, sought the reclusive Scott out for conversation during his European tour after Ellen's death, and incorporated into his own philosophy Carlyle's theory that great men embodied the spirit and feelings of their time. But as Carlyle's animus toward democracy as a violation of moral order became increasingly strident after 1840, his writing appealed more to southern conservatives and less to Emerson and other New England Transcendentalists. Many southerners interpreted Carlyle's dismissal of the abolitionist movement as "twaddle" to be an endorsement of southern culture, along with his characterization of the American North as "shot through with atheism, decadence, and self-indulgence."[51]

Also important in the formation of southern culture, the historical novelist Walter Scott (1771–1832) generated nostalgia for the old clans of the Scottish Highlands—a nostalgia to which Scotch-Irish immigrants to America and their offspring were especially prone. Scott's romantic celebration of the cultural nationalism of the Scottish clans and their moral superiority to English Saxons contributed to conceptions of southern manhood and to dreams of the South as an independent nation. Scott's depictions of medieval chivalry in some of his novels also contributed to romantic visions of the South. Southern planters borrowed Scott's term for the knightly class, "The Chivalry," for themselves and adopted his use of the archaic term "Southron" for southerner. A few plantation owners even hosted jousting tournaments based on passages from *Ivanhoe*.[52]

In his study of southern romanticism, historian Michael O'Brien warned against simplistic readings of Scott and also against simplistic interpretations of the southern readers who found Scott congenial. O'Brien argued that Scott was an eminently modern writer who "thought it right to remember and shed a gentlemanly tear" over Scottish chieftains and medieval courts but who also accepted their disappearance, believed in progress, and finally preferred the civilities and comforts of modern life to the brutish violence that he acknowledged as a characteristic of the past. Scott's southern readers felt similarly, O'Brien argued. Their defense and practice of slavery were not antiquated vestiges of premodern society, as some historians maintain, but essential to the vision of how many southerners thought modern America should develop. Southern planters crafted a society in which slave labor facilitated manufacture and in which the advantages of a market economy were wedded to a hierarchical social order saturated with Christian symbolism. This construction of a nation-state on the basis of a synthetic and deliberately crafted vision of culture was hardly medieval; indeed, its approach to human labor, racial division of society, and nostalgia for racial purity anticipated Nazi Germany. In O'Brien's words, "It was all too modern."[53]

Other historians agreed. Historian Scott Poole argued, "South Carolina, and much of the Old South, embodied the Janus face of modernity." Modern ideas about property ownership and capital investment shaped southern concepts of slave ownership and the leading men of the South crafted an ideology drawn from conservative romanticism to incorporate slavery as an essential element of southern culture. If their "respect for land and mastery" invoked sentimental visions of the past, their deliberate effort "to shape a public culture that would exhibit the values of hierarchy, prescriptive tradition, and liberty" was thoroughly modern.[54]

Romanticism led to the self-consciousness about culture out of which southern nationalism emerged. O'Brien called the southerners' strategic way of thinking about their lifeways an "act of synthesis, the step that brought components into a relationship that the Southerners of 1840 agreed to call Southern culture."[55] With biblical symbols of creation, fall, and redemption at hand, romanticism enabled southerners to forge symbolic connections between Christianity and southern honor, social order, and slaveholding. Thus Satan came to symbolize the North and its perceived atheism, arrogance, and rebellion against the divine order of society. And the Christian South became a living embodiment of Christ's work of overcoming evil and restoring moral virtue.

In sum, then, Protestant romantics, both North and South, deployed symbols of creation, fall, and redemption to portray nature, history, and American society. And as moody, intuitive people, romantics on both sides of the Mason-Dixon line struggled with feelings of disappointment and lost innocence, and looked for some kind of redemption. Sentimentalists simply depended more than other romantics on nostalgia for the past, and were less willing to examine the dissonance between their feelings and reality. Insofar as they could not think beyond their feelings, sentimentalists could be like the characters in Melville's *Pierre* (1852) whose romantic visions of how things should be enabled the cruelty and violence of their social world.

Sentimental Family Values

Sentimental conceptions of Christian culture were (and still are) deeply gendered; they define and limit many of the opportunities American society offers for women's equality and leadership. American women seeking equality and leadership have often found themselves engaged with sentimental ideals of womanhood, sometimes embracing those ideals as indirect means of influence and power, sometimes risking censure by circumventing them. Such difficulties have diminished dramatically in recent years, not because sentimentalism has disappeared, but because many women and men have become more self-conscious about the conventions of sentimental behavior and more skillful and fair-minded in handling them.

In nineteenth-century America, romantic commitment to an underlying spirit connecting humanity, nature, and God encouraged some Protestants to claim that differences in the behaviors of men and women were natural, and hence divinely ordained. The sentimental tendency to equate feeling with reality only exaggerated this willingness to naturalize gender difference. Sentimental romantics invested the gendered elements already present in Protestant theology with a new kind of cultural reality.

For example, in *Women's Suffrage: The Reform against Nature* (1868), Horace Bushnell argued that women were particularly receptive to religious influence because of their natural capacity for "delicate feeling and bright insight." The "facility and grace of movement" with which nature endowed women symbolized the beauty of divine grace, Bushnell thought. Indeed, he claimed that man is to woman as law is to gospel and that woman's nature was the "more effective" aspect "of the divine power; that which is the power of God unto salvation."[56]

Like other formulators of sentimental Christianity, Bushnell discerned a special correspondence between woman and Christ that involved compassion and suffering along with grace and beauty. Bushnell believed that self-sacrifice came naturally to women as part of their special correspondence to Christ and gave them real emotional influence within the home. While a father, who governs by reason, might earn the "respect of his children," Bushnell believed that a mother's love was so compelling that it inevitably won the "ineradicable, inexpugnable possession of the life of her sons and daughters." One important source of this compulsive love was self-denial. Through self-denial, a mother "fastens a feeling so deep in the child," Bushnell wrote, that she elicits reverence and obedience.[57]

Bushnell was not alone in drawing a correspondence between divine and motherly love. The famous Brooklyn preacher Henry Ward Beecher described the maternal sentiments of God who "pardons like a mother" and "kisses" her child's "offence into everlasting forgetfulness." As Beecher explained in 1858, "God Almighty is the mother, and the soul is the tired child; and he folds it in his arms, and dispels its fears, and lulls it to repose, saying, 'Sleep, my darling; sleep. It is I who watch thee.'"[58]

Such sentimental ideas about God and motherhood affirmed the religious importance of the home; descriptions of God as a forgiving mother, and womanhood as essentially Christ-like, called attention to the home as a center of Christian life. This emphasis on the religious atmosphere of the home in turn helped to legitimate the growing separation between family and work and the increasingly bifurcated association, especially among the middle class, of women with family and men with work. Although they recast it in terms of their own concerns about culture and modern life, proponents of this sentimental construction of gender roles drew on a long-standing commitment to family life that had been a crucial part of Protestant thought since the sixteenth century.

In his calls for religious revitalization in the sixteenth century, Martin Luther criticized the idealization of monastic life that separated Christians from the intimacies and responsibilities of marriage and parenting, and encouraged Christians to develop their religious vocations in the context of family life. Building on Luther's enthusiasm for domestic life, many reformers joined belief in the importance of family worship and religious instruction with skepticism about the authority of priests and their power to conduct absolution and atonement through sacraments. In England, the positive thrust of Puritan strategies for reform centered on "well-ordered households" as building blocks of a Christian society. In Milton's *Paradise Lost*, Adam and Eve were both the family and the state, and this emphasis on the importance of the family is one of the major keys to understanding Milton's vision of how human society ought to be organized. Other Puritans agreed. As William Gouge wrote in the manual of domestic life in 1622, "a family is a little Church, and a little Common-wealth." It is also "a schoole," he added, "wherein the first principle and ground of government and subjection are learned: whereby men are fitted to greater matters in Church or Common-wealth."[59]

More than two centuries later, Bushnell's best-known work, *A Discourse on Christian Nurture*, published originally in 1847, and in expanded and more widely read form in 1861, represented a major reformulation of this Protestant emphasis on family life. Criticizing the emphasis revival preachers placed on the dramatic transformation of "new birth," and the thoroughgoing corruption of original sin, Bushnell took the view that goodness was inherent in human nature and that children ought to be brought up to think of themselves as Christian and never differently. Critical of Calvinist churches that fostered "no element of genial warmth and love about the child" and gave "religion rather a forbidding aspect," Bushnell warned parents that some churches might even impede Christian nurture. He urged parents to take responsibility for nurturing their children's moral development and decide which churches and doctrines they should subscribe to (and which not) to supplement the Christian nurture their children received at home.[60]

Bushnell's romantic and sentimental celebration of the home as the center of Christian nurture coincided with major changes in industrialization and the development of a market economy. In colonial America, a society without factories, hospitals, monasteries, or cathedrals, Protestant homes had operated as centers of economic production and also as welfare institutions. Seventeenth- and many eighteenth-century Americans raised, grew, produced, and prepared food at home and made clothes, furniture, soap, and candles at home. Apprentices, servants, orphans, single people, old people, and people with mental disorders lived at home, they gave birth and died at home, and housewives nursed the sick and dispensed medicine, food, and clothing at home. Over time, the home declined in importance as a supplier of goods and emerged as the chief place where goods produced by others were consumed. As a national economy developed in the early nineteenth century, increasing industrial production and domestic consumption coincided with growing cultural emphasis on gender role differentiation. Traditional Protestant investment in the home as a center for religious life coincided with its diminishment as a center of economic production and its enlargement as a center of culture and consumption. The sentimental romantic linkage between Christianity and nature, and between Christian nurture and domesticity, contributed to this shift. It also coincided with a new attitude toward the impersonal brutality of economic production as something that could not be helped, but could be placed outside the sacred precincts of Christian homes.

In its trajectory over time, sentimental romanticism helped Protestants translate the symbols and stories of Christianity into secular terms, defining moral thought more and more in terms of nature, nation, and home, and less and less in terms of the sacraments, the church, and theological doctrine. During the nineteenth century, affluent, educated men in many parts of the country developed professional, managerial, and investment skills and married women who devoted themselves to their families and to benevolent work. Outside this increasingly well-established commercial and professional class, self-sufficient farmers had a hard time making ends meet, immigrants and poor natives worked in factories or as servants, and adventurous young people, especially men, often moved west.

New opportunities for homesteading and commerce drew many people into the Ohio River valley, through the Erie Canal, up and down the Mississippi, and across the Mississippi into western territories acquired by the United States. Protestants from Germany and Scandinavia established farms and built towns west of the Mississippi where the preservation of languages and customs from old countries provided some insulation from American culture. But the consumerist lifestyle sustained by sentimental Christianity became increasingly powerful in shaping American culture across the continent. As an influential representative of that lifestyle, Bushnell visited in the Midwest and spent the year 1856 as president pro tempore of the University of California, during which time he planned the Berkeley campus.

In the South, numerous small manufacturing industries developed, agricultural operations fed textile mills in the North and in Britain, and slaves provided much of the labor, enabling investors, attorneys, and land owners to cultivate a genteel home life. While southerners staunchly defended their family values, northern critics took them to task for the destructive effects of the slave system on family ties. In her enormously popular antislavery novel, *Uncle Tom's Cabin* (1852), the New England writer Harriet Beecher Stowe (1811–1896) condemned slavery in terms of its harmful effects on family life, separating husbands from wives, and parents from children, and corrupting the moral characters of slaveholders and their families. Stowe represented slavery as a destroyer of the natural order of Christian family life in which wives and children belonged to their husbands and fathers. At one point in the novel, George Harris says to his wife during their escape from slavery to Canada, "O Eliza! if these people only knew what a blessing it is for a man to feel that his wife and child belong to *him*! I've often wondered to see that men could call their wives and children *their own* fretting and worrying about anything else. Why, I feel rich and strong, though we have nothing but our bare hands."[61]

Southern writers responded to Stowe's work with a defense of slavery based on many of the same principles of Christian nurture and romantic domesticity that Stowe used to condemn it. Phyllis Eastman's *Aunt Phillis's Cabin; or, Southern Life as It Is* (1852) and John W. Page's *Uncle Robin in his Cabin in Virginia and Tom without One in Boston* (1853) defended southern life for its reverence and protection of the Christian family, which these authors, like Stowe, celebrated as the mainstay of Christian life.[62] For southern defenders of sentimental culture, the family values of the South had more warmth and more integrity than those espoused by liberal reformers from the North.

Romanticism developed differently in the South than in the North and partisans on both sides parted ways over slavery and its relationship to Christian society. Yet dispute over whether or not slavery had a justifiable place within a Christian nation obscured the underlying similarities between North and South and the role that romanticism—especially sentimental romanticism—played in constructing the cultural and religious terrain over which the two sides fought. At the most basic level, romantic thinking about nature, gender, and family life helped Americans construct cultural frameworks that joined disparate components of social life together. Romanticism coated ideas about nationhood with a kind of transcendental paste to which other beliefs and components of culture adhered. Subjective, symbolic interpretations of Protestant thought made sense to many Americans, especially when a transcendental view of consciousness offered assurance that symbols of loss and redemption were applicable to nature, history, and American society. Emotional feelings associated with loss and hope of redemption were finally not isolating or idiosyncratic, but shared experiences that religious leaders could shape and politicians exploit. Among the various components of sentimental Christianity, the family values component exerted special force as a means of gathering social conservatives from different doctrinal traditions, and as means of rallying political commitment to America's identity as a Christian nation.

The Political Legacy of Sentimental Religion

Romantic Christian visions of culture played defining roles in the development of many modern nation-states and the United States is no exception. Many Americans today want a president who can articulate, in a synthetic and compelling way, the romantic symbols of cultural loss and promise of recovery and redemption. The application of these symbols within American politics reached a new level of sophistication during the election of 1980, when Ronald Reagan used his considerable skill as an actor to express the nostalgia people felt for the way they thought America had been prior to the Vietnam War, and to represent, through his own humanity and manly grace, America's rebirth as a strong and virtuous nation. Although critics complained about damage to the environment, public health, and education under Reagan, his ability to stand as a symbol of moral virtue and promise for the future enabled him to withstand and even transcend criticism. Reagan's vision of the struggle for human freedom represented by the conflict between the United States and the Soviet Union, which he characterized as an Evil Empire, also played a role in his effectiveness in galvanizing support for his office. Perhaps without fully realizing what he was doing, Reagan revitalized sentimental romantic visions of American nationalism that had developed in the nineteenth century and recast them in the context of cold war politics.

After the Soviet Union disintegrated, the maelstrom of anger and disgust that erupted over Bill Clinton's affair with Monica Lewinski advanced the sentimentalism of American politics and contributed to further conservative control of American symbols. Europeans who could not understand why Americans were so obsessed with Clinton's private life did not appreciate the extent to which his ability to implement policy depended on his persuasiveness as an embodiment of the moral virtue that is such a crucial component of the American story of fall and redemption. Admission of past sins was one thing and even a potential asset, as George W. Bush later learned, insofar as a president's personal story seemed to represent the promise of redemption so crucial to American civil religion. But being caught and publicly humiliated for a serious lapse in personal morality while in office seemed to imperil the nation, however well he administered government bureaucracy. In the context of escalating international tension and impeachment proceedings against him, his adversaries' success in exploiting his failure to respect the symbols of office only reinforced the authority and legitimacy of those symbols.

Republican strategists took a lesson from this moral crisis and re-presented George W. Bush as an icon of moral virtue who had recovered from his fall into alcoholism through repentance, conversion, and adherence to conservative Christian values and was thereby equipped to defend American strength and integrity against the excesses and corruptions of liberalism. More self-consciously than ever before—and more cynically, critics would add—the Republicans deployed the synthetic, romantic formulation of American culture to their advantage. Bush's resolute personality and evocative descriptions of the "axis of evil" threatening America reaffirmed the mythic framework of the romantic American story by envisioning triumph over terrorism in religious and moral terms and by galvanizing support from the Christian Right in his crusade to save the the nation and spread American values throughout the world. Capitalizing on the grief and anger caused by the disasters of 9/11, Bush often displayed an intuitive sense of how his Presidency might represent a turning point in the history of the world that would revitalize America's covenant relationship with God. Despite serious miscalculations, setbacks, and failures in implementing policies, and strong arguments that the policies themselves worked against the best interests of the American people, Bush wielded considerable romantic, religious, and political power, at least for a time.

The emotional attractions of the American story of fall and redemption enabled Republicans to synthesize disparate components of cultural formation. The sentimental construction of the story muted real conflicts of interest between multinational corporations and American workers, between pharmaceutical companies and American consumers, between health-care insurance companies and both doctors and patients, and between American mineral and real estate developers on one hand and people concerned about the protection of environmental resources on the other. While muting these real economic and environmental conflicts, Republicans turned up the volume on religious differences between conservatives and everyone else. Bush's display of religious feeling and his moral opposition to gay marriage, abortion rights, and stem cell research were more than means of recognizing a base of supporters. They were also effective means of reasserting the connection between nationhood and conservative Christianity and of casting liberalism as a dangerous source of infidelity and immorality.

The line of development between Puritan ideas of good and evil and George W. Bush's War on Terrorism not only reveals the sentimentality of conservative religious nationalism but also the secularizing trend characteristic of the larger history of Protestant experience. Three centuries after Puritans interpreted evil as rebellion against God and warned of the dangers of failing to live up to a covenant relationship with God, American romantics pushed the symbolic meaning of American history further, burying religious meaning more deeply and completely within secular reality. In the early twenty-first century, sophisticated media and spin strategies enabled politicians and conservative religious leaders to orchestrate the rites of cultural catharsis and synthesis with great skill and proficiently.

The election of 1980 brought many religious conservatives from the South into the Republican Party and mobilized them to political action through Reagan's success in revitalizing the conservative and sentimental romantic ideal of a Christian nation. While economic and demographic trends contributed to the Republican Party's attraction to southern voters and to the South's political strength, Reagan's vision of Morning in America reawakened the conservative vision of nationhood that emerged in the South during the nineteenth century. In claiming that America had defeated Communism, stigmatizing liberals for their misguided belief in big government, and announcing that America would recover her birthright as the shining republic specially favored by God, Reagan almost sounded like he was saying the North and its arrogant, liberal, unreligious social reformers would be defeated and the battle for a redeemer nation won after all.

Of course, there were important differences between romantic conservatism in the Confederacy in the nineteenth century and the romantic conservatism of Reagan and his evangelical successor, George

W. Bush. Not least, assent to the legal system prohibiting and punishing overt forms of political and economic discrimination based on race became firmer and more widespread as southern evangelicals and their allies took over the Party that created and supported the Emancipation Proclamation. Many of those evangelicals took pains to express themselves in racially inclusive terms; more than a few expressed regret for the racist history of southern white evangelicalism. As a leading spokesman for the conservative Christian Coalition observed apologetically in the 1990s, "the religious conservative movement" in America has "been hamstrung by the painful legacy of Jim Crow, a history which remains shackled to their culture like a ball and chain." According to Coalition leader Ralph Reed, conservative white evangelicals must offer "genuine, public repentance for past racism" in order to "build bridges with the African-American community."[63]

"The African-American community" is itself a powerful romantic synthesis of disparate groups and cultural forces, and one that critics of political conservatism have often invoked in support of democracy and racial justice. For example, in his book, *Democracy Matters* (2004), cultural critic Cornel West argued that "much of prophetic Christianity in America stems from the prophetic black church tradition." This prophetic African American religious voice could be heard outside of church as well, according to West, in expressions of spiritual insight into ordinary life similar to those of the American Transcendentalists. Thus West linked "Louis Armstrong and Bessie Smith, Duke Ellington and Ma Rainey, John Coltrane and Sarah Vaughan" to "the deep democratic tradition in America" represented by Emerson and Melville. While recognizing that these black artists lived in the racial underbelly of the American society in a way that Emerson and Melville did not, West portrayed the connection among prophetic romantics, black and white, as more honest and vibrant than the connection Ralph Reed hoped to forge between religiously conservative blacks and the white evangelical movement. "Like Emerson," according to West, the "great blues and jazz musicians are eloquent connoisseurs of individuality in their improvisational arts and experimental lives." And "like Melville, they engage in deep-sea diving beneath the apparent American sunshine."[64]

Notes

1. Mary Bushnell Cheney, ed., *Life and Letters of Horace Bushnell* (New York: Harper & Brothers, 1880), quotation from p. 208; Conrad Cherry, *Nature and Religious Imagination: From Edwards to Bushnell* (Philadelphia: Fortress

Press, 1980), pp. 158–187. For Coleridge's importance in the South, see Michael O'Brien, *Rethinking the South: Essays in Intellectual History* (Baltimore: Johns Hopkins University Press, 1988), pp. 54–55. Thanks to Art Remillard and Lee Willis for bibliography on southern romanticism.

2. William Wordsworth, *The Prelude* (1814), Book 9, lines 143–165, quoted and discussed in M. H. Abrams, *Natural Supernaturalism: Tradition and Revolution in Romantic Literature* (New York: W. W. Norton, 1971), quotations from pp. 118, 111.

3. Abrams, *Natural Supernaturalism*, pp. 11–70, quotations from p. 12.

4. Emily Dickinson, *The Complete Poems of Emily Dickinson*, ed. Thomas H. Johnson (Boston: Little, Brown, 1960), poem 959, quotations from pp. 448–449.

5. Harry S. Stout, *Upon the Altar of the Nation: A Moral History of the American Civil War* (New York: Viking, 2006).

6. F. O. Matthiessen, *American Renaissance: Art and Expression in the Age of Emerson and Whitman* (New York: Oxford University Press, 1941).

7. Ralph Waldo Emerson, "Self-Reliance," in *The Essential Writings of Ralph Waldo Emerson*, ed. Brooks Atkinson (New York: Modern Library, 2000), quotation from p. 138.

8. Samuel Taylor Coleridge, *Aids to Reflection*, ed. James Marsh (Burlington: C. Goodrich, 1829; orig. 1825); Kenneth Walter Cameron, *Emerson the Essayist: An Outline of His Philosophical Development through 1836 with Special Emphasis on the Sources and Interpretation of Nature*, vol. 1 (Hartford: Transcendental Books, 1945).

9. For discussion of the American tendency to fuse religious and political values, see Mark Noll, *America's God: From Jonathan Edwards to Abraham Lincoln* (New York: Oxford University Press, 2002).

10. Mary Kupiec Cayton, *Emerson's Emergence: Self and Society in the Transformation of New England, 1800–1845* (Chapel Hill: University of North Carolina Press, 1989); Emerson, "Self-Reliance," Atkinson, *Essential Writings*, quotation from p. 145.

11. Emerson, "Self-Reliance," Atkinson, *Essential Writings*, quotations from pp. 133, 140, 146; italics mine.

12. Emerson, "Nature," Atkinson, *Essential Writings*, quotations from pp. 3, 6.

13. Emerson, "Nature," Atkinson, *Essential Writings*, quotations from pp. 6–7.

14. Emerson, "Threnody," Atkinson, *Essential Writings*, quotations from second stanza line 7, fourth stanza lines 17 and 18, line 6 from the end of seventh stanza, pp. 699, 701, 781; Cayton, *Emerson's Emergence*, p. 219.

15. Emerson, "Experience," Atkinson, *Essential Writings*, quotations from pp. 325, 310.

16. Anne C. Rose, *Transcendentalism as a Social Movement, 1830–1850* (New Haven: Yale University Press, 1981), pp. 1–37.

17. William Blake, "Milton" (1804), *Blake: Complete Writings*, ed. Geoffrey Keynes (Oxford: Oxford University Press, 1966), "Preface," line 8, quotation from p. 481.

18. Orestes A. Brownson, "Rights of the Temporal," *Brownson's Quarterly Review* 22 (October 1860): 496, quoted in Joseph P. Chinnici, ed., *Devotion to the Holy Spirit in American Catholicism* (New York: Paulist Press, 1985), p. 8.

19. Emerson, epigram to "Heroism," Atkinson, *Essentail Essays*, p. 225.

20. Thomas A. Tweed, *The American Encounter with Buddhism, 1844–1912: Victorian Culture and the Limits of Dissent* (Bloomington: Indiana University Press, 1992).

21. Rose, *Transcendentalism*, pp. 117–128, quotation from p. 122.

22. J. Edward Schamberger, "The Influence of Dugald Stewart and Richard Price on Emerson's Concept of the 'Reason': A Reassessment," ESQ 18:3 (1972), pp. 179–183. Also see Sheldon W. Liebman, "The Origins of Emerson's Early Poetics: His Reading in the Scottish Common Sense Critics," *American Literature* 45 (March 1973–January 1974): 23–33.

23. Dickinson, *Complete Poems*, poem 324, quotations from p. 153.

24. Jay Leyda, ed., *The Years and Hours of Emily Dickinson*, 2 vols. (New Haven: Yale University Press, 1960), vol. 1, p. 136.

25. "Emily Dickinson to Abiah Root, 7 & 17 May, 1850," "To Abiah Root, 29 January, 1850," and "To Austin Dickinson, 16 November, 1851," *The Letters of Emily Dickinson*, ed. Thomas H. Johnson, 2 vols. (Cambridge: Harvard University Press, 1958), quotations from vol. 1, pp. 97, 89, 158.

26. Dickinson, *Complete Poems*, poem 533, quotations from p. 260.

27. Dickinson, *Complete Poems*, poem 1387, quotations from pp. 595–596.

28. Dickinson, *Complete Poems*, poem 303, quotation from p. 143.

29. Dickinson, *Complete Poems*, poem 789, quotations from pp. 220–221.

30. Dickinson, *Complete Poems*, poem 632, quotations from pp. 312–313.

31. Herman Melville, *Typee*, reprinted in *The Portable Melville*, ed. Jay Leyda (New York: Viking Press, 1952), pp. 10–339, quotations from pp. 270, 271.

32. Leslie E. Sheldon, "Messianic Power and Satanic Decay: Milton in *Moby-Dick*," in *Melville & Milton: An Edition and Analysis of Melville's Annotations on Milton*, ed. Robin Grey (Pittsburgh: Duquesne University Press, 2004), pp. 25–46; Herman Melville, *Moby-Dick or, The Whale*, ed. Charles Feidelson Jr. (Indianapolis: Bobbs-Merrill Company, 1964), quotations from chapter 133, p. 689.

33. Clare L. Sparks, *Hunting Captain Ahab: Psychological Warfare and the Melville Revival* (Kent, OH: Kent State University Press, 2001), pp. 139–180. Also see Grey, *Melville & Milton*; and Giles Gunn, *The Interpretation of Otherness: Literature, Religion, and the American Imagination* (New York: Oxford University Press, 1979), pp. 159–174.

34. Melville, *Moby-Dick*, quotations from chapter 10, p. 82.

35. Walt Whitman, *Specimen Days* (1892) in *Whitman: Poetry and Prose* (New York: Library of America, 1996), quotations from p. 748.

36. Whitman, *Specimen Days*, quotations from pp. 757, 787–788.

37. Jeffrey Stout, *Democracy & Tradition* (Princeton: Princeton University Press, 2004); Walt Whitman, *Democratic Vistas* (1892) in *Whitman: Poetry and Prose*, quotations from p. 971.

38. In an account of her religious experiences later edited and published by her husband, Sarah Edwards described several days of religious ecstasy in 1742. When another church member expressed concern that Sarah would expire from the intensity of her experience, Sarah responded that she "should be willing to die in darkness and horror, if it was most for the glory of God." Later admirers of Sarah's piety used "willingness to die for the glory of God" as evidence of a person's grace. Sarah Edwards' first-person narrative is preserved in Sereno Edwards Dwight, "Memoirs of Jonathan Edwards," in *The Works of Jonathan Edwards, A.M.*, ed. Dwight, 2 vols. (London, 1840), vol. 1, pp. civ–cxii.

39. Dickinson, *Complete Poems*, poem 1445, quotation from p. 614.

40. Elizabeth Stuart Phelps, *The Gates Ajar* (Cambridge: Harvard University Press, 1964), pp. 75, 84, 92, 95, 124, 95, quotations from pp. 9, 89, 94–95, 84.

41. Gary Laderman, *The Sacred Remains: American Attitudes Toward Death, 1799–1883* (New Haven: Yale University Press, 1999).

42. Horace Bushnell, "Our Obligations to the Dead," reprinted in *The American Evangelicals, 1800–1900*, ed. William G. McLoughlin (New York: Harper & Row, 1968), pp. 142–157, quotations from pp. 145, 148–149, 147.

43. Bushnell, "Obligations to the Dead," quotations from pp. 149, 153.

44. Stewart Winger, *Lincoln, Religion, and Romantic Cultural Politics* (Dekalb: Northern Illinois University Press, 2003), quotation from p. 202.

45. Winger, *Lincoln*, pp. 183–208.

46. "Handbill Replying to Charges of Infidelity," July 31, 1846, in *The Collected Works of Abraham Lincoln*, ed. Roy P. Basler, 8 vols. (New Brunswick: Rutgers University Press, 1953–1955), vol. 1, p. 382; Don E. Fehrenbacher, ed., *Speeches and Writings* by Abraham Lincoln, 2 vols. (New York: Literary Classics of the United States, 1989), vol. 1, p. 139, quoted in Winger, *Lincoln*, 198.

47. Charles Reagan Wilson, *Baptized in Blood: The Religion of the Lost Cause, 1865–1920* (Athens: University of Georgia Press, 1980), quotations from p. 45.

48. G. W. Featherstonhaugh, *Excursion through the Slave States*, 2 vols. (London: 1844), vol. 2, pp. 340–342, quoted in Rollin G. Osterweis, *Romanticism and Nationalism in the Old South* (New Haven: Yale University Press, 1949), p. 141.

49. Frederick Douglass, "Narrative of the Life of Frederick Douglass, an American Slave" (1845), *Autobiographies*, ed. Henry Louis Gates (New York: Library of America, 1994), quotations from pp. 68–69.

Douglass drew a distinction between the slaveholder whose punitive outbursts reflected his low status with respect to other slave owners and the more consistent master who was "a birthright member of the slaveholding oligarchy." Douglass found in both types "all the love of domination, the pride of mastery, and the swagger of authority." But the newcomer to slaveholding (who, if religious, was more likely to be an evangelical than a romantic Anglican) "lacked the vital elements of consistency. He could be cruel; but his methods of showing it were cowardly, and evinced his meanness rather than his spirit." Douglass observed further that the patrician men born into slaveholding families made better masters than lower-born men of smaller spirit. "Slaves are not insensible to the whole-souled characteristics of a generous, dashing slaveholder, who is fearless of consequences," Douglass wrote, "they prefer a master of this bold and daring kind." Frederick Douglass, "My Bondage and My Freedom" (1855), *Autobiographies*, quotations from pp. 248–249.

50. T. L. McBryde, "A Sermon for the Times," *Keowee Courier*, January 26, 1861; "The First Abolitionist," *Keowee Courier*, March 30, 1861; "Yankee Heresy," *Confederate Baptist*, November 11, 1863; all quoted in W. Scott Poole, *Never Surrender: Confederate Memory and Conservatism in the South Carolina Upcountry* (Athens: University of Georgia Press, 2004), pp. 44–45. Also see Christine Leigh Heyrman, *Southern Cross: The Beginnings of the Bible Belt* (New York: Knopf, 1997).

51. Poole, *Never Surrender*, pp. 4–5, quotations from p. 4; Michael Moran, "Thomas Carlyle," in *The Encyclopedia of Philosophy*, vol. 2 (New York: Macmillan Publishing, 1967), pp. 23–25.

52. Osterweis, *Romanticism*, pp. 46–47.

53. O'Brien, *Rethinking the South*, quotations from pp. 55, 37.

54. Poole, *Never Surrender*, quotations from pp. 24–25.

55. O'Brien, *Rethinking the South*, quotation from p. 55.

56. Horace Bushnell, *Women's Suffrage: The Reform against Nature* (New York: 1868), quotations from pp. 86, 50–57.

57. Bushnell, *Women's Suffrage*, quotations from p. 171.

58. Henry Ward Beecher and Edna Dean Proctor, *Life Thoughts, Gathered from the Extemporaneous Discourses of Henry Ward Beecher* (Boston: 1859), quotations from pp. 5, 31.

59. William Gouge, *Of Domestical Duties* (London: 1622), quotations from pp. 16–17.

60. Horace Bushnell, *Christian Nurture* (New Haven: Yale University Press, 1967; reprint of 1861 ed.; orig. 1847), quotations from pp. 39–40.

61. Harriet Beecher Stowe, *Uncle Tom's Cabin* (New York: Bantam Dell, 1981), quotation from p. 212.

62. Thanks to Lee Willis for calling these novels to my attention.

63. Ralph Reed, *Active Faith: How Christians Are Changing the Soul of American Politics* (New York: Free Press, 1996), quotations from pp. 276–277.

64. Cornel West, *Democracy Matters: Winning the Fight against Imperialism* (New York: Penguin Press, 2004), quotations from pp. 91–92.

Chapter 4

Religious Expectations for Science

The romantic impulse to revere nature as the signature of God imbued investigations of nature with pious feeling and moral purpose. Romantic interest in the correspondence between mind and nature enveloped nature in idealism, enabling Protestants to work around skepticism about the factuality of biblical events by embracing the symbolism of the Bible as a template for understanding nature and history. Romantic appeals to the presence of God in nature and history kept doubt and skepticism at bay, preserved the authority of the Bible as a repository of sacred symbols and meaningful stories, and allowed scientific investigation to proceed under the cover of an encompassing religious idealism.

Protestants often affirmed science as part of a larger disposition toward earthly life as a realm of moral discovery, instruction, and action. Beginning in sixteenth-century Europe long before the emergence of romanticism, Protestants endorsed the study of nature as one way of affirming their belief in God's all-encompassing power. Especially in the Reformed tradition associated with John Calvin, commitment to the discernment of divine purpose in the material world instilled confidence in the harmony between natural philosophy and Christian faith. Along with the pleasure many Protestants derived from investigating natural phenomena, belief that nature proclaimed the wisdom of God and confirmed the purpose of creation revealed in the Bible encouraged exploration.

Scientific Investigation in Protestant Culture

Protestant confidence in the harmony between natural philosophy and Christian faith can be traced to the influence of John Calvin's interpreter, assistant, and successor in Geneva, Theodore Beza (1519–1605), who argued that both nature and scripture witnessed to the truths of biblical revelation, whether or not the student who contemplated them was one of God's elected saints. Christian leaders ought to encourage free investigations of nature uninhibited by ecclesiastical authority, Beza argued, because discovery of God's hand in nature was a legitimate beginning point for faith, as well as a form of worship for those who already believed.

According to historian Jeffrey Mallinson, "Beza and his students constantly affirmed the value of scholarship independent of overt theological considerations." An opposing stream of thought "hostile to secular knowledge" also existed within the Calvinist tradition, Mallinson noted, but in Geneva, where the early English Protestants who laid the groundwork for the Puritan movement spent their exile during the reign of the Catholic Queen Mary, Beza's more embracing approach to secular knowledge took hold. For Beza and his English and American successors, "science, or natural philosophy, was to follow its own proper method, theoretically free from theological concerns."[1]

Among English colonists in America, several leading ministers pursued scientific interests. In Boston in 1683, Increase Mather established a scientific society for the purpose of observing and discussing natural phenomenon. Mather's son Cotton, also a minister, carried on a lively correspondence with members of the Royal Society in London who welcomed his "observations on Natural subjects" and packages of fossil specimens gathered from the New World, and elected him to membership in the society in 1713. In *The Christian Philosopher* (1721), the younger Mather argued that scientific investigation of nature supported reverence for God. Far from being an inducement to atheism, he attested, "every Part of the *Universe* is continually *pouring in* something for the *confuting* of it." Indeed, the exercise of reason upon nature stimulated religious activity, Mather believed, and every part of the universe could be profitably studied without jeopardizing piety. As he put it with characteristic flourish, "Never does one endued with *Reason* do any thing more evidently *reasonable*, than when he makes every thing that occurs to him in the vast Fabrick of the World, an *Incentive* to some agreeable Efforts and Salleys of *Religion*."[2]

Cotton Mather's ultimately religious understanding of science corresponded with that of the English Protestant philosopher, Roger Bacon (1214–1292), who celebrated empirical investigation as a means of discovering the order of nature laid out by God at the time of creation. Along the same lines as those endorsed by Theodore Beza, Bacon and his numerous followers interpreted the intricacy, beauty, and remarkable functioning of natural phenomena as evidence of God's hand and intelligent design.[3] In the seventeenth and eighteenth centuries, Protestants

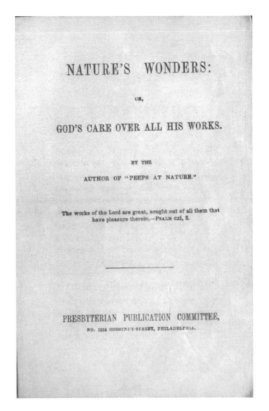

NATURE'S WONDERS:

OR,

GOD'S CARE OVER ALL HIS WORKS.

BY THE

AUTHOR OF "PEEPS AT NATURE."

The works of the Lord are great, sought out of all them that have pleasure therein.—PSALM cxi, 2.

PRESBYTERIAN PUBLICATION COMMITTEE,

NO. 1334 CHESTNUT STREET, PHILADELPHIA.

Nature's Wonders. Courtesy of Shaping the Values of Youth digital collection, Michigan State University.

in England, Scotland, and America conducted countless investigations of nature under the liberating assumption that whatever they discovered about the material world would ultimately glorify God and harmonize with the principles of Christian religion revealed in the Bible. Scientific discoveries in anatomy, physics, and earth sciences extended knowledge of the natural world, and its independence from ecclesiastical doctrine and oversight. Although some skeptics chipped away at the authority of the Bible by questioning the factual truth of miracles described there, many Protestants forged ahead with their quests for objective evidence, confident that investigating nature was a moral and even worshipful enterprise sanctioned by God.

This Protestant sense of liberty to investigate nature depended on the ancient concept of secondary causation, which ministers often interpreted to mean that God, as prime mover, had set the world going in regular ways and certain directions that human beings could generally rely on and study for edification. To suggest otherwise, explained the

New England Puritan minister Urian Oakes in a sermon delivered in 1677, "would be to suppose that the Lord hath set up an order and course in nature in vain, and given to second causes a sufficiency in their kind, for action, to no purpose." Respect for God's omnipotence as primary cause enabled people to act with confidence that ordinary nature could be trusted, for the most part, to be ordinary. "Though the Lord is pleased sometimes, upon great and important occasions, to leave the ordinary road of providence and act beyond and above the usual, stated course of things," Oakes explained, "yet it is not to be imagined that He should ordinarily dispense with the course and methods of His ordinary providence."[4]

The point of Oakes' sermon was that God controlled everything, even what appeared to be chance, "according to His own good pleasure." Consequently, Christians could be confident that all apparent injustices and unexplained sufferings were part of God's plan, however obscure that plan might seem to them at difficult moments. Trust in God's con-

A New Picture-Book. Courtesy of Shaping the Values of Youth digital collection, Michigan State University.

stant watchfulness over everything empowered believers to reason vigorously and act boldly, encouraging them to overcome setbacks and not feel defeated, even as respect for God's watchfulness instilled vigilance over one's own thoughts and fear of behaving badly. Commitment to God's transcendent authority imputed a kind of objectivity to interior life analogous to the objectivity characteristic of the material world. Christian pilgrimages through life involved careful scrutiny of both these realms, along with trust in the all-encompassing presence of God.

Confidence that everything human beings discovered was part of God's plan prevailed in many American colleges and schools well into the nineteenth century. Within certain limits associated with concern for social order and restraint of sinful behavior, this confidence encouraged intellectual curiosity, experimental knowledge, activist engagement in the world, and social reform. But even as American Protestants were expanding science education as part of a larger mission to spread Protestant culture and establish an educated citizenry, new discoveries in geology and paleontology caused many of them to look at the creation stories in the Bible in a new light, and against a new background of fossil evidence. When theories of natural selection and environmental adaptation began to take hold among scientists and their followers in the late nineteenth century, and evidence to support these biological theories continued to accumulate, belief in creation and natural order fell under suspicion. Ironically, beliefs in God's creation of nature and nature's intelligent design had helped to propel the investigations of nature that eventually challenged these beliefs, leaving Protestants in the difficult position of having either to rethink their cosmology or defend their religion against the scientific discoveries they had done so much to promote.

While naturalists in the eighteenth and nineteenth centuries made discoveries in geology and biology that challenged the factuality of biblical accounts of creation and divine providence, scholars undertook critical analysis of the Bible in a similar spirit of systematic inquiry. Their rigorous inspections of scriptural texts identified multiple layers of editorial revision in the Old Testament and raised questions about the authority of many New Testament passages. Mutually reinforcing discoveries in natural science and biblical criticism commanded increasing attention in the course of the nineteenth century, forcing Protestants to reformulate their understanding of both the Bible and the natural world.

In some ways, romantic idealism contributed to the forward momentum of these investigations. Romantic idealism about nature also worked to soften the distinction between primary and secondary causation that had helped propel earlier Protestants into scientific research; many romantic Americans imagined God as a force within creation rather than as the transcendent Creator who allowed nature to operate with a degree of independence. Liberal Protestants often interpreted evolution in terms of this pantheistic understanding of God, until forces of social upheaval and injustice forced them to confront questions about why nature was so violent and wasteful, and why human history appeared not to be progressing but rather descending into chaos and destruction. Even as Protestant faith generated some of the cultural hospitality to science out of which important new discoveries about the natural world emerged, Protestants found scientific discoveries challenging their Christian beliefs. Disturbed by this irony, some Americans worked to reconstruct Protestant theology to fit the demands of the new naturalism. Others denounced theories that seemed to force the issue between science and faith, arguing, at least in some cases, that these troublesome theories must be unscientific as well as irreligious since they challenged belief in God. The turmoil over science in which Americans today are still embroiled reflects the considerable extent to which Protestant faith has traditionally been linked to the confidence that science would glorify God. It also reflects the difficulty Protestants have in holding on to respect for science as one of the defining elements of their religious tradition.

In the twentieth century, fundamentalists resisted pantheistic interpretations of God along with evolutionary theories, espousing premillennialist ideas of global destruction and pointing to global warfare, corruption, and license as signs of the apocalyptic end of time prophesied in the book of Revelation. Still other Protestants, with no taste for apocalyptic scenarios, worked to embrace both science and Christian faith by returning to the distinction between God and the world maintained by Luther, Calvin, Augustine, and other Christian and Jewish thinkers. For Protestants who resisted both the romantic identification of God with nature and history and the fundamentalist belief in the factuality of the Bible, the problem of evil was easier to handle, at least with respect to God's culpability. They could explain violence, waste, and hatred as forces that people had to learn to transform in order to become the full human beings God intended. But these "neo-orthodox" and "neo-liberal" Protestants had to cope with the consequences of loyalty to a religious tradition that had once inspired grand visions of Christian faith supported by scientific evidence.

William James (1842–1910)

A strong supporter of both religion and science and an important contributor to both, the psychologist and moral philosopher William James exemplified the liberal Protestant effort to make the best of the diminishment of Christianity's power with respect to science. James' emphasis on human responsibility preserved the distinction between God and the world, and coincided with his readiness to reformulate Protestant religious thought in the light of new scientific discoveries. As he reformulated classic Protestant doctrines of justification by faith in light of evolutionary biology, his confidence in the ultimate compatibility of religion and science demonstrated the vigorous courage and world-affirming optimism of the Protestant spirit. At the same time, however, his efforts to preserve a place for religious experience in a world coming to be dominated by science also revealed an element of intellectual desperation

William James. National Portrait Gallery, Smithsonian Institution, Washington, D.C./Art Resource, N.Y.

that even James' ebullient Protestant spirit could not fully resolve or suppress.

James' fascination with evolutionary biology stimulated his interest in the varieties of religious experience and his appreciation of the importance of religious pluralism for the vitality and betterment of human society. His belief in the importance of individual variation for understanding all aspects of life, including religious life, led him to investigate mysticism and conversion in a variety of different religions, including Methodist and Holiness traditions, Christian Science and New Thought, Catholicism and Russian Orthodoxy, as well as in the archetypal journey of religious conversion familiar to Reformed Protestants from John Bunyan's Puritan classic, *The Pilgrim's Progress*. In his investigations into religion, James took experiences of a reality beyond ordinary consciousness seriously. Founder of the American branch of the Society for Psychical Research, he believed that evidence for supernatural phenomena might eventually be produced, arguing that, while there was no scientific evidence to prove claims to the existence of supernatural phenomena, there was no scientific reason to dismiss them either. But in claiming scientific open-mindedness with respect to religious claims, James bypassed the basic requirement of science that scientific theory be developed on the basis of evidence that could be tested and replicated. James' unscientific reasoning in support of psychical research reflected the strenuous nature of his effort to legitimate mystical experience. It also reflected the willful optimism characteristic of liberal Protestantism and the heroic efforts made by many liberal Protestants to handle growing unease about the meaning of life and the many pressures science was exerting on religion.

Natural Selection and the Will to Believe

James' approach to religion, science, and moral philosophy reflected his engagement with ideas about biological evolution advanced by the British naturalist Charles Darwin (1809–1882), especially Darwin's theory of natural selection. In *The Origin of Species* (1859), Darwin argued that organisms adapted to their environments and that the most successful ones reproduced over generations, while others died out. James applied this theory to human beings, arguing that they, too, interacted with their environments and that human evolution depended on the success of these interactions. He emphasized the role of individual variation in the evolutionary process, arguing for the importance of individual genius in human history and the need for society to recognize individual genius in order for evolution to occur. When society "adopts and preserves the great man," James argued in 1880, rather than sending him to a madhouse or destroying his influence in some other way, that man "acts as a ferment" on society, "and changes its constitution, just as the advent of a new zoological species changes the faunal and floral equilibrium of the region in which it appears."[5]

Darwin's focus on the means, or efficient causes, of evolution attracted James, as did the open-endedness of Darwin's theory of natural selection. As historian James Moore pointed out, Darwin's conception of "historical process" as something "unique, creative, and unrepeatable" corresponded in certain respects to the emphasis on the importance of history in Christian thought, especially in classic expressions of Reformed Protestantism. In contrast to "the Platonic universe of Louis Agassiz"—a famous naturalist of the nineteenth century who believed that everything in nature replicated ideal, pre-existing forms that never changed—"For Darwin as for [orthodox Protestant] Christians," Moore argued, "the world is a real historical place; its events are a meaningful and unrepeatable sequence; its purpose includes human beings but is not fully realized in them."[6]

Darwin developed his ideas about variation and natural selection in the context of a Protestant worldview. In six editions of the last chapter of *The Origin of Species* (1859–1872), Darwin concluded that natural selection "accords better with what we know of the laws impressed on matter by the Creator" than with theories of special creation that posited the existence of distinct and immutable forms of life. "When I view all beings not as special creations," Darwin wrote in the 1872 edition, "but as the lineal descendants of some few beings which lived long before the first bed of the Cambrian system was deposited, they seem to me to become ennobled." Along similar lines, Darwin argued that because "natural selection works solely by and for the good of each being, all corporeal and mental endowments will tend to progress towards perfection." The last sentence of *Origin* bore witness to Darwin's appreciation of the splendor of this process. "There is a grandeur in this view of life," Darwin concluded, "having been originally breathed by the Creator into a few forms or into one; and that, whilst this planet has gone cycling on according to the fixed law of gravity, from so simple a beginning endless forms most beautiful and most wonderful have been, and are, being evolved."[7]

Darwin's confidence in the existence of a Creator and his enthusiasm for the splendor of life wavered. By the end of his life, reflection on the suffering and wastefulness of life undermined his belief in the existence of God and led him to consider that existence uncertain. Yet he did not question the ability of human societies to develop moral behaviors that rose above the brutal competition for survival. Although progress was not inevitable, Darwin believed that both nature and history had progressed over time and that civilized nations adhered to moral principles far more advanced than simple expressions of the will to survive.[8]

Some aspects of Darwin's theory coexisted with that of the British philosopher Herbert Spencer (1820–1903), who coined the term "survival of the fittest," which Darwin inserted as part of the title of the fourth chapter on "Natural Selection" in the fifth edition of *Origin* in 1869.[9] Although he borrowed Spencer's phrase, Darwin claimed that Spencer's ideas "have not been of any use to me" and that "His deductive manner of treating every subject is wholly opposed to my frame of mind." In addition to focusing on the gathering of empirical evidence— as Spencer did not—Darwin was primarily concerned with biological development, and not with sociology, which was Spencer's main interest. Yet he shared some of Spencer's Victorian assumptions about the superiority of British culture and the Anglo-Saxon race. For Spencer, the power of the British Empire illustrated the inexorable principle of "survival of the fittest," and ought to be tempered with altruism and commitment to peace and fair play.

James strongly opposed Spencer's "social Darwinism" because its fatalistic view of human behavior left no room for individual inspiration as a source of creative adaptation and social betterment. In James' view, Spencer's deterministic approach to evolution was misguided; Spencer failed to appreciate the open-ended nature of life and overlooked the important role that individual genius played in human society. James found Spencer's reduction of consciousness to an automatic mechanism of cognition repugnant. "The knower is not simply a mirror," James wrote in a review of Spencer's work, "passively reflecting an order that he comes upon and finds simply existing. The knower is an actor," James insisted. Ideas "help to *make* the truth which they declare. In other words, there belongs to the mind, from its birth upwards, a spontaneity, a vote."[10]

James' interpretation of Protestant theology, along with his approach to religion more generally, derived from his own weathering of despair and personal discovery of the important role that belief could play in improving individual life. In 1870, closing in on thirty years of age without having ever held a job or found a vocation to sustain him, James wrote in his diary, "Today I about touched bottom." To his brother Henry, he confessed to feeling that all of life was against him: "It seems to me that all a man has to depend on in this world, is, in the last resort, mere brute power of resistance."[11]

In this sorry state, James succumbed to an attack of panic, "just as if it came out of the darkness." Along with "a horrible fear of my own existence," there appeared in his mind "the image of an epileptic patient whom I had seen in the asylum, a black-haired youth with greenish skin, entirely idiotic" who "sat there like a sort of sculptured Egyptian cat or Peruvian mummy, moving nothing but his black eyes and looking absolutely non-human." Recognizing the image as a representation of his own sorry state, James wrote, "There was such a horror of him, and such a perception of my own merely momentary discrepancy from him, that it was as if something hitherto solid within my breast gave way entirely, and I became a mass of quivering fear." The event "was like a revelation," he wrote, and seemed to have "a religious bearing." In addition to the sheer intensity of the experience making it feel religious, old habits of religious practice enabled him to weather it: "the fear was so invasive and powerful that if I had not clung to scripture-texts like 'The eternal God is my refuge,' etc., 'Come unto me, all ye that labor and are heavy-laden,' etc., 'I am the resurrection and the life,' etc., I think I should have grown really insane."[12]

James published this account of his brush with madness in his classic study of religious psychology, *Varieties of Religious Experience* (1902), where he disguised it as a report from a French "correspondent." He included it along with other reports of melancholy, desperation, and religious terror, in a chapter entitled "The Sick Soul," which laid the groundwork for discussion, in subsequent chapters, of conversion as an act of healing resolution that Christians described as an experience of grace. In his own life, James did not undergo the kind of conversion associated with evangelical Protestantism. But he did find the impetus to recover from his sick soul in the writings of the French philosopher Charles Renouvier (1815–1903), who argued against the fatalistic view that universal laws governed human life, maintaining instead that the moral judgments people made drove real historical change. Reading Renouvier helped convince James that he had to act decisively to improve his attitude and relationship to life.[13]

James' approach to religion derived from a deep-seated respect for Protestant faith, the intellectual stimulus of evolutionary biology, and personal experience of surmounting despair. His insistence that knowledge and belief constructed experience, and ought to be recognized as activities that could change the world, reflected both his affirmation of the core principles of Protestant theology as well as the influence of evolutionary theories of adaptation and natural selection on his thinking. His understanding of Protestant theology also reflected the influence of his father, Henry James Sr., whose religious views proceeded along some of the same lines as Emerson's. The elder James defined sin as the pernicious illusion of self-sufficiency. Salvation, according to the elder James, was the individual's overcoming of that illusion through commitment to the well-being of the human race.[14] Like Emerson, Henry James Sr. believed that moral virtue came to expression through individual consciousness; truly inspired individuals sensed their connection to their fellow human beings, and acted in behalf of this larger society.

Self-discipline and productivity as a researcher in human psychology brought Willaim to a professorship at Harvard, where he spent much of the 1880s constructing a theory of the emotions. In the 1890s, he turned to broader philosophical and ethical issues to work out a moral philosophy that reflected his personal success in overcoming lassitude and despair, as well as his psychological interpretation of Protestant theology. In "The Will to Believe" (1896), his most famous essay in moral philosophy, James reformulated distinctive aspects of Protestant theology in terms of a proposal for cherishing human life, securing individual happiness, and improving the welfare of society.

Delivering the essay as an address to the Philosophical Clubs of Yale and Brown universities, James announced his intention of addressing the most "vital subjects" of Reformed Protestant belief. After bantering about "Harvard freethinking" come to "old orthodox" Yale, he promised to deliver "something like a sermon on justification by faith," by which he meant, at least initially, "an essay in justification *of* faith, a defense of our right to adopt a believing attitude in religious matters."[15]

Clearing the ground for this defense, James distinguished between live beliefs and dead ones. "For us Protestants," he wrote, the option "to believe in masses and holy water" was dead; "these means of salvation seem such foregone impossibilities" that they stimulated little interest or possibility of action. But if masses and holy water were not live options for him and his Protestant audience, that might change if they were surrounded by Catholic believers. In many cases, "the *prestige*" associated with certain beliefs, not any "inner clearness" in apprehending them, motivated assent to them. Most of our beliefs were socially agreeable and intellectually fuzzy, James argued, and there was nothing wrong with that. Only when situations forced people to make moral choices did the need for inner clarity arise.[16]

Seeking to avoid error was equally common and, in most cases, nothing to be ashamed of either. Unless the need to actively pursue the truth about something was forced upon us, James argued, the safe, conservative inclination to avoid error worked best in ordinary life as well as in scientific work: "wherever there is no forced option, the dispassionately judicial intellect with no pet hypothesis, saving us, as it does, from dupery at any rate, ought to be our ideal." At the most important moments in life, however, people found themselves in situations where "momentous" decisions were forced upon them without having all the objective evidence they needed to make a fully informed choice about which was right. Some of these situations included moments of deciding whether to believe in God or not.[17]

James invoked the famous "wager" described by the French philosopher Blaise Pascal, who bet on God's existence. Although he agreed with Pascal's decision to wager that God existed, James placed his bet for different reasons. Pascal had rationalized that belief in God was the best bet since that belief would not affect your eternal prospects if it turned out you were wrong, while those prospects would be dim if it turned out that God did exist, and you had chosen not to believe. James, on the other hand, threw in with God because belief in God made him happier and more productive than unbelief. Linking faith in God to the more general claim that life was meaningful and worth living, James thought that when circumstances forced people to decide whether or not life was worth living, faith was "our own active good-will, as if evidence might be forever withheld from us unless we met the hypothesis half-way."[18]

James did not tie this active goodwill to affiliation with any particular church or to any special doctrine of divine revelation or scriptural inerrancy. Rather, he understood active goodwill as an expression of the vitality that drove the whole evolutionary process, including the creation of new varieties of religious experience. Thus James affirmed the diversity of religious beliefs in terms of the natural process of variation essential to evolution. At the same time, he suggested that the classic doctrines of Protestant faith might be rejuvenated with the infusion of new ideas about the relationship between faith and biological vitality. If the playful words at the beginning of "The Will to Believe" can be taken seriously, James hoped that the pollen of Harvard freethinking spread around old orthodox Yale might produce fruitful, new adaptive ways of thinking about religious life.

James' did more than offer a justification *for* faith; his essay also reformulated the doctrine of justification *by* faith. By implication, James agreed with Luther that faith "justified" individuals, making them right with God. And he followed Calvin and the Reformed Protestant tradition in arguing that faith made possible the kind of good work that contributed to the betterment of the world. Thus James' understanding of faith as an active disposition to meet life half-way reflected a Calvinist understanding of religious life as moral action as well a Calvinist sense that religious assurance was a matter of hopefulness, but not certainty, about the future.[19]

James believed that behavior created mood—we are sad because we cry, and happy because we laugh, as he argued in his scientific work, *Principles of Psychology* (1890). He also believed that changing one's behavior could be difficult and that the willful resolve to pull oneself together required a process like conversion. Thus while James highlighted the importance of individual resolve, he also believed that the impetus for it often came from the deepest recess of individual consciousness and probably from a source beyond that.

James' reformulation of Protestant ideas in the context of Darwinian evolution coincided with his rejection of monistic views of divine omnipotence that represented "the world as one unit of absolute fact." In *Varieties*, James made it clear that he thought monistic views of divine providence forced the conclusion that "evil, like everything else, must have its foundation in God." The God people clung to, who made a positive difference in people's lives, could not be a perpetrator of evil, James insisted. At the same time, James respected the power of belief in an "absolute world-ruler" as a stimulus for moral action. In an attempt to deal with these conflicting ideas, he invoked scientific language to exempt God from evil by projecting God's power to rule the world into the future, conceptualizing faith as a "*real hypothesis*"—not simply a summation of existing knowledge but a belief about reality that predicted new results and stimulated new discoveries. Defining faith as an active ingredient in the realization of God and his goodness on earth, James characterized faith as a hypothesis with predictive power for the future. Once again, James invoked the open-ended spirit of scientific inquiry to create a belief—in this case, in the usefulness of human faith to God—in a negative way, with no evidence. "Who knows whether the faithfulness of individuals here below," James wondered, "may not actually help God in turn to be more effectively faithful to his own greater tasks?"[20]

While James understood religious faith as a process of active engagement in bringing religious expectations to reality, other Americans in the Reformed Protestant tradition demanded more certainty. James had emerged from his struggle with despair willing to give himself to life, willing to accept the uncertainty of life's outcome and to embrace that uncertainty as a catalyst for creative action. Other Protestants worked through the problem of religious assurance differently. Faced with challenges to religious belief in the modern era, many conservative Protestants wanted assurance that the outcome of life was settled and that their traditional conceptions of God and salvation were correct. From their perspective, the idea that life was open-ended contradicted the Bible and their understanding of Protestant faith. Thus while James found Darwin's theory of natural selection and its emphasis on the importance of individual variation in the process of evolution a stimulus for reformulating the "old orthodox" doctrines of justification, sanctification, and assurance, some conservatives saw Darwin's theory as a threat to faith and believed that it ought to be rejected outright.

Competing Protestant Expectations about Science

While Darwin and his close readers defined science in narrow procedural terms as a method of generating and verifying explanations of natural events, many other Protestants situated investigations of nature more firmly within a framework of religious belief that divine intelligence could be discovered in all aspects of nature. In the spirit of this Baconian outlook, many conservative Protestants believed in the important place of empirical science in Christian life. But in wedding empirical investigation to claims about divine purpose and final causation, religious conservatives headed down a path different from that of modern scientists who established methods of investigation based on open-ended inquiry and empirical validation and who eschewed questions of final causation and the intellectual constraints such questions entailed.

As a proponent of the scientific method, James emphasized the importance of empirical validation for scientific theories about reality and often treated religious claims about the divine purpose of creation as statements about final causation—and hence as nonscientific. At the same time, however, he thought that religious beliefs were "the most interesting and valuable things" about people and should be regarded "with tenderness and tolerance so long as they are not intolerant themselves."[21] He also kept the door open for evidence of supernatural phenomena. With the strenuous nature of James' effort to keep religion in conversation with science as a point of comparison, we can understand how more conservative American Protestants, who expected new discoveries in science to confirm their beliefs in biblical revelation, might have come to the conclusion that science had betrayed them.

New Arguments in Defense of Biblical Authority

Early stirrings of the conservative religious and political movement that later came to be known as fundamentalism emerged at the same time William James was beginning to work out his pragmatic approach to the relationship between religion and science. At a meeting of the

Evangelical Alliance in New York City in 1873, a split developed between liberal and conservative evangelicals over the relationship between biblical accounts of creation and scientific discoveries in geology and paleontology. Paleontologists had discovered fossil records indicating that the earth was much older than previously thought, and much older than the Bible seemed to indicate. Some evangelicals had tried to reconcile this inconsistency by interpreting each of the six days of biblical creation as a large number of years and laying out world history in terms of large periods of time, or dispensations. Evolutionary biology posed additional challenges, such as how to harmonize biblical accounts of the creation of separate and immutable forms of life with the transformation of species through adaptation to new environments and the development of human beings from more primitive forms of life. While liberals were content to read the stories in Genesis symbolically as moral fables, others insisted that, as the inspired word of God, the Bible was completely accurate and that alleged discrepancies between the Bible and science resulted from the fallibility and incompleteness of human understanding. This religious investment in the factuality of the Bible became a defining element of fundamentalism.

Some evangelical leaders agreed with the President of the College of New Jersey (Princeton), James McCosh, who argued in 1873 that evolution was not a threat to the Bible because "both reveal order in the world" and "those who view development in the proper light see in it only a form or manifestation of law." Others followed the more conservative Presbyterian Charles Hodge of Princeton Theological Seminary who responded to McCosh's concession to evolution by taking a hard position against it. "Is development an intellectual process guided by God," Hodge asked in response to those willing to entertain evolutionary theory, "or is it a blind process of unintelligible, unconscious force, which knows no end and adopts no means?" Hodge correctly discerned that evolutionary biologists denied that nature operated by intellectual design.[22]

Along with their hostility to evolution, Hodge and his colleagues at Princeton viewed German universities as major antagonists. Researchers in Germany led the way in the "higher criticism" of the Bible, with its analysis of different layers of editorial commentary in the Old Testament and investigation of the authenticity of the gospels. Germany was also a principal source of liberal theology and romantic philosophy. Hodge criticized the German theologian Friedrich Schleiermacher for attempting to shift the essence of Christianity in a romantic direction, away from Biblical principle to human emotion. Working to resist this romantic shift, Hodge declared in his *Systematic Theology* of 1874 that, "The infallibility and divine authority of the Scriptures are due to the fact that they are the word of God."

Hodge's use of the term "fact" represented a newly conceived defense of biblical authority and a departure from the classic Presbyterian commitment to the importance of the Spirit's "inward work." In the standard formulation of Presbyterian doctrine represented in the Westminster Confession of 1647, "assurance of the infallible truth" of scripture derived from "the inward work of the Holy Spirit, bearing witness by and with the Word in our hearts." As historian Ernest Sandeen explained, Hodge "substituted a *doctrine* of inspiration for the *witness* of the Spirit." In his antipathy to romantic feeling as a basis for Christian life, Hodge presented the Spirit's inspiration of the Bible as an objective fact supporting a logical argument about the Bible's authority, rather than as a reference to the Spirit's engagement of the believer's subjectivity in imparting assurance of the Bible's truth.[23]

Hodge's followers at Princeton hardened this doctrinaire position further in response to inconsistencies in biblical texts uncovered by scholars, many of whom worked in German universities. In 1881, Archibald Alexander Hodge (son of Charles) and his colleague Benjamin B. Warfield redefined the meaning of scripture's "infallible truth" to mean factual inerrancy, insisting that the *words* of the Bible—not just the thoughts behind the words—were mutually consistent and literally, factually true. Defending the inerrancy of the Bible against claims made by German scholars about discrepancies and inconsistencies, Hodge and Warfield argued that copyists had introduced errors into the texts that biblical scholars studied. In a way similar to James' idea that certain claims may be legitimate if they cannot be proven wrong, Hodge and Warfield challenged scholars to find any error in the Bible's "original autograph," should that document ever be discovered.[24]

Rigid defense of the Bible as a factual document that could stand up to empirical investigation became an important ingredient in the fundamentalist movement of the twentieth century. For fundamentalists, the Bible was not only a beacon of light in a dark and confused world, but a document whose moral principles were clearly laid out and whose descriptions of nature, history, and the future of the world were superior to anything natural scientists could produce. As far as fundamentalists were concerned, their defense of the Bible met the challenges of modern science and biblical criticism. It also reflected the enormous pressure they felt modern science and biblical criticism exerting on their outlook on the world, as evidenced by their readiness to reformulate the truth of the Bible—in defiance of centuries of non-literal Bible reading—in terms of a set of factual propositions and by their readiness to equate Christian faith with assent to these propositions.

Fundamentalism as a Political Movement Hostile to Evolution

Fundamentalists got their name from their adherence to teachings that conservative Protestants in the Reformed tradition regarded as fundamental to biblical principal and authority. Militant opposition to modern culture at the end of the First World War prompted these religious conservatives to join together in an organized political effort to restore the moral values of America and expunge liberalism from Protestant churches. Fundamentalist opposition to the teaching of evolution in public schools became the centerpiece of a political battle to save American culture from moral ruin. In this political movement to defend the authority of the Bible and the moral values of American culture, "evolution became a symbol" of the massive threat facing Christian civilization.[25]

As historian George Marsden showed, fundamentalism did not emerge as a political movement until 1918, although many of the religious ideas supporting the movement had been formulated earlier. As a religiously militant political movement, fundamentalism echoed other calls to mobilization and massive armament during the First World War. Many who joined the movement came from premillennialist Protestant traditions in which believers anticipated a catastrophic world struggle before the Second Coming of Christ. Many premillennialists saw signs that the end of days had begun in the upheaval, destruction, brutality, and global crisis of the First World War. Amidst the largest war the world had ever seen, the militant rhetoric of premillennialist culture became more politically directed and the apocalyptic imagery of the book of Revelation acquired new relevance. Fundamentalists talked of marching to battle against modern culture in the name of their heavenly King.

Before the war, conservative opponents of evolution had not used military imagery to express their religious views. More concerned to separate themselves from modern culture than wage battle against it, conservative Protestants prior to 1918 tended toward pacifism. Marsden cited numerous illustrations to show how suddenly conservative religious endorsement of American participation in the war had occurred. For example, in 1918, after years of political quietism, the Moody Bible Institute's *Christian Workers Magazine* called readers to shoulder "our responsibility to God as the executioners of His avenging justice."[26]

Conservative Protestants mobilized to stop the moral collapse that seemed to have occurred in Germany from happening in America. Militant conservatives blamed Germany's behavior in the war on the liberal theology and biblical criticism flowing out of its universities, and connected these pernicious influences with Darwin's theory of evolution, which they interpreted as an insidious form of atheism. With rhetorical and organizational strategies forged in the context of the militaristic fervor and catastrophic violence of the world war, militantly conservative Protestants banded together after the war to expel liberals from their denominations and to rid American culture of modernism epitomized by the teaching of evolution in public schools.

The Scopes Trial

Between 1921 and 1929, fundamentalists proposed legislative changes in twenty states to bar the teaching of evolution from public schools. In the early 1920s, the first legal victories for antievolutionists occurred in Oklahoma, where the legislature prohibited the use of textbooks that incorporated evolution, and in Florida, where the legislature resolved that teaching evolution was "improper and subversive." In 1925, Tennessee passed a bill that made teaching evolution a crime. In 1926, Mississippi passed a similar bill, and Arkansas followed suit in 1928.[27]

In 1925, soon after the Tennessee bill passed into law, the newly formed American Civil Liberties Union (ACLU) in New York City approached John Scopes, a science teacher and athletic coach in Dayton, Tennessee, who agreed to test the constitutionality of the new law by standing trial for teaching evolution in a Tennessee high school. The ACLU hired the well-known Chicago attorney Clarence Darrow to represent Scopes. The State brought in William Jennings Bryan, three-time contender for the presidency of the United States and the best-known spokesman for the fundamentalist cause, to prosecute Scopes. The trial attracted enormous publicity, and stands today as a major landmark in the history of American fundamentalism.

Darrow did not dispute the charge that Scopes had broken Tennessee law, but took the opportunity of a sensational courtroom confrontation to put fundamentalist arguments against evolution on trial. In a high-handed and transparent effort to expose what he obviously regarded as the stupidity of fundamentalist reasoning, Darrow called Bryan to the stand and grilled him on his views of creation. Although the jury convicted Scopes after only nine minutes of deliberation, many of Darrow's admirers thought that he had humiliated Bryan and succeeded in discrediting fundamentalism. When Bryan died five days later, observers wondered if Bryan's desperate efforts to explain his religion and its approach to science had caused his heart to fail.

Confusion about the implications of Bryan's testimony contributed to the false impression among liberals that fundamentalism had been defeated in the Scopes trial. As historian of religion and science Ronald Numbers showed, Darrow thought all fundamentalists believed the earth was only 6,000 years old, that creation took place in six twenty-four-hour days, and that by getting Bryan to testify that he did not believe in such a young earth or quick creation, he had exposed Bryan's hypocrisy and the preposterous nature of fundamentalist beliefs. Under Darrow's questioning, Bryan testified that he did not believe the earth was created in six literal days of twenty-four hours each. He testified that he "wouldn't attempt to" say exactly how long ago the earth had been created and acknowledged that "It might have continued for millions of years." Although he "would not attempt to argue as against anybody who wanted to believe in literal days," Bryan resorted to his "impression" that the six days of creation described in Genesis referred to "periods" of time, not literal twenty-four-hour days.[28]

Bryan had expressed similar views before, and his views corresponded with those of many fundamentalists. In 1925, only a small minority of fundamentalists, most of whom were Seventh-Day Adventists, maintained that God created the earth in six literal days 6,000 years ago. Most fundamentalists of the time believed differently, that Genesis included two creation accounts, one describing an initial creation in which God made the earth and all nonhuman life forms, and a later event, 6,000 years ago, in which God created Adam and Eve. Bryan represented a third group, "an influential minority" of fundamentalists, according to Numbers, who "chose to accommodate the fossil evidence by reading the 'days' of Genesis as vast geological ages."[29]

Darrow and his supporters overlooked the diversity of opinion within fundamentalism and apparently had no idea that fundamentalists wanted to respect science. Nor did they realize that fundamentalists took seriously the task of squaring empirical evidence with their understanding of biblical authority. Because fundamentalists believed that the Bible's description of creation was scientifically valid, they simply could not accept evolution as a valid scientific theory.

Creation Science

Fundamentalists did not retreat in shame after the Scopes trial, as many liberal commentators supposed. They continued to work for state laws against the teaching of evolution through the 1920s, then redirected their energies toward local school boards, where they were and continue to this day to be remarkably effective. The grassroots opposition to the teaching of evolution in public schools remains a political force to reckon with in many states. Efforts on the part of religious conservatives to create scientific alternatives to evolutionary theory have not abated over the years, but only increased. Today, fundamentalists have gained sympathy and political and financial support from a broad range of religious conservatives who want public instruction in science to incorporate respect for religious teachings.

As far as the vast majority of scientists are concerned, the empirical evidence for evolution is overwhelming, and fundamentalists have had little success in gaining a hearing among scientists. The whole enterprise of biology rests on evolutionary theory, and evidence for natural selection and environmental adaptation in the development of life continues to accumulate. To take one example of a recent discovery supporting evolutionary theory, in research published in 2004, Anders Moller and Tibor Szep showed that female barn swallows who migrated back and forth between South Africa and Denmark preferred males with elongated tail feathers. In response to this preference, the overall length of male tail feathers in this population increased by 10 percent during the short period of two decades. During that time, diminished vegetation in the Sahara favored the survival of the strongest males, who had to cross over the desert on their way to Denmark. The researchers theorized that "the males' tails act as advertising for good genes because males must be in good health to spend the energy growing them." Thus the swallows quickly adapted to dramatic change in their environment through a process of natural selection.[30] Thousands of studies such as this provide evidence that life forms mutate in response to their environments and that the most adaptive mutations succeed in reproducing.

Overlooking mountains of evidence in support of evolutionary biology, fundamentalists developed a rhetorical strategy that equated belief in the authority of the Bible with opposition to evolution. They argued that the Bible was not on trial because it was the revealed truth of God. *Evolution* was on trial, and should be judged against the standard of God's revealed truth, which fundamentalists believed they clearly discerned. This appeal to the Bible as the arbiter of scientific theory reflected the pressure science exerted on Protestant thinking and the willingness of militant conservatives to deploy the Bible to defeat evolutionary theory. In their battles against evolution and modern culture, fundamentalists simplified the religious and historical complexity of the Bible and made it a document of legal defense against modern ideas and behaviors they found offensive.

Cartoon of Two Schools. Harper's Weekly, August 30, 1873. Courtesy of Florida State University.

By simplifying the literary, moral, and theological textures of the Bible in their efforts to defend divine creation, fundamentalists succeeded in setting the terms of debate over science for many religious conservatives who were drawn into religious discussions about evolution on fundamentalist terms. In his analysis of the remarkable popularity of antievolutionism in the United States, Numbers described the well-funded and highly effective political effort to galvanize opposition to the teaching of evolution in public schools: hard-core opponents of evolution gained power, called attention to the importance of the issue, and established the pattern of debate for religious conservatives. In the 1960s, the young-earthers of the Seventh-Day Adventist Church founded a Geoscience Research Institute to promote studies in geology and paleontology that confirmed the account of creation described in Genesis and conformed to the teachings of Ellen White, the founder of Adventism who witnessed God's creation of the world in a vision. While Adventists disputed with each other over the meaning of the fossil record, with some maintaining that the creation of life in six days described in Genesis should not be taken literally, Adventist writings in support of the factuality of Genesis attracted a considerable following among conservative evangelicals and contributed to the revival of "creation science" in the late-twentieth century.

Fundamentalist insistence that proponents of evolution could not be Christian affected the development of Holiness and Pentecostal churches in the twentieth and early twenty-first centuries. In spite of their strong commitment to religious healing and theological emphasis on the heart over matters of the head, Holiness and Pentecostal leaders allied many of their teachings, schools, and churches with fundamentalist opposition to evolution. Other evangelicals were drawn into discussion of evolution on fundamentalist terms, which declared evolution on trial against the revealed truth of God. Even though many of these evangelicals did not think of themselves as fundamentalists, they found themselves caught in a rhetorical strategy that fundamentalists had established. Willing to admit the explanatory power of evolutionary theory, but not willing to relinquish the truth claims of the Bible or the Bible's relevance to the debate over evolution, many evangelicals found themselves searching for a theistic approach to evolution. Whatever intellectual confusion this situation reflected, it also reflected the powerful influence of fundamentalist rhetoric among evangelical Christians, the political character of the fundamentalist movement, and the challenge evolutionary biology posed, and continues to pose, for many American Christians.

Protestant Naturalism

The strange customs and Catholic or Jewish affiliation of many immigrants from southern and eastern Europe disturbed many old stock Protestants in the United States in the late nineteenth and early twentieth centuries, fueling pseudoscientific ideas about the superiority of the Anglo-Saxon race, its natural affinity with the Protestant religion and leading role in the evolutionary progress of human society. In the hands of some moralists, appeals to scientific language about race bolstered the notion that white Anglo-Saxon Protestants represented the pinnacle of Christian civilization and served as a model for other groups to emulate. Emboldened by this sort of rhetoric, an increasingly powerful class of wealthy industrialists opposed all forms of work regulation and labor organization, controlled political machines, supervised hospitals, colleges, and universities, and established exclusive clubs. Their wealth and political power challenged earlier conceptions of democratic individualism as did the growing numbers of poor people upon whose labor the industrialists depended.

While new immigrants faced discrimination in the United States, African Americans suffered the worst. White Protestants often looked down on blacks despite the fervent allegiance to Christian belief and worship that many blacks expressed. Devotion to Christ did not keep southern blacks from being lynched in the South, terrorized by the Ku Klux Klan, or humiliated by Jim Crow laws passed in southern states to prevent inter-racial mixing except in highly controlled situations that enforced white superiority. Racism was a growing force in the North as well, as millions of blacks immigrated from the South to northern cities in the late nine-teenth and early twentieth centuries to escape southern poverty and per-secution. Although some succeeded in overcoming formidable obstacles to education and economic opportunity, many did not. In response to the emerging problem of race, which to some extent replaced but also grew out of the older problem of slavery, white Protestants often turned to science, or to what passed for science, for help in thinking about race. Beginning in the late nineteenth century, a growing number of professional social scientists identified racial distinctions among different groups of human beings, even measuring the sizes of people's heads to determine intelligence, and developed scientific-sounding theories to explain what they believed to be the superiority of the Anglo-Saxon race.

The Myth of "Social Darwinism"

The ideas of Herbert Spencer played a major role in constructing these theories about race as they did in shaping American Protestant conceptions of evolution; Spencer's ideas about evolution were better understood and more often invoked in the United States than those of Charles Darwin. Like Darwin, Spencer believed that human beings evolved from more primitive forms of life, but unlike Darwin, who built his theories on meticulous observation of plants and animals in different environments, Spencer deduced his theories from a first principle, which he named "The Persistence of Force." Spencer assumed that matter was indestructible and, like time and space, beyond comprehension. Driven by an inscrutable underlying force, evolution was, for Spencer, essen-tially a thermodynamic process characterized by "the integration of matter and dissipation of motion." Along with a stabilizing dissipation of motion, this integrative process could be discerned in the evolution of human thought and civilization, Spencer believed, as well as in nature: "in the integrations of advancing Language, Science, and Art, we see reflected certain integrations of advancing human structure, individual and social."[31]

Spencer joined these mechanistic principles to an altruistic philos-ophy, arguing that humanity was reaching a new stage of maturity characterized by cooperation and sympathy. Combining belief in the existence of an inexorable force with hope for its ultimately positive and humane effects, he believed that human beings were capable of controlling the violence of their own natural tendencies and applying human intelligence to the violent forces of life. Arguing that "the possibility of a higher civilization depends wholly on the cessation of militarization and the growth of industrialization," Spencer was highly critical of the imperialism of his own British society. In 1876, he gathered English friends together in the hope "of doing something towards checking the aggressive tendencies displayed by us all over the world—sending, as pioneers, missionaries of 'the religion of love,' and then picking quarrels with native races and taking possessions of their lands."[32]

Spencer's philosophy achieved more popularity in the United States than in his homeland, perhaps because of the way idealism about science and industry in this country had become linked to evangelical faith in America as the center of religious and social progress. Spencer's ideas reached America before Darwin's and conditioned the reception of Darwin's work to a considerable extent; William James repeatedly found it necessary to challenge Spencer's ideas and explain why he thought Spencer's linkage of evolution and philosophical determinism wrongheaded. Spencer's work helped establish an equation between evolution and progress in the minds of some Protestants that made it difficult to grasp the challenge to assumptions about inevitable progress, or any other sort of determinism, posed by biological studies of evolution. To be sure, this challenge is easier to see today than it was in the nineteenth century, when the basic ideas of organic evolution were still being worked out, when Americans took God's hand in establishing natural order more for granted, and when the vogue of Herbert Spencer's philosophy encouraged uncritical faith in the linkage between evolution and progress.

Although Spencer was an agnostic who believed that the underlying force behind evolution was unknowable, many of the liberal Protestants attracted to his sweeping determinism identified the prime mover of evolution with the biblical God, the same God who had enabled their own good fortune and cultural attainments. Among the first to embrace Spencer's philosophy and graft it onto biblical theology, the famous Brooklyn preacher Henry Ward Beecher (1813–1887) linked God to nature and evolution in a way that made historical progress a natural outcome of evolution. In 1885, he proclaimed that God not only "created matter" and "gave to it its laws," but also "impressed upon it that tendency which has brought forth the almost infinite results on the globe, and wrought them into a perfect system." For Beecher, evolution was "that tendency" which "by inherent laws gradually builded itself" into "a universe so adjusted that it left by the way the poorest things, and steadily wrought toward more complex, ingenious, and beautiful results!"[33]

As a young man, Beecher looked to nature as a model for understanding human society, using trees as a metaphor for the organization and organic growth of human society. "Society grows," he opined in a collection of sermons and essays published in 1855, "as trees do, by rings. There are innumerable circles formed, by mutual attraction."[34] When Spencer's effort to project evolutionary progress onto human society captured Beecher's attention fifteen years later, he enlisted E. L. Youmans, Spencer's promoter and leading disciple in the United States, as a consultant to a group of local preachers Beecher gathered in New York for weekly meetings to discuss Spencer's theory and its implications for Protestant theology. Beecher's own success as a celebrity preacher derived from his fusion of Spencer's ideas about progress in human society with sentimental Christianity.

Beecher's religion involved commitment to social reform as well as confidence in liberal Protestant values, perceptions, and people. The mock slave auction he organized in Plymouth drew considerable attention, as did his efforts to fight the spread of slavery by raising money for guns—nicknamed "Beecher's Bibles"—to help government officers enforce antislavery laws in Kansas prior to the Civil War. Beecher's growing investment in Spencer's evolutionary philosophy supported his commitment to social reform as well as a certain sense of complacency that made the affluence and prestige he enjoyed seem natural.[35]

In his belief that he had an obligation, as a minister of Christ and representative of a powerful Protestant elite, "to speak on every side of political life," Beecher contributed to the equation between patriotism and evangelical Protantism and to the idea that being American was a sacred enterprise, like a religion itself.[36] The language of evolution enabled Beecher to impute scientific validity to older ideas about divine providence and America's special relationship to God and, in so doing, make the moral righteousness of America, and the superiority of her religious leaders, seem almost inevitable. Beecher exemplifies the bridge between sentimental romanticism and Spencer's philosophy of evolution, the steady undermining of earlier Protestant emphases on the transcendence of God, and the drift among proponents of liberal theology toward social conservatism.

As historian Sidney Mead argued, the rhetoric of evolution helped to fuel a patriotic religion, developed in concert with the teachings of Protestant churches, based on belief in "the destiny of America, under God, to be fulfilled by perfecting the democratic way of life for the example and betterment of all mankind." This "amalgamation" of Christianity and Americanism sanctioned a free-market economy, unrestrained industrial development, individual accumulation of wealth, and

The celebrated preacher, Henry Ward Beecher, took a romantic approach to the integration of Christianity and evolution. Courtesy of the Library of Congress.

political and economic expansionism. Senator Albert J. Beveridge of Indiana celebrated this religion of America in the most grandiose terms in a speech defending the annexation of the Philippines in 1900. God "has marked the American people as His chosen Nation to finally lead in the regeneration of the world," Beveridge proclaimed. "This divine mission," he went on, "holds for us all the profit, all the glory, all the happiness possible to man." God had bestowed great responsibility as well as many material rewards on the American people: "The judgment of the Master is upon us: 'Ye have been faithful over a few things; I will make you ruler over many things.'"[37]

Building on Mead's critical view of this religious outlook, historian Martin Marty emphasized the racist character of the evolutionary rhetoric employed by Americans who promoted the idea of America as a Protestant empire destined to play a leading role in moving the world toward the reign of Christ on earth. Calling attention to the subordination of Native

Americans and African Americans in this vision of America as a Protestant Empire, Marty quoted the nineteenth-century historian of American religion, Robert Baird, to illustrate his point. "In a word," Baird wrote in 1844, "our national character is that of the Anglo Saxon race."[38]

The racism implicit in evangelical conceptions of American destiny became increasingly explicit through association with scientific (or allegedly scientific) theories of evolution and racial difference. The term "race" was commonplace in nineteenth-century discussions about nature; Darwin used it as a synonym for species variation in an extended title for *The Origin of Species*, which read, *By Means of Natural Selection or the Preservation of Favored Races in the Struggle for Life*. In addition to its use in differentiating flora and fauna, race caught on as a way of categorizing different groups of people. The prevalence of racial lingo in evolutionary theory contributed to its appeal as a means of classifying different groups of people according to their "natural" characteristics.

Nineteenth-century fascination with the concept of race lent credence to the popular interpretations of the biblical story of Ham, Noah's son consigned to slavery, along with all of his descendants, after seeing the nakedness of his drunken father (Genesis 9:20–27). In the South, white Protestants often welcomed scientific-sounding language about racial difference for its support of biblical evidence and justification for slavery. In many cases, white Protestants opposed to slavery also accepted racial categories derived from evolutionary theory, employing those categories to distinguish themselves from African Americans on the grounds of racial difference. Even among African Americans themselves, the myth of Ham, supported by allegedly scientific theories about the inferiority of the African "race," gained a hearing as an explanation for the misfortunes they suffered.[39]

At the end of nineteenth century, as concern mounted over problems associated with urban industrialization and immigration, evangelical leaders like Josiah Strong proclaimed the superiority of the Anglo-Saxon race as the hope of mankind and appealed to Christianity, science, and economic success to back his claim. Strong's view of racial evolution involved a forward-looking, even open-ended, element that appealed to progressives. He attributed the superiority of the Anglo-Saxon race not to its purity, but to "its highly mixed origin," including "Celt and Gaul, Welshman and Irishman, Frisian and Flamand, French Huguenot and German Palatine," as well as "Saxon and Norman and Dane." Claiming that the "new Anglo-Saxon race of the New World" would surpass anything known before, Strong quoted Spencer's claim that further "mixture of the allied varieties of the Aryan race" promised to yield "a type of man more plastic, more adaptable, more capable of undergoing the modifications needful for complete social life." For Strong, the religious, political, and economic institutions of the United States were destined to further stimulate the growth of this robustly adaptive race. While in Britain, "the union of Church and State tends strongly to paralyze some of the members of the body of Christ," in the United States "there is no such influence to destroy spiritual life and power. Here, also," Strong wrote, "has been evolved the form of government consistent with the largest possible civil liberty. Furthermore," he went on, "the marked characteristics of this race are being here emphasized most," especially one of "the most striking features of the Anglo-Saxon," namely, "his money-making power."[40]

By appealing to their common roots and investment in political and economic freedom, Strong encouraged evangelicals who disagreed with each other about whether to interpret the Bible literally or symbolically to find common ground as guardians of the moral values of American culture. As Secretary of the Evangelical Alliance, the nondenominational group that brought evangelical leaders from the North and South together for important meetings in 1887, 1889, and 1893, Strong played a major role in generating concern for social causes among conservative as well as liberal evangelicals.[41] Framing his arguments for social activism in terms of evolutionary theory, especially that of Herbert Spencer, Strong combined appeals to the principles of religious and political liberty with references to underlying, biological forces of nature.

To realize their bright future, Strong believed, American Protestants needed to gain control over the perils that threatened to overpower them. These perils included the immigration of foreigners unaccustomed to American liberty and the fast-growing influence of the Roman Catholic Church with its religious authoritarianism and hostility to religious freedom and separation of church and state. Strong worried that Catholicism would undermine the strength of the American public school system and its ability to inculcate Protestant values. He also included Mormonism with its "ecclesiastical despotism" and "designs" against the United States in his list of threats to the country, along with secularism, intemperance, socialism, materialism and luxuriousness, and last but not least, the weakness of Protestant influence in America's fast-growing cities.[42]

In the final years of the nineteenth century, Strong and his allies formed an evangelical cohort of old stock Protestants with ties to government, education, and industry intent on strengthening the establishment of Protestant leadership in American society. This alliance did not involve the legal establishment of any particular church, as the Anglican

Church had once been established in Virginia or the Congregationalist had once been established in Massachusetts. The alliance of affluent Americans of British and northern European stock at the end of the century was a *de facto* establishment of Protestant leaders and interlocking social, political, and commercial institutions, bolstered by rhetoric derived from evolutionary theory. In addition to recognizing the prominence of an older Protestant elite, the alliance incorporated a new professional class eager to wed evangelical Christianity to new developments in social science.

Progressives had outgrown romantic sentimentality about nature; they appealed to Christianity and social science to control nature and soften the consequences of man's natural brutality to man. Just as Herbert Spencer criticized British imperialists who failed to rein in their natural greed for power, many American progressives worked to address the social problems created by fast-paced industrial growth and the unrestrained indulgence of human nature's "survival of the fittest" mentality. Business tycoons John D. Rockefeller and Andrew Carnegie turned to Christianity and social science to improve society and attend to some of the destructive effects of the dog-eat-dog world of industrial capitalism, while steadfastly and even brutally opposing labor unions and government regulation of working conditions and employment policies as obstacles to financial success. A "gospel of wealth" rationalized disparity between rich and poor in terms of the responsibility rich people had as stewards of wealth and philanthropists able to help many people and contribute to the betterment of society as a whole.[43]

Historian Robert Bannister showed that if the Rockefellers, Carnegie, and other wealthy Protestant philanthropists occasionally tossed around terms like "survival of the fittest," they were well aware that "social Darwinist" was an odious label applied to ruthless business people and hardly thought it captured the full range of their activities in the world, which included unprecedented contributions to humanitarian causes. Bannister also showed how the meaning of the term "social Darwinism" expanded over time to become a negative epithet to castigate proponents of social engineering with whom one disagreed—like the Nazis who wanted to redesign society to preserve racial purity and produce fitter people. Writing in 1979, long before Enron executive Jeffrey Skilling would endorse "survival of the fittest" and "the selfish gene," Bannister argued that Rockefeller and Carnegie knew better than to call themselves social Darwinists. But Bannister did not question the influence of evolutionary thinking on these liberal Protestants. These modernists used naturalistic, evolutionary rhetoric to describe the brutalities of modern society and believed in Christian stewardship of society as an adequate and realistic response.[44]

The wealthy philanthropists of the early twentieth century invested in universities, hospitals, libraries, and centers for music and art as means of social engineering aimed at advancing the progressive evolution of society. They regarded themselves not only as businessmen endowed with natural ability to compete but also as Christians with a moral obligation to contribute to the uplift of society in a manner proportionate to their good fortune. Hostile to governmental regulation of business and labor, they undertook philanthropy as stewards of wealth with the means and foresight to construct a better society and ameliorate the disadvantages suffered by other people in the inevitable competition for wealth.

In their efforts to establish or enlarge universities, hospitals, libraries, and centers for music and art, the Rockefellers and Carnegie transformed the older concept of Christian benevolence, which had animated a tremendous amount of evangelical activism in the nineteenth century, into a new scientific conception of philanthropy that proved highly influential in shaping American ideas about the moral stewardship of wealth and the meaning of a good society. As historian Judith Sealander showed, these modern donors used the term "scientific giving" to describe a new form of philanthropy that was systematic and strategic in its aim to alter the working order of society. In wanting to do more than respond here and there by giving alms to hardship cases in a "retail" manner, they constructed a new form of giving directed at social problems in a "wholesale" way. These pioneers of "scientific philanthropy," especially the Rockefellers, led the way in establishing new expectations for giving among a new class of extremely wealthy families. They also shaped some of the contours of modern American society, pouring unprecedented sums of money into private foundations. "Between 1900 and 1930," Sealander wrote, "scientific giving very significantly 'helped along' change in three areas: American education, medicine, and the promotion of social science."[45]

By the end of the nineteenth century, "scientific thinking" had emerged as a powerful new way to analyze the ills of society and construct agendas for social reform. In philanthropy, education, and politics, "scientific thinking" began to eclipse "Providence" as a means of conceptualizing the future of American society. But in important respects the two overlapped; among progressives, both "Providence" and "scientific thinking" implied optimistic visions of the future, and both involved ambitious programs of social reform. Both enjoyed considerable vogue among Protestant leaders, including those who opposed government regulation, like the Rockefellers and Carnegie, as well as those who admired socialism. Challenges to scientific thinking did develop in the United Stated after World War I through the fundamentalist movement and also among liberals whose distress over the carnage of the war and concern about instability and pessimism in Europe led them to challenge the arrogance of thinking that western civilization and Christianity were equivalent and that science and technology would diminish or even erase human sin. But enthusiasm for social progress still persisted in many American Protestant circles through the 1920s and 1930s, outweighing pessimism about American society and continuing to motivate efforts to resolve social problems by scientific thinking.

To a considerable extent, then, enthusiasm for scientific thinking coincided with, and even replaced, the religious language of Providence among progressive Christians in the late nineteenth and early twentieth centuries. Scientific language applied to society had the advantage of being open to Jews and secular intellectuals as well as evangelical Protestants. A new culture of professional neutrality allowed for more diverse forms of leadership and for a new level of discourse about the problems facing American society. At the same time, Protestant visions of a holy commonwealth and an evangelical sense of responsibility for social progress and reform were often implicit in the application of science to the problems of American society.

Science seemed to offer a way to realize Protestant visions of America, replacing romantic devotion to nature with an even more materialistic interpretation of Christianity. In important respects, faith in science was built into the bedrock of the Reformed Protestant tradition and its emphasis on the importance of empirical evidence for Christian revelation in nature. Some of the consequences of this faith are ironic, to say the least, and more than a few American Protestants have come to lament the unrestricted power they ceded to science.

Writing in 1988, Protestant sociologist Robert Wuthnow expressed concern about the "kind of mythic quality about science to which we link ourselves as a nation when we view such 'advances' as space launches, mechanical heart transplants, and the latest generation of American-produced home computers." Wuthnow argued that the objectivity of our increasingly scientific and technological world made that world appear natural and the forces behind it Godlike in their power to construct and determine reality. He accurately predicted that global competition for technological supremacy would only increase and suggested that Americans had yet to fully confront the dilemma of living in a high-tech world that their religious faith in science had helped to create.[46]

The Social Gospel

Evolutionary thinking shaped the "social gospel," one of the most influential religious movements in the early twentieth century and foremost expressions of modern evangelical reform. The chief exponent of the movement, Walter Rauschenbusch (1861–1918), argued that Jesus' proclamation of the kingdom of God was the central message of the New Testament and that pious hope of individual salvation was not all that being Christian involved, especially in the modern world; followers of Jesus were obligated to work toward transforming the social structures of this world to bring about the kingdom on earth. Along with enthusiasm for economic reform and eagerness to translate gospel imperatives into social policy, Rauschenbusch embraced evolution as a modern formulation of Reformed Protestant belief in divine Providence. As he explained simply, evolution ought to be interpreted in Christian terms: "Translate the evolutionary theories into religious faith, and you have the doctrine of the Kingdom of God." As historian Gary Dorrien suggested, Rauschenbusch's concept of evolution derived more from the idealism of the German philosopher Georg Wilhelm Friedrich Hegel than from the scientific discoveries of Charles Darwin. Rauschenbusch was committed to an idealism about historical progress that involved Christian reform of industrial society and the alleviation of suffering and poverty.[47]

The son of a strict German Baptist Professor at Rochester Theological Seminary in upstate New York, Rauschenbusch studied both in Germany and in the United States. He encountered Darwin's ideas as a student at the University of Rochester, where his physiology teacher presented natural selection as a way of understanding nature and science that was compatible with Christian theology. A conversion experience as a young man and a lifelong commitment to prayer and personal experience of Christ coexisted with his respect for science and gave his idealism about history a personal thrust. Idealism about history as the realm where God's will came to expression over time enabled him to accept scientific analyses of the Bible that identified layers of editorial revision, multiple voices and perspectives, and isolated some accounts of the ministry of Jesus as more historical than others, without losing faith in the moral and spiritual truths revealed through the Bible. Protestant idealism about history also conditioned Rauschenbusch's exposure to the revolutionary social philosophy of Karl Marx and his appropriation of several important elements of Marx's philosophy. Although he rejected the materialistic vision of history and religion at the core of Marx's determinism, he appreciated Marx's analysis of capitalism, class struggle, and the future transformation of society. Investment in personal experience of Christ and idealism about history enabled Rauschenbusch to challenge Marx's atheism and to set his revolutionary political philosophy within a Christian framework.

In 1885 and newly ordained, Rauschenbusch took charge of the Second German Baptist Church of New York City on Tenth Avenue in Hell's Kitchen, where exposure to the grueling poverty of German immigrants disturbed him deeply and forced him to think through the implications of the gospel with respect to the people of his church. Rauschenbusch drew admiration from John D. Rockefeller for his work with German immigrants. He also met Richard Ely (1854–1943), an Episcopalian with a German doctorate in economics, and supported Ely's program of social Christianity, which involved commitment to labor unions and to Henry George's proposal for a single tax on land value appreciation to pay for improved public facilities and lessen the growing division between rich and poor. Rauschenbusch joined the ranks of a growing number of American Protestants who called for the estab-lishment of a Christian form of socialism that would protect working people from ruthless exploitation and bring the moral values represented by the kingdom of God to bear on economic and political policy.

Rauschenbusch died in 1918, the same year that Germany signed the Armistice document bringing a temporary halt to war, and the same year that fundamentalism emerged in the United States as a militant political movement aimed at purging liberals from religious institutions and bringing an end to the teaching of evolution in public schools. Champions of the social gospel continued to define progress toward social justice as the unfolding realization of God's will in history and to support social policies aimed at bringing that progress about. But after World War I, they had to defend their enthusiasm for social science, socialist leanings, and liberal interpretations of scripture against fundamentalists. They also had to rethink their optimism about social progress in relation to the waste of life in World War I and the ongoing cycles of domination and revenge that continued to undermine stability and progress in the world. Proponents of social Christianity became increasingly focused on world peace, international order, and hopes for the League of Nations. Their understanding of Jesus as an emissary of peace drew many adher-ents and continued to hold sway in many Protestant institutions and in ecumenical organizations where Protestants cooperated with Catholics, Jews, and others in efforts to alleviate suffering and improve society.

Neo-Orthodox and Neo-Liberal Theologies

In the 1930s, resistance to the evolutionary optimism of the social gospel and to the social gospel's reliance on political institutions and economic policy to move American society closer to the kingdom of God came under fire from Protestants who called for a more transcendent interpretation of the kingdom and a more realistic assessment of modern society and its institutions. In 1932, the newly appointed Professor of Applied Christianity at Union Theological Seminary, Reinhold Niebuhr, blasted the idea that governments could embody Jesus' love and ridiculed social gospel visions of the kingdom of God as hopelessly sentimental and idealist. "In spite of the disillusionment of World War I, the average liberal Protestant is still convinced that the Kingdom of God is gradually approaching," he wrote disparagingly. Americans were particularly susceptible to this naïve belief, he argued, and he criticized liberal Protestants, unfairly, for overlooking the evils that surrounded them. "The evolutionary optimism of the eighteenth and nineteenth centuries, and the sentimentalism of the moral and social problem in romanticism, have affected religious idealism with particular force in America," he wrote in *Moral Man and Immoral Society*, obscuring "the brutality which is the inevitable concomitant of vitality."

In rejecting the evolutionary idealisms associated with Spencer, Hegel, and their American followers, Niebuhr embraced a form of realism more in line with the cold facts of science. His linkage of vitality with brutality and his belief that "society must always remain something of the jungle, which indeed it is, something of the world of nature," suggests the powerful hold that depictions of the violent aspects of Darwin's theory of natural selection exerted on neo-orthodox thought. Niebuhr's emphasis on the need for hard knowledge of "how to use the forces of nature to defeat nature, how to use force in order to establish justice" reflected a muscular, crusader form of Christianity as well as the persistent legacy of the social gospel's interpretation of Christianity in terms of social justice. Niebuhr did not disguise the extent to which empirical realism undermined traditional Christian beliefs in supernatural reality and forced him to reconceptualize the meaning of Christian faith. "The truest visions of religion are illusions," he wrote, "which may be partially realized by being resolutely believed. For what religion believes to be true," he went on, pursuing a line of thought much like that of William James, "may become true if its truth is not doubted."[48]

Reinhold's younger brother, the ethicist and historian of American Protestantism, H. Richard Niebuhr (1894–1962), took a similar position in his 1937 publication, *The Kingdom of God in America*. Recognizing the Faustian bargains liberal Protestants made first with romanticism and then with scientific naturalism, the younger Niebuhr denounced the "evolutionary" interpretation of God's relation to humanity as a distortion of Christianity: "it reconciled God and man by deifying the latter and humanizing the former." He also denounced the equation of Protestant Christianity with American culture constructed by nineteenth-century evangelicals, taking issue with the fusion of religious ideas about the kingdom of God with American culture, politics, and science. "Christianity, democracy, Americanism, the English language and culture, the growth of industry and science, American institutions— these are all confounded and confused," he complained. "The contemplation of their own righteousness filled Americans with such lofty and enthusiastic sentiments that they readily identified it with the righteousness of God." In the spirit of a modern day Jeremiah, he denounced the sense of "divine favoritism" that led many American Protestants to think that the Kingdom of God was "a human possession," which they owned and could translate into capital growth and technological prowess, rather than "a permanent revolution" in the hearts of Christians. He also perceived an invidious connection between the racism of American Protestant thought and its investment in scientific thought, industry, and technology. "It is in particular the kingdom of the Anglo-Saxon race," he wrote sarcastically, "which is destined to bring light to the gentiles by means of lamps manufactured in America."[49]

As a foil to linkage between American culture and the kingdom of God promoted by nineteenth-century evangelicals and their social gospel heirs, Richard Niebuhr held up the theology of Jonathan Edwards for admiration. He highlighted Edwards' insistence on the inscrutability of God, Edwards' juxtaposition between the grandeur of God and the puniness of humanity, Edwards' insight into the vulnerability and monstrous self-centeredness of human beings, and Edwards' respect for suffering and sacrifice. But if Niebuhr admired the "radical monotheism" of Edwards, the two men understood the relationship between faith and evidence drawn from nature and history differently. While Edwards understood God's control of nature and human events as an intellectual certainty borne out in science and history, Niebuhr embraced faith in the providence of God despite the evidence of science and history. Thus Niebuhr cited "a great phrase" from the philosopher of science, Alfred North Whitehead (1861–1947), to describe the difficult journey modern believers who took science and history seriously had to make to reconstruct religious faith. Alluding to the apparent absence of God in modern science, Whitehead wrote that, in the modern world, faith required a "transition from God the void to God the enemy and from God the enemy to God the companion."[50]

If scientific theories about biological evolution and the origin of the universe raised the specter of God as nonexistent or inhumane, fear of The Bomb that haunted Americans after World War II made that specter an obsession Protestants had to make sense of one way or another. While evolutionary biologists and astrophysicists described the origins and development of life in a radically different way than the Old Testament, the destructive potential of the technologies derived from new discoveries in physics and engineering challenged confidence in sentimental beliefs about evolutionary progress and the loving nature of God. American Protestants faced a crisis. Their religious heritage predisposed them to embrace science and expect science to bear out the truths of theology and the Bible. They could reject or refuse to consider some of discoveries of modern science, as fundamentalists did, and argue that proponents of evolutionary biology had strayed into atheism. They could struggle for ways of reconceptualizing the meaning of God, and redefine God as the "ultimate concern" or "God above God" manifest in the depths of human expression, as some neo-liberal theologians did.[51] Or they could say, "God is dead," and take up Christian life from there.

Proponents of the death-of-God movement among liberal Protestants after World War II viewed themselves as being honest about reality. Their conceptions of reality were deeply influenced by science and modern technology. "The death of God is not an intellectual cry of merely iconoclastic value," wrote French American theologian Gabriel Vahanian in 1960. "God's absence, or the death of God itself, has become what a man directly experiences." This experience of God as void was the result of modern Protestant faith in science and in the world that science and technology had created. In a telling metaphor, Vahanian wrote, "God became but an appendix to the marvels and wonders of a scientific universe."[52]

The modern theological concept of "the death of God" originated with the German existentialist Friedrich Nietzsche (1844–1900), who was an admirer of Emerson. Nietzsche suggested that human beings had created a transcendent God to supercede the many gods of nature and then killed that transcendent God because he saw too deeply into their own ugly nature.[53] For radical Protestants in the United States after World War II, death-of-God theology reflected the fear they felt in a world threatened by nuclear holocaust and also the emptiness they associated with the burgeoning materialism and technology of American culture. For them, saying that God was dead was a way of declaring that the equations between Christianity and American materialism, patriotic supremacy, and technological achievement were wrong and that the God many Americans worshipped was really an idol. In an important way, these theologians saw themselves as carrying forward the Niebuhrs' critique of Protestant assumptions about the special connection between Christianity and American culture.

Embedded within their iconoclastic denunciations, death-of-God theologians expressed the sense that something redemptive lay beneath their efforts to clear the house of idols. For example, in 1980, the death-of-God theologian Thomas J. J. Altizer wrote of "a pure and total grace" manifest in "moments when speech and vision have most fully been given us" and linked this grace to "the disintegration of all unique interior identity." In a way reminiscent of Emerson and perhaps of Jonathan Edwards as well, Altizer wrote, "It is an illusion, and a demonic and perverse illusion, that a common humanity is simply that humanity which seems to be at hand, or which is most visible or most audible in a mass culture and a mass society." But if the technological artifice and hyper-realism of mass culture served as a foil against which the absence of what Christians used to call the presence of God could be measured, it also offered new ways to experience such presence. For example, "One of the greatest gifts of our technological age is that it is now possible for the first time for each of us to listen to music alone." Thus it was in solitude, Altizer thought, as Emerson did, that the individual confronts the "not me." For Altizer, "total presence" involved something at once more profound and more objective than individual subjectivity. "The very absence of self-consciousness in our deepest and most actual moments," he wrote, "is a decisive sign of the identity of that common humanity which has dawned in our time."[54]

Not all Protestants understood the meaning of death-of-God theology or confronted the implications of the neo-liberal theologies upon which death-of-God theologians built their religious thought. Nevertheless, many American Protestants in the twentieth and twenty-first centuries sought experiences of "total presence" akin to what Altizer described and many identified those experiences with the biblical God and power of the Holy Spirit. Not all Protestants were as critical of the idea that God had a special relationship to America as the neo-liberals and their successors. But in the late twentieth century, Protestants on the conservative end of the spectrum also became increasingly critical of American culture and the role of science and technology in American society. If liberals tended to be more concerned about promoting social justice, multiculturalism, and the environment, while conservatives tended to be more concerned about denouncing homosexuality and abortion, science and technology played major roles in the problems both groups identified.

Conclusion

American Protestants faced a daunting array of challenges in the late nineteenth and early twentieth centuries as they turned to science and technology to solve problems and expand opportunities for wealth and progress. The booming population growth of urban centers stimulated industrial development, and vice versa, especially in the Northeast and Midwest, as poor Catholic and Jewish immigrants from southern and eastern Europe poured into New York, Chicago, and Detroit, along with blacks from the American South seeking a better life in the North. Jammed into ghettos with poor sanitation, little protection, abysmal working conditions, no laws against child labor until the 1920s, and no guarantees, before the 1930s, of a minimum wage or social security, the growing numbers of urban poor challenged easy optimism about America as a land of freedom and opportunity.

Efforts to come to terms with science have shaped Protestant experience and defined how American Protestants have understood religious life in the modern world. Protestant respect for the evidences of God's hand in nature and history contributed to widespread American interest in science prior to the twentieth century and laid important groundwork for the vast infrastructure supporting scientific investigation and achievement that developed in the United States since that time. In the context of this massive investment in science and technology, religious challenges to evolutionary biology and other religiously controversial areas of science led to battles between religion and science that earlier Protestants could never have imagined. In the United States today, Protestant efforts to insulate religion from critical inquiry and impose religious limits on science education are better organized and more effective than ever before, even as scientific language, imagery, and the fruits of scientific research thoroughly permeate American life. While conservative defenders of biblical authority have attacked the basic principles of evolutionary biology more vigorously and effectively in the United States than anywhere else in the world, the success they have enjoyed has resulted, at least in part, from strategic use of the latest media technologies and social scientific strategies to rally supporters, stage demonstrations, and lobby government officials.

Even the practice of piety has come to reflect the power of science technology. Over the course of the twentieth century, prayer became more a system of communications technology like telegraph, radio, telephone, and eventually, high speed internet connection through which appeals for divine assistance could be made and less a means of meditating on unworthiness in the sight of God, as it had often been for Puritans. Experiences of conversion, sanctification, and healing were like jolts, bolts, and currents of electricity. Visions, raptures, and translations to heaven were like photographs, movies, and journeys into space that paid obeisance to the dynamics and factuality of those technologies.[55]

Conservatives often defended their faith against the threat of modernism and its embrace of science with claims about salvation, atonement, personal immortality, and the virgin birth and resurrection of Jesus that appeared to compete for allegiance with the objectivity prized by scientists. Thus conservative writer J. Gresham Machen (1881–1937), who wanted to raise faith in the Bible above any competition with science, declared the Bible to be an "infallible rule of faith and practice." No real evidence against that infallibility had ever come to light, he thought; claims that the Bible contained errors could all be shown to derive from mistaken readings by inherently sinful mortals. Rejecting the liberal tendency to conceptualize grace as an experience that enabled people to live better lives, Machen hammered at the objective reality of Christ and his sacrificial atonement. "Faith is essentially dogmatic," Machen argued, "you cannot remove the element of intellectual assent from it." He encouraged Protestants to separate God, Christ, and the Bible into an intellectual realm that empirical skepticism and human experience could not alter, making intellectual assent to an objective reality beyond human experience the crucial test of faith: "it is not the faith which saves the Christian," Machen wrote, perhaps with William James in mind, "but the object of the faith."[56]

If liberal Protestants have put more effort into incorporating higher criticism of the Bible, new discoveries about nature and new information about human behavior developed through the social sciences into their understanding of Christian faith, they have also confronted dilemmas created, in part, through their own enthusiasm for science and technology. Faced with the grim realities of world war, endemic poverty, environmental degradation, and threats of nuclear catastrophe, neoliberals emphasized the hubris in connecting the will of God to American prosperity, scientific achievement, and technological advance. While they have disagreed with conservatives on many issues, liberals and neoliberals have also been preoccupied with science and its offshoots and struggled to come to some understanding of the relationship between scientific realities and religious belief.

Romantic Protestants in the nineteenth century played an important role in this history. Their naturalistic "new theology" laid the groundwork for many new forms of religious expression in the twentieth century, including important developments in feminist theology and nature spirituality and in the appreciation of Native American and Asian religions. Nineteenth-century proponents of the "new theology" rejected orthodox interpretations of divine transcendence, predestination, and original sin as too harsh and puritanical and embraced evolution as the means through which a loving God expressed his creative wisdom progressively. Interpreting the meaning of evolution in terms of romantic idealism about nature as a symbol of spirit and its development through history, proponents of this theology had a hard time coming to terms with the challenges to assumptions about nature's goodness and harmonious design posed by evolutionary biology. Critics of this "new theology" argued, and not without reason, that it limited God's transcendence. Machen attacked liberal theology on precisely this point. "In modern liberalism," he complained in 1923, the "sharp distinction between God and world is broken down, and the name 'God' applied to the mighty world process itself."[57]

Competing ideas about the nature and meaning of evolution confused many of the debates between religious liberals eager to think about Christianity in terms of Herbert Spencer's philosophy and conservatives who thought of evolution in Darwinian terms and resisted it. Disputes over the question of how Protestant belief should be interpreted in light of modern science muddied the waters further, making it difficult for people to hear each other, much less come to agreement. Although his position is not without its problems and fallacious strategies, William James offered a mediating point of view that continues to attract adherents. His acceptance of both biological evolution and Protestant theology, and willingness to think about each in light of the other, reflects the commitment to empirical investigation and reasoning that has characterized the mainstreams of Reformed Protestant thought since the sixteenth century, as well as commitment to the distinction between God and nature important throughout the history of Christian thought.

While James argued that religious belief should not be tied to materialism in nature, other Protestants—both liberals and conservatives—clung to the idea that nature would always supply evidence of the existence and wisdom of God that everybody could see. While James worked to separate religious thought and experience from the materialism of nature, many others remained wedded to belief in God's hand or spirit in nature. Faced with new discoveries in geology, biology, and physics, many Protestants grasped for ways to keep nature holy, or at least under control and comprehensible as part of God's intelligent design.

James resisted the concept of destiny as well as the tendency to secularize nature. His exposure to Darwin led to his understanding of life as an open-ended process and his affirmation of the open-endedness of life rekindled his Christian faith. His justification for faith coincided with his resistance to the idea that God was an irresistibly predetermining power. While some liberal Protestants viewed God as the Absolute moving forward through time, generating higher forms of life in nature and social progress in history, James was less idealistic about both nature and history and resisted the tendency to equate God with "world process itself." But unlike conservative Protestants who also resisted that pantheistic tendency, James preferred to think of intelligent design as something that human beings might work out together in the future, rather than as something predetermined and preexisting.

James' investment in the future coincided with his affirmation of religious pluralism, which he championed for the opportunities it provided for individual genius and for its role in the construction of better societies and advancement of human welfare. If he did not fully appreciate the dangers of demagoguery and the blinding power over others that individual geniuses could exert, or the futility of keeping science open to supernatural claims, his openness to religious pluralism and individual genius was an important Protestant contribution to American life.

Notes

1. In the seventeenth century, Separatists in Amsterdam represented the antisecular "trend in Protestant education" most clearly. Jeffrey Mallinson, *Faith, Reason, and Revelation in Theodore Beza* (Oxford: Oxford University Press, 2003), pp. 23, 177–187, quotations from p. 238.

2. Cotton Mather, "Letter to John Woodward" and *The Christian Philosopher*, excerpted in *Cotton Mather: Selections*, ed. Kenneth B. Murdock (New York: Hafner Publishing, 1926), quotations from pp. xxi, 350, 352.

3. Theodore Dwight Bozeman, *Protestants in an Age of Science* (Chapel Hill: University of North Carolina Press, 1977).

4. Urian Oakes, "The Sovereign Efficacy of Divine Providence," September 10, 1677, proposition 2.

5. William James, "Great Men, Great Thoughts, and the Environment," in *The Will to Believe* (New York: Longmans, Green, 1897), p. 140; Jonathan Schull, "Selection—James's Principal Principle," in *Reinterpreting the Legacy of William James*, ed. Margaret E. Donnelly (Washington, DC: American Psychological Association, 1992), pp. 139–151, quotation from p. 150.

6. James R. Moore, *The Post-Darwinian Controversies: A Study of the Protestant Struggle to Come to Terms with Darwin in Great Britain and America 1870–1900* (Cambridge: Cambridge University Press, 2003; orig. 1979), quotations from p. 308.

7. Charles Darwin, *The Origin of Species by Means of Natural Selection; Or the Preservation of Favored Races in the Struggle for Life*, 6th ed. (New York: Modern Library, 1998), quotations from pp. 647–648.

8. Moore, *Post-Darwinian Controversies*, pp. 157–161; T. A. Goude, "Darwin, Charles Robert," in *Encyclopedia of Philosophy*, ed. Paul Edwards, 8 vols. (New York: Macmillan Publishers, 1967), vol. 2, pp. 294–295.

9. Gillian Beer, "Introduction," in *The Origin of Species*, ed. Gillian Beer (New York: Oxford University Press, 1996); Charles Darwin, *The Autobiography of Charles Darwin, 1809–1882, with Original Omissions Restored*, ed. Nora Barlow (New York: Harcourt, Brace & World, 1958), p. 109; Moore, *Post-Darwinian Controversies*, p. 162; Herbert Spencer, *Autobiography*, 2 vols. (London: Williams and Norgate, 1904), vol. 2, pp. 374–378.

10. Quoted in R.W.B. Lewis, *The Jameses: A Family Narrative* (New York: Farrar, Straus and Giroux, 1991), p. 282.

11. Quoted in R.W.B. Lewis, *The Jameses*, p. 216.

12. William James, *Varieties of Religious Experience: A Study in Human Nature* (New York: New American Library, 1958; orig. 1902), pp. 135–136.

13. George Boas, "Renouvier, Charles Bernard," in *The Encyclopedia of Philosophy*, ed. Paul Edwards, 8 vols. (New York: Macmillan Publishing, 1972; orig. 1967), vol. 8, pp. 180–182.

14. Giles Gunn, ed., *Henry James, Senior: A Selection of His Writings*, (Chicago: American Library Association, 1974).

15. William James, "The Will to Believe," *Essays on Faith and Morals* (Cleveland: Meridian Books, 1962), pp. 32–62, quotations from p. 32.

16. James, "The Will to Believe," quotations from p. 40.

17. James, "The Will to Believe," quotations from pp. 52–53, 57.

18. James, "The Will to Believe," quotations from pp. 60, 59.

19. Both Luther and Calvin argued that godly work, holiness, and sanctification were the result of the faith in the redeeming power of Christ's love that justified sinners, making them right with God, and they accused the Catholic Church of inverting the truth by making holiness and good works the precondition of justification. While Luther equated holiness with believers' awareness of their own sinfulness and not with any moral reconstitution, Calvin and his followers argued that holiness derived from an internal moral change in believers, and that justification by faith enabled sinners to become moral agents capable of humbly following God's will.

20. James, *Varieties*, quotations from pp. 115, 390, 391.

21. James, *Varieties*, quotations from p. 338.

22. George M. Marsden, *Fundamentalism and American Culture: The Shaping of Twentieth-Century Evangelicalism, 1870–1925* (New York: Oxford University Press, 1980), quotations from p. 19; Philip Schaff and S. Irenaeus Prime, eds., *History, Essays, Orations, and Other Documents of the Sixth General Conference of the Evangelical Alliance, Held in New York, October 2–12, 1873* (New York, 1874), pp. 264–275, 317–23.

23. Ernest R. Sandeen, *The Roots of Fundamentalism: British and American Millenarianism, 1800–1930* (Chicago: University of Chicago Press, 1970), quotations from pp. 118, 119. Italics are mine.

24. Archibald Alexander and Benjamin B. Warfield, "Inspiration," *Presbyterian Review* 2 (April 1881): 226–246, quotation from p. 242.

25. Marsden, *Fundamentalism*, quotation from p. 149.

26. Marsden, *Fundamentalism*, quotation from p. 150.

27. Ronald L. Numbers, *Darwinism Comes to America* (Cambridge: Harvard University Press, 1998), pp. 77–78, 88, quotation from p. 78.

28. Numbers, *Darwinism*, quotations from p. 80.

29. Numbers, *Darwinism*, quotations from p. 81.

30. Carl Zimmer, "Sexier Posterior Evolves Almost Overnight," *New York Times*, November 30, 2004, quotation from D1.

31. Herbert Spencer, *First Principles* (New York: D. Appleton and Company, 1896), quotations from pp. 539, 318–319.

32. Herbert Spencer, *Autobiography*, 2 vols. (London: Williams and Norgate, 1904), quotation from vol. 2, p. 374.

33. Henry Ward Beecher, *Evolution and Religion* (New York: Fords, Howard, & Hulbert, 1885), pp. 113, 115, quoted in Moore, *Post-Darwinian Controversies*, p. 221; also see p. 92.

34. Henry Ward Beecher, *Star Papers; Or Experiences of Art and Nature* (New York: 1855), quotation from p. 194.

35. Henry F. May, *Protestant Churches and Industrial America* (New York: Harper & Row, 1949), p. 91.

Beecher's religious outlook involved a blend of looking forward and backward that illustrates the difficulty involved in attempting to pin down what it meant to be a liberal Protestant in the late nineteenth century. Beecher was liberal in the sense of not being confined to orthodox or authoritarian principles and also in his commitment to helping to bring about a new social order unlike anything in the past. On the other hand, he was conservative in his allegiance to a social class defined by Puritan ancestry and expectations of cultural dominance and public leadership. In a famous but oversimplified statement describing the conservative impact of Beecher and his fellow clergymen, historian Henry F. May wrote in 1949, "In 1876 Protestantism presented a massive, almost unbroken front in its defense of the status quo." (p. 91.)

36. Henry Ward Beecher quoted in Martin E. Marty, *Righteous Empire: The Protestant Experience in America* (New York: Harper & Row, 1970), p. 147.

37. Sidney E. Mead, *The Lively Experiment: The Shaping of Christianity in America* (New York: Harper & Row, 1976; orig. 1963), quotations from pp. 135, 136, 153–154. Also see Arthur M. Schlesinger, "A Critical Period in American Protestantism, 1875–1900," *Massachusetts Historical Society Proceedings* 44 (June 1932): 523–548.

38. Marty, *Righteous Empire*, quotation from p. 23.

39. Sylvester Johnson, *The Myth of Ham in Nineteenth-Century American Christianity: Race, Heathens, and the People of God* (New York: Palgrave Macmillan, 2004).

40. Josiah Strong, *Our Country: Its Possible Future and Its Present Crisis*, rev. ed. (New York: Baker & Taylor, 1891; orig. 1895), quotations from pp. 219–220.

41. Robert T. Handy, *A Christian America: Protestant Hopes and Historical Realities*, rev. ed. (New York: Oxford University Press, 1984; orig. 1971), p. 136.

42. Strong, *Our Country*, pp. x–xviii.

43. Historian Richard Hofstadter quoted business celebrities John D. Rockefeller and Andrew Carnegie to illustrate their belief that success in business reflected scientific and moral principles. "The growth of a large business is merely a survival of the fittest," John D. Rockefeller told Sunday-school students. "[I]t is merely the working-out of a law of nature and a law of God." Andrew Carnegie, author of *The Gospel of Wealth*, expressed himself similarly on at least one occasion, declaring competition to be a "law" of evolution and social progress that "insures the survival of the fittest in every department." John D. Rockefeller and Andrew Carnegie quoted in Richard Hofstadter, *Social Darwinism in American Thought*, rev. ed. (Boston: Beacon Press, 1955; orig. 1944), pp. 45–46.

44. Against Hofstadter, Bannister maintained that no self-proclaimed proponent of "social Darwinism" ever existed. Critics of unrestrained capitalism created the term as a way of deploring the moral philosophy of business tycoons like the Rockefellers and Carnegie. "The so-called conservative social Darwinists of the 1880s (laissez-faire liberals, utilitarians, and the like) were, *as social Darwinists*, the invention of their opponents to the left," Bannister complained. Once invented, the term caught on as a negative epithet for a variety of other groups. "Eventually, the label was used not merely to caricature the 'let-alone-philosophy' (as it was termed), but to denigrate programs of other state activists one happened to oppose, whether New Liberals, fellow socialists, or eugenicists." Robert C. Bannister, *Social Darwinism: Science and Myth in Anglo-American Social Thought* (Philadelphia: Temple University Press, 1989; orig. 1979), quotations from p. xi.

45. Judith Sealander, "Curing Evils at Their Source: The Arrival of Scientific Giving," in *Charity, Philanthropy, and Civility in American History*, ed. Lawrence J. Friedman and Mark D. McGarvie (Cambridge: Cambridge University Press, 2003), pp. 217–239, quotation from p. 230.

46. Robert Wuthnow, *The Restructuring of American Religion: Society and Faith since World War II* (Princeton: Princeton University Press, 1988), quotation from p. 286.

47. Walter Rauschenbusch, *Christianizing the Social Order* (New York: Macmillan, 1912), p. 121, quoted in Gary Dorrien, *The Making of American Liberal Theology: Idealism, Realism, and Modernity 1900–1950* (Louisville: Westminster John Knox Press, 2003), p. 110.

48. Reinhold Niebuhr, *Moral Man and Immoral Society: A Study in Ethics and Politics* (New York: Charles Scribners' Sons, 1932), quotations from pp. 79, 81.

49. H. Richard Niebuhr, *The Kingdom of God in America* (New York: Harper & Row, 1937), quotations from pp. 191, 179.

50. Alfred North Whitehead, *Religion in the Making* (New York: 1926), p. 16, quoted in Niebuhr, *Kingdom of God*, p. 192.

Whitehead's thought illustrates the effort made by philosophers of religion in the twentieth century to reconcile religion and science. Whitehead developed much of his philosophy in the United States after moving to Harvard in 1924 and becoming more closely acquainted with the work of William James.

Whitehead understood all of life as a thoroughly interconnected evolutionary process in which previous life events conditioned new ones. Like James, he resisted the idea of defining God as the source of vitality—what Aristotle called the Prime Mover—because that conceptualization made God responsible for evil as well as good: "He is then the supreme author of the play, and to Him must therefore be ascribed its shortcomings as well as its success." Arguing that value comes about through a concretizing process of limitation and exclusion, Whitehead proposed that God be conceived as a Principle of Concretion involved in the emergence of new events out of conditions established by previous events. "God is not concrete," Whitehead believed, "but He is the ground for concrete actuality." The principle Whitehead discerned within the production of concrete life events was a principle of exclusion, and vitality itself or its source. This principle of exclusion, not sheer vitality, established value. If God "be conceived as the supreme ground for limitation," as Whitehead thought he should, "it stands in His very nature to divide Good from Evil, and to establish Reason 'within her dominions supreme.'" Alfred North Whitehead, *Science and the Modern World* (New York: Free Press, 1925), quotations from pp. 174, 178–179.

51. See, for example, Paul Tillich, *The Courage to Be* (New Haven: Yale University Press, 1952).

52. Gabriel Vahanian, *The Death of God: The Culture of Our Post-Christian Era* (New York: George Braziller, 1961; orig. 1957), quotations from pp. 187, 181.

53. Friedrich Nietzsche, *Thus Spake Zarathustra*, part 4, chap. 67, in *The Philosophy of Nietzsche* (New York: Modern Library, 1954), pp. 264–267.

54. Thomas J. J. Altizer, *Total Presence: The Language of Jesus and the Language of Today* (New York: Seabury Press, 1980), quotations from pp. 104–105; see Ralph Waldo Emerson, "Nature" (1836), in *The Essential Writings of Ralph Waldo Emerson*, ed. Brooks Atkinson (New York: Modern Library, 2000), pp. 5–7.

55. Amanda Porterfield, *Healing in the History of Christianity* (New York: Oxford University Press, 2005).

56. J. Gresham Machen, *Christianity and Liberalism* (Grand Rapids: William B. Eerdmans, 1923), quotations from pp. 142–143.

57. Machen, *Christianity and Liberalism*, quotation from p. 63.

Chapter 5

Equality and the End of Protestantism

A merican society changed dramatically after the Second World War in response to numerous factors including the Civil Rights movement, the Vietnam War, the cold war, new immigration policies, and the resurgence of feminism. New media technologies, increasingly sophisticated marketing strategies, and a developing global economy all impacted American society and religious life profoundly. At the same time, persistent tensions within American society prompted the resurgence of old conflicts, shaping American responses to new events in familiar ways. Long-standing tendencies to portray America as a special, superior nation threatened by internal betrayals and evil forces abroad characterized American political rhetoric and popular culture in the wake of new countercultural protests, fears of nuclear Armageddon, and terrorist attacks. Concern about the inequalities in American society also preoccupied many people, and conflict over how to explain and respond to these inequalities fell into familiar grooves of disagreement.[1]

The culture wars that engaged Americans after 1960 emerged out of several centuries of American debate about the proper relationship between individual freedom and social order. At the time the United States was formed, that debate was partially resolved in constitutional guarantees of freedom of religion, speech, press, and assembly and in the principle of equality proclaimed in the Declaration of Independence as a basis for social order. Although Americans disagreed about who should be equal and how far equality should extend, the principle of equality provided a basis for law and government. Enlightenment faith in human reason and, behind that, Reformed Protestant attention to individual conscience as the best and truest source of social order informed this principle of equality.

Appeal to the principle of equality as a solution to the problematic relationship between individual freedom and social order was not fully worked out in the founding of the republic, as the compromise on slavery made clear. In many ways, equality is still being worked out in America and the relationship between individual freedom and social order is still the central cultural problem that many Americans struggle with. New forms of this problem came to expression after 1960 as a result of a variety of new forces and events, but they had roots in historic tensions within American Protestant culture at the end of the eighteenth century, when the American republic was founded.

In the American colonies and early republic of the United States at the end of the eighteenth century, political philosophies based on natural reason and the principle of equality coexisted with visions of the kingdom of God as a model for social order. Both reflected Protestant experience of the world and Protestant ideas about society and Christian morality. But political philosophies based on natural reason were secular and humanistic while visions of the kingdom of God involved supernatural claims and expectations. Although the two ways of thinking were not entirely incompatible and many Americans ascribed to both, they represented two different trajectories that Protestant thought would take in the United States, trajectories that would play a major role in dividing Americans against one another in the late twentieth and early twenty-first centuries.

Equality in the History of Protestant Thought

The principle of equality came to expression among Protestants in England, America, and Scotland during the seventeenth and eighteenth centuries through the influence of the Puritan writer John Milton (1608–1674), the political philosopher John Locke (1632–1704), and many others who shared their worldviews. In his defense of freedom of the press and arguments in support of the overthrow of oppressive monarchs, Milton argued for political liberty on the basis of his understanding of Reformed Protestant theology and its emphasis on individual conscience and moral agency. Locke developed Milton's understanding of political liberty further in his "Essay on Toleration" (1667), arguing that the sole business of government was the "peace, safety, or security of the people" and that laws with any other purpose constituted "meddling." In Locke's theory, the ideal of the "godly prince" held up by Martin Luther as the guarantor of a virtuous state no longer applied. Locke wanted citizens to be the guarantors of virtue. To fulfill that responsibility citizens needed to be free to pursue their own interests, able to defend their interests but restrained from infringing on the rights of others, and educated in the pro-social implications of enlightened self-interest.[2]

Locke's assertion in his 1681 "Religion" essay, "That there is a God and what that God is nothing can discover to us nor judge in us but natural reason," carried forward earlier Protestant efforts to define religious life apart from miraculous claims. It was also an assertion of confidence in the God-given natural ability of individuals to reason and make moral judgments, which in Locke's opinion, as in Milton's, magistrates respectful of God were obligated to respect. As Locke argued in his 1667 "Essay on Toleration," a magistrate "can right me against my neighbor, but cannot defend me against my God." The magistrate has "no more certain or more infallible knowledge of the way to attain" a right relationship to God "than I myself," Locke insisted, "where we are both *equally* inquirers, both *equally* subjects."[3]

Milton and Locke were only the most articulate spokesmen for the principle of equality developed out of this Anglo-Protestant understanding of man's relationship to God. While more socially conservative Christians believed in the need for more thoroughgoing magisterial authority, the idea of equality among men based on their relationship to a sovereign God was the basis of a strong argument for political liberty that resonated with many American patriots. In the pamphlet *Common Sense*, which galvanized support for independence when it appeared in January 1776, Thomas Paine (1737–1809) argued that monarchy was no more defensible than papacy: "For monarchy in every instance is the Popery of government." Along with condemnation of monarchy for its "degradation and lessening of ourselves," Paine rejected "hereditary succession" as "an insult and imposition on posterity." Individuals might deserve honor for their accomplishments, he maintained, but every generation had to earn its own honor: "For all men being originally equals, no *one* by *birth* could have a right to set up his own family in perpetual preference to all others for ever." As these sentiments came to expression in the Declaration of Independence, published six months after *Common Sense*, the argument for revolution derived from the principle of equality, which in turn derived from Protestant rejection of the Church of Rome, commitment to the priesthood of all believers, and belief in the Bible's endorsement of the rights, dignity, and importance of individuals.[4]

The principle of equality coexisted in the minds of many American patriots with the classical ideal of a virtuous republic and its hierarchical understanding of government and social order.[5] Newspapers and political pamphlets at the time of the Revolution and formation of the early Republic were filled with admiration for the civilizations of ancient Greece and Rome, and with idealism about a new American republic that would embody the virtues of ancient Greek city-states governed by cadres of educated citizens. Champions of American republicanism pointed to the ancient Greek city-states of Athens, Sparta, and Thebes as models for the new United States and cited the ancient Roman writers Cicero, Virgil, and Tacitus as political philosophers whose conceptions of a virtuous republic could be realized in America. These ancient philosophers and many of their eighteenth-century admirers defined a virtuous state in terms of a stable social hierarchy governed by an educated class and dependent on the willingness of all members of the society to sacrifice their own interests for the public good.[6]

Because discussion of the classical republican ideal dominated the political press, interpreters have sometimes underestimated the influence of Lockean thought. In a study of Locke's influence in America, historian Jerome Huyler argued that while Americans disagreed sharply with each other about how far freedom and equality should extend, Locke's influence was ubiquitous and taken for granted as part of a common worldview many shared. Americans quoted Cicero and Tacitus more than they quoted Locke because their attraction to these ancient writers required some explanation; their own worldviews overlapped with that of Locke more than with those of Cicero and Tacitus.

Compounding the tendency among historians to minimize Locke's influence, Huyler argued further, critics of modern liberalism have sometimes distorted Locke's worldview and misunderstood his ideas, making him into an advocate of unrestrained self-interest and unrestrained capitalism, which he was not.[7] Locke had an almost Calvinist sense of the depth of human acquisitiveness, and awareness of the dangers that acquisitiveness posed to social order. Like his intellectual heir James Madison, Locke thought forceful, preemptive attempts to restrain human liberty created worse problems than liberty did and that education and moral reasoning tempered natural acquisitiveness; enlightened self-interest offered a better means to social order and peace than repression.

Madison was under no illusion that religious freedom would guarantee moral virtue or ensure responsible citizenship. Nevertheless, he believed religious freedom was a better option than religious establishment because it encouraged the engagement and development of individual conscience, whence he thought moral virtue and responsible citizenship derived. The case against establishment was overwhelming as far as Madison was concerned; Christianity's "legal establishment" had "been on trial" for fifteen centuries and was "more or less" a disaster for the faith "in all places." As a better alternative to the legal establishment of Christianity, government that endorsed "the duty of every man to render to the Creator such homage and such only as he believes to be acceptable to him," Madison argued, would promote respect for law, decrease religious violence, and stimulate moral virtue and the growth and vitality of the Christian religion.[8]

For Madison and Locke, religious freedom not only meant that all religions were equal in the eyes of the law, so far as government support was concerned, but also that a kind of golden rule applied to different forms of religious beliefs. Each individual owed others who believed differently the same degree of respect they would like for themselves, and with good reason, as far as civility and sociability were concerned. As Locke put the issue in his "Essay on Toleration," "If I observe the Friday with the Mahomedan, or the Saturday with the Jew, or the Sunday with the Christian," none "of these, if they be done sincerely and out of conscience," will "of itself make me" a "worse neighbor" except if "I will, out of pride or overweeningness of my own opinion, and a secret conceit of my own infallibility, taking to myself something of a godlike power, force and compel others to be of my mind, or censure or malign them if they are not."[9]

Not all American Protestants agreed with this reasoning. The prohibition against religious establishment in the First Amendment applied at the federal level only and the men who ratified the Amendment understood that some states in the union would preserve or create established churches. Religious leaders in Massachusetts, the stronghold of New England Puritanism, managed to hold off disestablishment until 1833. But if not everyone agreed on the meaning of equality with respect to religious freedom, the principle of equality offered a pragmatic approach to conflict avoidance. It also involved a social ethic derived from Protestant ideas about the importance of individual moral conscience and the priesthood of all believers. Indeed, as an expression of the principle of equality, respect for religious difference constituted a certain completion of Protestant idealism with respect to freedom of conscience. As such, it contributed to the decline in Protestant animosity toward other religions and to the dissolution of Protestantism itself as a distinctive and coherent religious tradition.

Visions of Heaven and Christ's Reign on Earth

Throughout American Protestant history, visions of heaven and the coming kingdom of God have complicated debate about equality and religious freedom. Along with meditations on heaven above, expectations of Christ's return for a 1,000-year reign before Satan's final defeat and depictions of a divine establishment of religion contributed to hopes that evil and injustice would be eradicated and goodness and justice ultimately prevail. Such visions also contributed to fears of future punishment and suffering and to fantasies of revenge and superiority. In appealing to supernatural agency to bring order out of darkness and evil and resolve all of life's problems, these visions complicated critical thinking about the future, drawing attention away from the kind of pragmatic reasoning needed to think through the relationship between individual freedom and social order and the implications of equality for American life.

Visions of heaven and Christ's millennial kingdom were not simply excuses for not thinking things through, however; they were means of expressing desires and aspirations that pressed beyond the limits of what social convention allowed some people to express more forthrightly. As historian Catherine Brekus showed in her study of female preachers in the eighteenth and early nineteenth centuries, the Second Coming of Christ was a favorite theme among women who defied conventional prohibitions against female preaching and gestured toward universal equality. In 1776, for example, Jemima Wilkinson, the farmer's daughter from Rhode Island who traveled around the northeast on horseback, calling herself the Public Universal Friend, dreamed of angels in white robes and gold crowns who came down to earth, "Bringing a sealed Pardon from the living god; and putting their trumpets to their mouths, proclaimed saying, Room, Room, Room, in the many Mansions of eternal glory for Thee and for everyone."[10]

Much as women made more room for themselves on earth by voicing their visions of heaven, African Americans pointed to heaven to denounce racial inequality. Measuring status in moral and spiritual terms rather than in terms of earthly wealth and prestige, more than a few evangelical preachers proclaimed a just deity who welcomed his faithful black servants into heaven and denied entrance to richer and more powerful white people. Along these lines, the ex-slave Frederick Douglass claimed, "Slaves knew enough of the orthodox theology of the time to consign all bad slaveholders to hell." Escaped slave John Anderson made the case for heavenly justice even more emphatically, "Some folks say slaveholders may be good Christians, but I can't and won't believe it, nor do I think that a slaveholder can get to heaven."[11]

Visions of Christ coming down to earth or of earthly life moving toward his kingdom were commonplace among American Protestants, reflecting fascination with biblical prophecy and Protestant belief in divine providence working its way out in human history. Although Protestants were hardly the first or only Christians to anticipate the coming of heaven to earth and the completion of God's plan for the world, Protestant theology encouraged such millenarian experiences in ways that Catholic theology did not. Catholic theology emphasized the prolongation of earth's separation from heaven and directed attention to the Church and its sacraments and saints as the means of passage and communication between the two. In their protests against the Catholic Church, many Protestants wanted to reconstruct society according to Christ's dictates, break the Church's unlawful hold on the keys to heaven, and join in the glorious momentum this rupture was setting into motion.

After encountering the revolutionary violence inspired by radical preachers claiming that Christ had returned to destroy all injustice and reveal prelates as swine, Martin Luther backed away from expectation of Christ's appearance on earth to endorse a more Catholic view of two kingdoms, one of heaven, the other of earthly kingdoms and princes to which Christians owed allegiance. John Calvin and others in the Reformed tradition resumed the millenarian effort to re-form society in anticipation of the coming kingdom, but often through authoritarian institutions that incorporated affirmations of equality before God within repressive systems of social hierarchy and enforced humility. In the American colonies, radical and unsettling forms of millenarian expectation often cropped up despite efforts by magistrates to keep chiliastic visions and other potentially disruptive religious forces in society under control. Disappointment and dissatisfaction during numerous crises in American colonial history fueled fears that the end times were near. Many American Protestants read John Foxe's popular *Acts and Monuments*, which linked the appearance of the Antichrist to the persecution of sixteenth-century English Protestants during Mary's reign, and emulated Foxe's strategy of reading apocalyptic signs within episodes of political crisis. Religious revivals prompted jubilant scenarios for faithful converts and vivid descriptions of hellfires awaiting sinners; many evangelicals involved in revivals during the eighteenth and nineteenth centuries thought that the millennium might be dawning in America.

Along similar lines, religious patriots linked the American Revolution with the dawning of the kingdom as prophesied in the Book of Revelation. After the battle of Lexington in 1775, Calvinist preacher Elisha Fish assured the Worcester Committee of Correspondence that "although men or devils, earth or hell, Antichrist or the dragon rages, the people of God may still triumph in Christ, the Captain of their salvation." In a 1779 essay in Philadelphia's *United States Magazine*, a writer from Delaware went further in identifying the "man child" born of the "woman in the wilderness" who escaped the dragon in the book of Revelation with the "faithful *and pious freemen*" of America, "preserved in infancy from the devouring *dragon of arbitrary power*."[12]

Such millenarian rhetoric bathed discussions of political liberty and republican virtue in a wash of religious idealism that promised to resolve whatever latent tensions there might be. The popularity of millenarian rhetoric about the Revolution and early Republic also underscored the Protestant character of the discussions and debates Americans had with each other about how the new nation should be formed; if Americans disagreed sharply with each other on many points, many shared important assumptions about the general course of history and its biblical template, the crucial role of the Protestant Reformation in the history of the world, and their own responsibility to help carry that history forward to completion.

Lockean patriots shared some of the same assumptions about the general course of history even if they did not expect supernatural intervention to transform human history. Although their vision of human society and its future was more secular, it was deeply informed by Protestant ideas about individual responsibility to a sovereign God. If Locke's closest followers in America were skeptical of belief in miracles, so were many earlier Protestant Reformers. If they threw their faith in on the side of natural reason, they were keenly aware of the power and dangers of self-interest as well. If they preferred the pleasures of human sociability to those of conversion, sociability may have appeared to them to be the better path to Christian virtue.

Lockean egalitarianism, patrician republicanism, and millenarian supernaturalism all coexisted and reflected the influence of Protestant religious and moral thought. A shared culture of Protestantism made it easier for people to ascribe to more than one of these conflicting emphases without necessarily being troubled by concern about their incompatibility. Overriding agreement about the importance of individual conscience and the illegitimacy of the Catholic Church and high-handed British treatment of the American colonies facilitated this coexistence. But while all three strands of thought coexisted in American Protestant culture, tensions among them about the implications of equality and the relationship between freedom and order fueled political conflict in the early republic and continued to do so afterward. These tensions shaped events leading to Civil War in the 1860s and to the conflict between modernism and fundamentalism in the early twentieth century. By the time of the culture wars of the late twentieth and early twenty-first centuries, when some of the same tensions erupted again, unresolved issues regarding equality and the relationship between individual freedom and social order had become intertwined with similar issues and debates around the world.

In America in the early nineteenth century, incompatibilities among Lockean, classical, and millenarian visions of society were temporarily muted during the resurgence of evangelicalism, which led to the growth of a national Protestant evangelical religion alongside the multiplicity of denominations and sects competing for adherents. Although not all evangelicals jumped on the patriotic bandwagon, many did, establishing ties with each other and with business and political leaders through the missionary movement, urban revivals, and the construction of a public school system that rivaled that of every other country in the world. In the eyes of many evangelical patriots, America was a Protestant nation with a mission to save the world, or at least lead it in a progressive direction. The meaning of the term "Protestant" became associated with this national project as much as with any particular church.[13]

The evangelical equation between Protestantism and Americanism was bound to fall apart. Increasing professionalism in education, health care, and social services, especially among those who were well educated, affluent, and active in public life, made many Protestants uncomfortable with conversion as a measure of moral virtue and with conceptions of biblical revelation that defied modern science. Liberal Protestants became more interested in reaching across to other religious traditions than in rescuing people from them.[14] As twentieth-century heirs of John Locke, they understood the thrust of Protestant faith more in terms of making the world a better place for everyone than in terms of the conversion of heathens and infidels to Christ.

One of the most influential of these twentieth-century Lockeans, the philosopher John Dewey (1859–1952), recast his enthusiasm for the best aspects of Protestant psychology and social ethics into "a common faith" he thought all human beings could share. This common faith centered on the principle of equality and required Christians to give up the "separation of sheep and goats; the saved and the lost; the elect and the mass" that evangelicals so often preached. True religious faith, according to Dewey, involved commitment instead to the unifying aspects of human experience, and to "the sweep and depth of the implications of natural human relations." Supernatural justifications for divisions among human beings got in the way of real faith, as far as he was concerned: "I cannot understand how any realization of the democratic ideal as a vital moral and spiritual ideal in human affairs is possible without surrender of the conception of the basic division to which supernatural Christianity is committed."[15]

Not every modernist who traced his or her religious heritage through the Protestant Reformation went so far as Dewey in embracing secular humanism as the proper domain of religious faith. Nevertheless, the tendency to see democracy and respect for equality and religious difference as expressions of Christian virtue was not uncommon among liberal Protestants. Meanwhile, growing numbers of Catholics and Jews were no less committed to America and her promise of freedom and equality. Their presence and sociability, many contributions to American society, and love of freedom and equality made them as American as anyone else. As Catholics and Jews in the twentieth century became increasingly confident about proclaiming their patriotism and contributions to American society, the harassment and condescending treatment that Protestants directed at Catholics and Jews lessened, especially in the context of American engagement and victory in the Second World War when Protestants, Catholics, and Jews fought together to defend these ideals.

Religious Pluralism in the Late Twentieth Century

By the time Will Herberg wrote *Protestant-Catholic-Jew* in 1955, American Catholics, Jews, and others in the United States unaffiliated with any Protestant church had contributed their own hopes and dreams, and their own religious and cultural sensibilities, to American national identity. They had also absorbed, or at least come to terms with, Protestant idealism about America and its inscription within patriotic rhetoric and feeling.

In the 1950s, this Protestant-inflected idealism about America worked in some respects as a unifying force represented by the flag and pledge of allegiance, which was amended in 1954 to include reference to God. In some respects, the added insistence on "one nation *under God*" represented a defensive, conservative turn that furthered rather than resolved splits in perceptions of the American nation and fueled dissension among Americans about what the relationship between religion and politics should be. This dissension had many components, not the least of which was the longstanding tension among Lockean, classical republican, and millenarian visions of American society. This historic conflict reemerged in the decades after World War II as Americans struggled to come to terms with new military, economic, political, and religious forces and with a population far more ethnically and religiously diverse than that of American colonists in 1776.

After 1965, when quotas imposed in 1890 and 1925 favoring European immigrants were lifted, the expanding U.S. economy and educational system beckoned new immigrants from Asia, Africa, and Latin America eager for better lives. The United States became more religiously and ethnically diverse and more like a global crossroads than ever before. By the end of the century, the increasing diversity of cuisines readily available in the United States had become a metaphor for cultural and religious pluralism and for the many opportunities individuals had to experience new ways of being religious. Salsa outstripped ketchup as a popular condiment and tandoori chicken, pad Thai tofu, and sushi surpassed the hamburger in appeal to many Americans, including some whose ancestors came over on the *Mayflower*.

New religious centers sprang up in many towns and cities. Hindu community centers added new texture to the fabric of American religious life, as did Vietnamese, Korean, and Theravada Buddhist temples, Sikh gurdwaras, and the presence of Islamic masjids in many American neighborhoods. In schools, workplaces, shopping centers, city streets, airports, and trains, American Protestants interacted more frequently and regularly than before with people born and raised in Hindu, Buddhist, and Muslim families.

Anglo-American and African American Protestants not only rubbed shoulders more frequently with Hindus, Buddhists, and Muslims after 1960, but also found their view of Christianity enlarged by the growing numbers of Christians from Asia and Latin America. Korean immigrants often arrived in the United States as Protestants, reflecting the sizable number of Presbyterian, Methodist, and Baptist churches in South Korea and the historic role played by American Protestant missionaries in helping to found churches and schools in Korea. Across the United States, Korean Presbyterians, Methodists, and Baptists worshiped in the Korean language and maintained respect for elders and other aspects of Korean culture. At the same time, English-speaking Presbyterians, Methodists, and Baptists worked to incorporate Korean Americans in their churches, seminaries, and outreach programs.

Latino immigrants altered the face of American Christianity even more thoroughly, embodying Catholicism in distinctive ways and bringing cultural diversity to many Protestant denominations. Arriving in growing numbers after 1965 to enlarge a long-established Latino presence in the United States, new immigrants from Latin America and the Caribbean represented a variety of different religious and cultural traditions, including Santeria, vodou, and Candomblé as well as devotion to numerous Madonnas embodying indigenous forms of popular Catholicism. Not least, Latinos made significant contributions to the fast-growing Pentecostal movement and its popularity as a major international phenomenon.

In response to these diverse manifestations of Christianity, and diverse manifestations of religion more generally, some American Protes-

Earnest prayer at the Southern Baptist Convention, 2006. Photo by Kent Harvill. Courtesy of Baptist Press.

tants worked to defend, strengthen, and clarify the boundaries between their beliefs and the beliefs of others. For many caught up against their wills in the process of cultural and religious diversification occurring in the United States after 1960, respect for other traditions was not easy to come by and the principle of equality competed poorly against fear, resentment, and concerns about social stability, moral order in society, and the preservation of white Protestant dominance. Radical religious visions about the end times, the appearance of the Antichrist, the separation of the elect, and the providentially destined role of America in the coming millennium played on those negative feelings.

As preachers, fiction writers, and filmmakers delved into such topics, stories about the end times and its present signs riveted the imaginations of many Americans. Tim LaHaye's popular *Left Behind* series of books described the remnant of struggling good people left behind to challenge the power of the Antichrist after the rapture removed many saints to heaven. These books tapped into general uneasiness about the future and left the impression that pagans were taking over the world. They also drew upon older Protestant images of the pope as the Antichrist and the Catholic Church as the whore of Babylon, as well as on more recent conceptions of the Soviet Union as an Evil Empire of godless communism. In one of the most popular books in the series, *The Remnant: On the Brink of Armageddon*, published by LaHaye and Jerry Jenkins in 2002, Rayford Steele, a former 747 pilot left behind after his wife and son departed in the rapture, leads the resistance movement against Nicolae Carpathia, the Global Community Supreme Potentate. This American hero defends the cause of heaven against the "Global Community" of pagan diversity and weakened manhood ruled over by a ruthless totalitarian dictator.[16]

Protestant Seekers Attracted to Hinduism and Buddhism

If a shrinking globe and increased awareness of religious diversity led some Americans to expect Armageddon, others were inspired to search for new ways to experience God. Despairing of the emptiness of traditional forms of worship or simply seeking new ways of feeling the transforming power of grace, these spiritually adventurous Protestants joined with equally adventurous Catholics and Jews to form a growing group of Americans that sociologist Wade Clark Roof called "seekers."[17] These Americans responded to the increasing variety of religious expression in the United States by exploring new religious practices and reconceptualizing their own beliefs about God in light of religious thinking and practice in other traditions. Traveling across the boundaries of different religious traditions in quest of spiritual enlightenment, assurance, and direction, experimenting with new forms of religious knowledge and practice, seekers became acquainted with various religious and ethnic cultures with a quickness and open-mindedness most of their grandparents would have found astonishing.

Hinduism and Buddhism attracted many of these spiritual explorers. The growing numbers of Asian immigrants to the United States contributed to seekers' attraction to Asian philosophies and to the seekers' growing familiarity with the meditation practices and material cultures associated with these philosophies and practices. But rubbing elbows with Asian Americans was not the only way Protestant seekers became acquainted with Hinduism and Buddhism. Within the tradition of

American Protestantism itself, a streak of fascination with Hindu and Buddhist scriptures dated back to the Transcendentalists of the mid-nineteenth century.[18] As pioneers of American spirituality, Henry David Thoreau translated the Buddhist *Lotus Sutra* and Ralph Waldo Emerson constructed a concept of the Oversoul partly from the Hindu Brahma, the ultimate creator God and absolute reality behind the many deities in the Hindu pantheon.

Nineteenth-century Transcendentalists approached Buddhist and Hindu scriptures through American Protestant ideas about the importance of subjective experience for Christian life as well as through their reading in German philosophy and English romantic literature. They had little understanding of the religious schools and monasteries where these scriptures were traditionally kept and studied in Asia, and even less understanding of popular religious devotions in Asia, which diverged significantly from elite monastic forms of spiritual practice associated with scriptural study. But if Transcendentalists like Emerson and Thoreau failed to grasp the "real" Hinduism or Buddhism, they were serious about the spiritual insights they perceived within Hindu and Buddhist scriptures and believed that these insights paralleled their own very Protestant desire to salvage spiritual experience from the impositions of ecclesiastical authority and from the hypocrisies, superficiality, and corruptions of conventional religion. Emerson and Thoreau were radical "Protestants" in their disdain for conventional forms of religious practice that seemed to them to deaden or mimic authentic religious experience, in their thirst for immediate experience of divine grace, and in their belief that Jesus called people to meet God with the same forthright spirit he embodied.

The distance between the Transcendentalists' worldview and that of the Lockeans of the Revolutionary era reflected the surge of romanticism that swept through American culture in the decades prior to the Civil War. Transcendentalists appealed to a higher, intuitive Reason above natural reason that opened the soul to natural beauty and poetic inspiration. But for all its bathing in romantic feeling, the principle of equality central to the Lockean worldview persisted among Transcendentalists. In his essay, "Self-Reliance," Emerson argued along Lockean lines that individual thought and integrity were the best guarantees of civil society and he complained about the decline in his day of "the law of consciousness" that characterized true individuality. "Consider whether you have satisfied your relations to father, mother, cousin, neighbor, town, cat and dog—whether any of these can upbraid you," Emerson demanded. "If any one imagines that this law is lax, let him keep its commandment one day." The discipline of self-reliance was not "mere antinomianism" as far as Emerson was concerned, any more than Locke's emphasis on self-interest was an endorsement of unrestrained capitalism. "I like the silent church before the service begins, better than any preaching," Emerson wrote in describing his respect for other individuals: "how chaste the persons look, begirt each one with a precinct or sanctuary!" He urged his readers to their own self-reliance as the best means to civil society, which he thought would be vastly improved if each person was ready to "stand in awe" of other individuals and their "communication with the internal ocean."[19]

Interest in Hinduism and Buddhism as a means to self-reliance persisted among a small minority of Americans during the late nineteenth and early twentieth centuries, then burst into flower in the 1950s when Beat poets like Allan Ginsberg and Gary Snyder seized upon Buddhism as an alternative to the materialism and uniformity of American culture and as a way to experience the flow of life in a direct and authentic way. A number of Protestant ministers and Catholic priests made pilgrimages to India during the 1950s and early 1960s to meet Hindu religious leaders and become better acquainted with Hindu beliefs and practices. Martin Luther King Jr. met with Mahatma Gandhi, the religious leader of the Indian independence movement, and this meeting led King to adopt Gandhi's strategy of nonviolence as a moral discipline that embodied the respect for self and others implicit in the principle of equality.[20]

During the Vietnam War, Buddhist appeals for peace attracted attention in the United States and, later on, Buddhist teachings contributed to the environmental movement and to new forms of psychotherapy. Buddhism appealed especially to seekers eager for spiritual insight but unwilling to undergo the emotional breakdown of conversion, participate in the childlike anticipation of heaven encouraged by some preachers, or engage in the defiance of modern scientific thinking built into fundamentalist readings of the Bible and conservative interpretations of biblical authority. Pop star Tina Turner's devotion to the eightfold path to enlightenment and the mind-opening effect of chanting the Lotus Sutra was just one example of this American fascination with Buddhism. Other American Protestants looked to Hinduism and Buddhism not to convert, but simply for assistance in pursuing their own quests for authentic self-reliance and encounter with the real forces of life. To further such enterprises, a number of theologians, philosophers, and translators stepped up to explain Asian religions in ways that met these modern western needs.

Among the most influential of the bridge builders between Protestant experience and Asian religions, the Japanese translator and philosopher D. T. Suzuki presented Zen Buddhism as a means to the end he thought many modern Protestants were seeking and as an antidote to the loss of confidence in traditional theism, which he perceived as a widespread modern phenomenon. He defined Zen enlightenment, or satori, as "the Absolute Present" and equated it with grace, which he understood as the living experience of Christian faith stripped of superstition and doctrinal rigidity. Zen could help modern Christians recover the authentic faith of Jesus, Suzuki believed, whereas conventional forms of theology often obscured what Jesus had actually been saying. Modern Christians failed to experience the Absolute Present as Jesus taught because they had been taught to think of God as having "many ethical and spiritual append-ages" and thus lost sight of what Suzuki called the "naked God," which Jesus experienced and embodied. This failure to experience God directly was related, Suzuki believed, to the failure of modern Christians to un-derstand their selves. Suzuki thought that modern Christians "hesitate to appear before" the naked God "also in their nakedness, that is, take hold of him in the Absolute Present." If they stepped out of the "dualistic garments" that created the illusion of their separation from God, Suzuki assured, "they will discover that their God is not other than the Absolute Present itself."[21]

Suzuki was acquainted with Emerson and the American Transcen-dentalists and with existentialism and other philosophic movements that liberal Protestants in the twentieth century turned to in order to make sense of modern life and keep their faith in God alive. Suzuki drew on theologian Paul Tillich's ideas about "the protestant principle" as a dialectic between no and yes, challenge and affirmation, that attracted many intellectuals in the United States after World War II. Like Tillich's "God beyond theism," Suzuki explained Zen satori as a way to the Ab-solute Presence behind all of the world's great religious traditions and forms of artistic expression and beyond the anthropomorphic deities celebrated in revivalism and fundamentalism. Following Suzuki's lead and that of other bridge builders between Christianity and Asian reli-gions, many American Protestants (along with many Catholics and Jews) came to respect Hinduism and Buddhism as alternative ways of experi-encing God, welcoming them as new additions to American religious life. As denominations with whose people Americans from many backgrounds might enjoy cordial and productive relations, Hinduism and Buddhism added to the Protestant-Catholic-Jew paradigm that had typified Ameri-can religious life in the 1950s.[22]

For more than a few Americans who traced their religious heritage through the Protestant Reformation, however, Hindu and Buddhist conceptions of God were the last things on their minds. If they shared desires for new and authentic forms of religious experience with seekers who explored Asian religions, more religiously conservative Americans looked within the evangelical traditions for powerful expressions of religious charisma. Instead of seeking spirituality in other traditions, they sought more direct encounters with the spirit of Jesus.

For these conservative evangelical seekers as for more boundariless liberal ones, Protestantism as a protest movement against the authoritarianism and corruption of the Catholic Church was a thing of the past. Many liberal and conservatives were post-Protestant both in shifting attention away from hostility toward Catholicism and in moving beyond conceptions of God and Christ formulated by Luther and Calvin. Those reformers called for an absolute obedience and faith in the will of God that could only be imparted through the grace of Christ. In building out from this conception of religious life, liberal seekers were post-Protestant in giving up the idea that Christ was the only way to God. Post-Protestant in a different way, many conservative Christians retained the reformers' belief that Christ was the only way to salvation but overlooked the reformers' objections to expectations of miracles and blessings of good fortune in return for faith.

Pentecostalism as a Post-Protestant Movement

Pentecostalism emerged in the United States at the turn of the twentieth century among revivalists eager to bring the healing power of God's spirit to people removed from traditional communities of religious support and beset by isolation, poverty, ill health, and other problems associated with urban industrialism. In some instances, the emotional intensity of early Pentecostal worship involved fellowship among whites, blacks, and Latinos who connected with each other across racial and cultural boundaries in electrifying experiences of the spirit of Christ. Even when they separated into racial groups, Pentecostals affirmed the gift of spiritual healing practiced by Jesus and his early followers and also the gift of speaking in tongues that marked the first Pentecost, described in the second chapter of Acts, when a tongue of fire descended from heaven as people from different regions joined together through fellowship in Christ.

In its revival preaching, emphasis on individual conversion, devotion to the Bible, and efforts to emulate the teachings of Jesus, Pentecostalism was an outgrowth of Protestant evangelicalism. As a global religious movement, it reflected the success of Protestant missionary outreach and the fruition of Protestant hopes for worldwide evangelization and spiritual renewal. At the same time, however, Pentecostals left behind certain aspects of classical Protestant thought and incorporated local forms of religious practice that reflected new intercultural encounters and forms of inspiration.

Pentecostals departed from classical forms of Protestant theology in their efforts to recover the spiritual gifts of healing and speaking in tongues that enlivened the early church, and in their absorption of indigenous forms of shamanism and spirit possession. Luther, Calvin, and their followers believed that miracles of healing and speaking in tongues marking the extraordinary time of Christ's appearance on earth had ceased at the end of the apostolic era. They objected to what they perceived as the Catholic Church's exploitation of superstitious devotion to saints, relics, and sacraments as agents of miraculous healing and sought to replace entreaties for miraculous cures and blessings with reflection on the sufferings and vicissitudes of life as occasions for repentance, worship, and alignment to the will of God. Luther and Calvin believed that sickness and misfortune were lessons in humility that helped individuals better understand their dependence on God and prepare for unmerited grace, not opportunities for negotiating with God and bargaining away misfortune. Christian prayer involved worshipful meditation on the transcendent sovereignty of God and honest reflection on one's sinfulness and need to be forgiven, not entreaties for miracles of healing and other special blessings.[23]

The reformers' denunciation of idolatrous attempts to bargain with God had only limited effect, of course, and many Protestants continued to pray for healings and other blessings whatever arguments Protestant theologians laid out against such practices. Prophecy, healing, and dramatic expressions of spirit intoxication had been part of Protestant life since the early sixteenth century, and as David Hall and other historians of "lived religion" have successfully demonstrated, this enthusiasm for supernatural experience continued unabated in colonial America.[24] Protestant experience in America has often incorporated forms of religious expression that Luther and Calvin would have condemned as magic or superstition. And even among those most adamant about not asking for miracles and focusing instead on pure worship of the transcendent sovereignty of God, American Protestants often had a hard time resisting efforts to barter with God and make providence unfold as they wanted it to.

To take one example of how tempting it has been to slip such manipulations into even the most dedicated efforts to conform entirely to God's will, New England Puritans declared days of public fasting with a clear view of the benefits to be derived from their repentance for sins. Although he would have recoiled in horror to be perceived as attempting to control or manipulate God, the influential Puritan minister Increase Mather argued that public declarations of faith would bring New England closer to God's side. Even if "there were not visible degeneracy amongst us, yet this renovation of covenant, might be of singular advantage," Mather argued in 1679. "Legalists and hypocrites" would be scared into "an outward reformation" that would "divert temporal judgments," while "they that are sincere, will thereby be engaged unto a more close and holy walking before the Lord, and so become more eminently blessings unto the societies and places whereto they do belong."[25]

In the revivals of the eighteenth century, evangelical preachers urged Americans to express desire for salvation and claim experiences of new birth much more forthrightly than Mather would ever have dared and encouraged people to expect concrete results. Erosion of strict Calvinist predestinarianism enabled evangelical preachers to ease up on orthodox resistance to petitioning God for special blessings. Lockean empiricism contributed to growing acceptance of free will among evangelicals, especially as it was disseminated and altered through Scottish common sense realism and Wesleyan Methodism, both of which made room for experience of supernatural realities in ways that Locke's skepticism about miracles did not. Growing acceptance of free will contributed to the success of revivalism and its increasingly straightforward demands that sinners accept responsibility for deciding to be saved.[26]

In the nineteenth century, widespread fascination with mesmerism, animal magnetism, and spiritual séances prompted still more aggressive efforts to obtain spiritual assistance in obtaining prosperity, health, communication with the dead, and other forms of proximity to heaven and its spiritual power. These popular nineteenth-century movements led to a rising interest in healing among revival preachers and participants, as did the ongoing infusion of African American practices of conjuring and spirit possession. The influence of Afro-Caribbean beliefs and practices on revivalism, especially after the Louisiana Purchase in 1803 stimulated travel through New Orleans and up the Mississippi, worked further among revivalists to erode the classic Protestant resistance to direct appeals for spiritual blessings. In the Southwest, devotional practices among Latinos also stimulated investment in spiritual healing within Protestant evangelicalism. Many of these coinciding forces and forms of religious expression came together in the multiracial Azusa Street revival in Los Angeles in 1906, sometimes identified as the birthplace of Pentecostalism.

In North America as well as in Africa, Latin America, and Europe in the twentieth and twenty-first centuries, Pentecostalism combined evangelical preaching, conversion, and adherence to biblical teaching with indigenous practices of spirit possession and spiritual healing. Historian Philip Jenkins estimated that there were hundreds of millions of Pentecostal-type Christians in 2002 and that the number would exceed one billion by 2050. In the "thought-world" of this new form of Christianity, Jenkins observed, "prophecy is an everyday reality, while faith-healing, exorcism, and dream-visions are all basic components of religious sensibility. For better or worse," Jenkins asserted, "the dominant churches of the future could have much in common with those of medieval or early modern European times."[27]

Although Jenkins suggested that Pentecostalism might be considered a kind of retrograde religion because of its enthusiasm for miracles, it may be more accurate to see it as a post-Protestant and thoroughly modern response to globalization. The Spirit's mobility, power of instantaneous communication, defiance of economic and political boundaries, and fondness for cultural borderlands reflect the increasing mobility and rootlessness of human societies, the rapid communication and dissemination of new ideas and practices, the growing prominence and commonality of borderland cultures, and the increasing permeability of economic and political boundaries, while also responding to problems that these trends generate. Pentecostalism may be similar to Christianity in medieval Europe in incorporating popular enthusiasm for miracles, but the rapid fusion of local and international cultures within Pentecostalism, the incorporation of new forms of media technology into worship, and references to electricity and high-speed communications technology to describe the work of the Spirit are more reflective of contemporary post-Protestant life than anything medieval.

Post-Protestant Aspects of Islam

As a major world tradition dating to the seventh century and embraced today by a significant portion of the world's population, Islam is completely independent of Protestant Christianity in many important respects. Yet Protestant thought contributed to the modern development of Islam through its role in the formation of democratic individualism, which influenced intellectuals in the Islamic world during the nineteenth and twentieth centuries who sought to modernize Islam and bring their cultures into greater alignment with the West. Today, liberal conceptions of Islam function less as a model to emulate than as a foil against which conservative Muslims construct alternative forms of government and sociability.

Inside the United States, Islam is a multifaceted religion, with immigrants from numerous places—Iran, Pakistan, Saudi Arabia, Indonesia, the Sudan, and elsewhere—bringing a variety of different cultural expressions of Islam along with different views about the relationship between Islam and Christianity, and different views about the relationship between religion and politics.[28] As the number of Islamic immigrants to the United States grew as a result of the change in immigration policy in 1965, many Protestants greeted these newcomers and their growing families in much the same way they greeted new Hindu and Buddhist immigrants—as members of another denomination in the panoply of world religions. Whether they were curious about Islamic life or simply willing to let Muslims do their thing, many American Protestants prior to 9/11 viewed Islam as one among many religions of the world, accepting it as an expression of the universal human quest for meaning and identity. Before the destruction of the World Trade Center in 2001, and the exploitation of that event by fundamentalists within both Christianity and Islam, as far as many Americans were concerned, Islam simply expanded the Protestant-Catholic-Jew paradigm they were used to without challenging the basic idea of compatibility between religious pluralism and civic union that this paradigm affirmed.

Protestants who took a more active, appreciative interest in Islam often found themselves drawn to Sufism, the mystical branch of Islam that first developed among Muslim ascetics in Persia in the seventh century, flourished afterward in a variety of different places, and played an important role in modern interpretations of Islam, especially in Turkey and Pakistan. Sufi mystics emphasized the believer's union with God and the ego's extinction in God in contrast to more legalistic interpretations of Islamic teaching that stressed the distance between God and humanity and strict conformity to religious law. Sufism made sense to American Protestants who viewed different religious traditions as different paths in the universal human quest for meaning and especially to those who took a Transcendental approach to their own religion, elevating mystical expression above conventional forms of religious practice and doctrines that encouraged group uniformity and submission to external authority. For many American seekers, Sufism offered a path to God and another way around some of the problems associated with traditional Christian forms of theism. As Harvard University's expert on Sufism, Annemarie Schimmel, explained in 1975, Sufis differentiated " 'wisdom that is with and from God' and is granted to the Gnostic by an act of divine grace, from normal knowledge." According to Schimmel, Sufis " 'tasted' (*dhauq*)" and "experienced new levels of revealed wisdom that were not to be attained by a scientific approach or by theological reasoning."[29]

A similar appreciation of Sufism developed among musicians who followed "the jazz route" to Islam. In Harlem in the 1940s and 1950s, an Islamic culture centered in clubs and restaurants run by Muslim immigrants from the Caribbean attracted African American musicians, including Charlie Parker, Dakota Staton, and the saxophonist John

Coltrane, whose famous composition, "A Love Supreme," reflected his encounter with Islamic mysticism in the Dar ul-Islam movement. As an African American branch of Sunni Islam, Dar ul-Islam offered a religious alternative to people familiar with evangelical Christianity but disgusted with its racism. For Coltrane and other musicians drawn to Islam at some point in their careers, as well as for those who joined the Dar ul-Islam movement as converts, the racially inclusive mysticism of Islam stood in clear opposition to the bad treatment and poor images of people of color that many converts to Islam associated with Protestant Christianity.[30]

Dar ul-Islam competed with the so-called Black Muslim movement associated with the Nation of Islam. Dar ul-Islam and the Nation of Islam were similar in their distrust of American government, commitment to black control of black communities, disaffection from evangelical Christianity, and general perception of Christianity as a racist religion that encouraged black submission to white masters. But converts to Dar ul-Islam carried cards identifying them as members of the international religion of Sunni Islam, the largest branch of Islam worldwide, known for its doctrine of universal brotherhood within the house of Islam. By contrast, Elijah Muhammad and other leaders of the Nation of Islam preached that whites were the product of a horrible series of experiments by Mr. Yakub, a black scientist, that Christianity was the religion developed by whites to enslave and humiliate blacks, and that "the white devils" would eventually be destroyed and blacks returned to their rightful position of authority. One of the best-known African American converts to Islam, Malcolm X (1925–1965), rose to prominence as a leader in the Nation of Islam, but rejected the racist interpretation of Islam preached by Elijah Muhammad in the early 1960s, especially after his pilgrimage to Mecca in 1964. After his conversion to Sunni Islam, his break with Elijah Muhammad and his subsequent assassination, Malcolm X was revered as a great leader and martyr by the people of Dar ul-Islam.[31]

Islam was a post-Protestant religion for many African American Muslims in the sense that they, or their parents, embraced Islam after some acquaintance with evangelical Christian organizations and partly in reaction to the racism they encountered in many Protestant churches and believers. African American Muslims who perceived Christianity as an instrument of black oppression had reasons for their perception. Many law-abiding white citizens, government officials, and upstanding members of white churches in the South through the 1960s appealed to patrician and romantic expressions of Christianity to oppose racial integration and justify segregating blacks in special schools, rest rooms, restaurants, hotels, and in the rear sections of busses, theaters, and churches. The white supremacist Ku Klux Klan, founded after the Civil War and revitalized in the 1920s, represented an extreme form of the belief shared by many white Protestants, especially in the South, that the Bible sanctioned racial segregation and white rule. In its conservative construction of Protestant values, the Klan was anti-Semitic and anti-Catholic, too.

While African American Muslims reacted against the racism of white evangelical Christianity, the millennialism of evangelical Christianity may have been a stepping-stone in their attraction to Islam. Visions of the kingdom of God, whether located in heaven, on earth, or in a wonderful fusion of the two, figure prominently in evangelical preaching today, as they have for several centuries. The tension between these powerful visions of how God's people should and will live on one hand, and the betrayal of those visions in the racism of white Christians on the other, led to a frustration of religious desire among many African Americans to which Islamic visions of a racially inclusive paradise offered relief.

With the growing population of Muslim immigrants after 1965 and the increasing interaction of Muslims from a variety of different cultures, Islam became more of a regular denomination in American society, ethnically diverse within itself but also identifiable to outsiders and thus comparable to Protestantism, Catholicism, and Judaism. The conception of religion inherent in the complicated process through which Islam became established as a kind of religious denomination in the United States derived from Protestant conceptions of denominationalism, which derived in turn from ideas promulgated among religious separatists in seventeenth-century England about the nature of the church as a variety of mutually respectful centers of worship and religious teaching independent of the state. In this sense, too, Islam in the United States at the end of the twentieth century carried a post-Protestant stamp.[32]

As conservative and radical movements within Islam became increasingly prominent worldwide, and debates raged around the world over the question of Islam's compatibility or incompatibility with democracy and between modernist and antimodernist views about the status of women in Islamic law, American Muslims made important contributions to these movements and debates. In academic circles, American Muslim women advanced discussions about gender and feminism in Islam and promoted strategic efforts to improve health and education for women worldwide. In social and political practice, as opponents of immorality and indecency, Muslims contributed to the conservatism of American society in the late twentieth and early twenty-first centuries. As staunch advocates of religious faith based on scriptural revelation, they also participated in the worldwide movement against secularism and modern liberalism.[33] In strikingly similar ways, Islamic devotion to the Qur'an as the revealed word of God paralleled literal interpretations of the Bible among Christian fundamentalists, and Islamist opposition to secularity and modern liberalism paralleled that of Christian conservatives.[34]

Islamist Fundamentalism in Relation to Christian Fundamentalism

At the most apparent level, the Islamist movement associated with Osama bin Laden and other militant jihadists stands in direct and violent opposition to Christian fundamentalism. Islamists declared a holy war on America, the birthplace and stronghold of Christian fundamentalism. And the religious hatred has been mutual, if the depiction of Islam as "a very evil and wicked religion" by the conservative Christian spokesman Franklin Graham in 2002 is any indication.[35] Those who agree with Graham view Islam as an enemy to Christianity, not as a denomination within the family of religions deserving of respect and accommodation. Dispute over Israel exacerbates this hostility. While militant Islamists challenge Israel's right to exist, Christian fundamentalists are often strong supporters of the State of Israel and her military defenses because of their belief that the Jews' return to Israel and rebuilding of the Temple will herald the Second Coming of Christ.

Beneath these obvious conflicts and mutual hatreds, Islamist militants and Christian fundamentalists have much in common. While Islamists view their religion as under siege from the West and seek to extend the influence of Islam worldwide and establish Islamic law in many countries, many Christian fundamentalists in the United States also view their religion as being under siege and seek to extend their religious values and political authority both at home and abroad. They share similar visions of history as heading toward religious victory for true believers and punishment for unbelievers. They both believe that the path of their own salvation lies in giving their lives to the glory of God and in the defeat of his enemies. Both regard their scriptures as the word of God and derive strict codes of conduct from them. Both have strict ideas about gender role differentiation, about the importance of female modesty, and women's important contribution to the furtherance of religion as mothers and wives. They believe that secularism and modern liberalism are antireligious and that many of the problems they face in attempting to establish their religion derive from the influence of these forces. Against liberals who endorse religious pluralism and emphasize respect for different opinions as essential to civil society, both Islamic and Christian fundamentalists press for greater cultural uniformity and moral purity.[36]

Fundamentalism as a Post-Protestant Movement

As a religious movement defined by opposition to modern liberalism, fundamentalism has become a way of being religious in the modern world, a global movement manifest beyond the borders of Protestant Christianity where it first emerged. In its reaction against the liberalism that emerged in the context of Protestant culture and Protestant ideas about individual conscience and personal agency, fundamentalism is a post-Protestant movement, at least in part. Although fundamentalists may still be "Protestant" in protesting what they perceive as the corruption of religious truth, this corruption is no longer defined in terms of the unjustifiable political imposition of religious authority. Ironically, in wanting to impose their religious values on society by political means, fundamentalists represent something like the kind of religious authority Protestantism was born to resist.

Clerical elitism and hypocrisy are not the challenges to religious truth fundamentalists are concerned about, nor is popular belief in healing miracles near the top of the list of what fundamentalists want to discourage, as it was for Protestant reformers. The enemies of fundamentalism are modern liberalism, secularization, religious pluralism, female autonomy, and acceptance of homosexuality. These expressions of individualism are products—not entirely, of course, but in important respects—of liberal Protestant thought and culture.

In its classical expressions, Protestants directed their opposition against what they perceived as corrupt and idolatrous exertions of religious authority in the Catholic Church, not against the forces of individualism and secularization, which they contributed to and helped to create. While fundamentalist Christians today would still agree with earlier Protestants in their positive emphasis on the sovereignty of God, the kingship of Christ, and the coming of the kingdom to earth, they approach these principles as doctrines to be defended against liberal interpretation and secular analysis, not as forces to be freed from clerical manipulation and political restraint.

The religious militancy that both Islamic and Christian fundamentalists share is not simply conservatism with respect to inherited religious tradition but strong reactionism. As opponents of modern secularism, both Islamic and Christian fundamentalists stand within the modern world, utilizing its language and technology in their combat against it. Both are similar to radical Protestants in the sixteenth century in their insistence on fulfilling God's will in the present and bringing the moral code of his kingdom to bear on ordinary life and history. Both are post-Protestant in their rejection of the modern liberalism that emerged out of Protestant cultures in the West.

Fundamentalist concerns about immorality often revolve around sex and gender. In the United States as well as in the Islamic world, religious fundamentalists regard public acceptance and displays of homosexuality as the height of immorality and social decadence. Violence, hunger, poverty, and corporate greed do not come close to exciting the kind of outrage that homosexuality, especially male homosexuality, excites among religious conservatives. Public displays of female flesh and sexuality also generate considerable animosity and seem to epitomize, from the fundamentalist perspective, what is wrong with America and the world. Prohibitions against sexual freedom are much stronger in many parts of the Islamic world than in the United States, but intense concern about sex and the violation of gender boundaries defines religious fundamentalism everywhere. At least part of what disturbs religious conservatives about homosexuality and women's public display of flesh are the challenges they pose to well-demarcated codes of heterosexual behavior that are perceived to be crucial to the bedrock of social order.

Americans live in an economy in which most women work for a living and many heads of families are women. Christian fundamentalists may not like this state of affairs, but it is a reality in which they participate. Equal pay for equal work is standard policy in government work and in many companies in the private sector, even if it is not always adhered to in practice. American women today have more autonomy and more economic freedom than their grandmothers and more autonomy and political freedom than most women in the Islamic world. At least partly because of women's greater equality in the United States today, Christian fundamentalist concerns about sex, gender, and female autonomy differ in many particulars from such fundamentalist concerns in the Islamic world, but the underlying issue of equality as it pertains to women is similarly troublesome.

Christian fundamentalism is not so much a reaction against the principles of human freedom, individuality, and equality as it is against expressions of those principles that conflict with conservative political values. Conservative white Christian support for the U.S. Supreme Court ruling in *Plessy v. Ferguson* (1896), that "separate but equal" facilities for whites and blacks complied with U.S. Constitution, showed that equality was hard to deny in principle and was even invoked as justification for a system of apartheid that was anything but equal in practice and not overturned until *Brown v. Board of Education in Topeka* in

1954. In terms of women's rights, *Roe v. Wade* (1973) upheld a woman's right to an abortion on the basis of her constitutional rights to liberty and equal treatment before the law. In numerous state and federal cases involving specific aspects of abortion, too detailed to go into here, conservative Christian opponents of *Roe* attempted to reverse that decision by appealing to the rights of a fetus to life, liberty, and equal treatment before the law. In this divisive and often bitter debate, the principle of equality has been upheld by fundamentalists, while its implications with respect to a woman's body and her right to end a pregnancy are disputed. For Christian fundamentalists engaged in this battle, more is at stake than the lives of the unborn. Women's sexual and reproductive freedoms conflict with fundamentalist belief in the authority of husbands over wives and the gender role differentiation implicit in conservative family values. Women's equality and freedom also threaten the classical republican image of America as a stable hierarchy organized around people (especially female people) willing to sacrifice their own interests for the public good.

Is Protestantism Finished?

In *The Kingdom of God in America* (1937), H. Richard Niebuhr, one of the most respected Protestant thinkers prior to World War II, defined American Protestantism in terms of commitments to "The Sovereignty of God," "The Kingship of Christ," and "The Coming Kingdom." In long chapters devoted to each of these themes in turn, Niebuhr took American Protestants to task for their tendencies to confuse God's rule, Christ's authority, and the coming kingdom with inflated views of their own righteousness and that of the American nation. He hoped American Protestants would recall their forgotten heritage embedded "in the great doctrines and traditions of the Christian past" and realize "that there was no way toward the coming kingdom save the way taken by a sovereign God through the reign of Jesus Christ."[37]

Today, the politically inflected imagery of divine kingship would appeal more to fundamentalists and Pentecostals than to the Christians in the more liberal denominations whose predecessors Niebuhr addressed. Especially after the feminist critique of sexist God-talk in the 1970s and 1980s pushed forward earlier ideas about the principle of equality central to modern liberalism, many liberal Protestants made efforts to avoid language about God and Christ that seemed to support patriarchal authority and women's inequality.[38] Attentive to God's concern for social justice and dignity of persons, Christians in those churches have become more attuned to language about the mystery of God, the presence of

Christ, and the companionship of Jesus than to language about the kingship of Christ and God's absolute sovereign rule.

The monarchical language about God so prominent in classical Protestant expression reflects the historical and political contexts in which early Protestantism arose as well as biblical language about Christ as the successor of the Davidic monarchy celebrated in the Old Testament. As historian Carlos Eire argued in an influential study, the reformation movements of the sixteenth century were not simply efforts to restore purity in religious practice but also political movements with grievances and claims to justice expressed through the medium of religion.[39] Appeals to the sovereignty of God and kingship of Christ in early Protestantism had the effect of demoting earthly princes and making room for more just and equitable forms of social order.

Emphasis on the coming kingdom set Protestants apart from Christians who adhered to official Catholic teaching about the separation of heaven and earth and postponement of Christ's coming reign of justice. However much they have disagreed about how and when it would come, Protestants have often attuned their religious beliefs and worship to expectations of the coming kingdom. Some have wanted to hold the world to the standards of heaven and, in effect, create the kingdom on earth. Others have held themselves and their churches to the standards of heaven while anticipating a cataclysmic judgment from heaven that would separate wheat from tares and purify the earth. Still others have attempted to bring the moral idealism of Christianity down to earth by reconceptualizing it in secular, pragmatic terms.

Seventeenth-century English Protestants committed to religious tolerance worked to translate Protestant values in ways that facilitated sociability and civic virtue. Milton, Locke, and others who shared their worldviews teased out principles of liberty, religious tolerance, and equality that shaped the thinking of Benjamin Franklin, Thomas Jefferson, James Madison, and other contributors to the construction of the U.S. government and legal system. All of these men understood the connections between Reformed Protestant religious thought and political equality. None of them thought that equality applied only to Protestants.

In his study of this "Lockean worldview" and its influence on American culture, Jerome Huyler took the pessimistic view that "Ultimately, Lockeanism did not triumph in the United States" because "we have never permitted it to work." From Huyler's perspective, Lockean liberalism was "challenged from the beginnings of American politics" by "forces that, however 'liberal' they may appear today, were anathema to the theory and practice propounded by some important eighteenth-century British and American Lockeans." For Huyler, some

Americans today mistakenly confuse Locke's conception of self-interest with unrestrained capitalism and moral relativism. Others, fearful of disorder and loss of status, argue that morality and social order have to be based on something stronger than equality.[40]

Huyler saw the glass as half empty. Although the liberal commitment to equality has not been fully realized in the United States, neither has it been without compelling power or influence. Relatively few Americans today would deny that the institutions of slavery and Jim Crow exert a shameful drag on the whole of American history or that these institutions made a mockery of the idea of "liberty and justice for all." If such consensus is not the same thing as racial equality, it nevertheless moves in that direction. Many Americans would also acknowledge that the principle of equality has contributed to the strength and well-being of American girls and women and to the opportunities they have to pursue to economic, professional, and educational interests.

To say that equality was stimulated by Protestant religious thought and that it emerged as a political philosophy in the context of Protestant cultures is not to argue that all proponents of equality have been Protestant, or that all Protestants have defended equality, or that equality belongs to Protestants in some special way. In fact, Protestants have not always been the most forward champions of equality. With influence far greater than the size of their population, Jews in the United States made major contributions to thinking about equality and its practical applications, especially with regard to the defense of separation of church and state as an essential means of preventing discrimination. As a Jew himself, Will Herberg called attention to the importance of secular ideologies among American Jews in the early twentieth century and to the "conviction, widely held though rarely articulated, that because the Western Jew achieved emancipation with the secularization of society, he can preserve his free and equal status only so long as culture and society remain secular."[41]

If members of minority and underrepresented groups have sometimes been quicker to embrace freedom and equality than Americans who trace their religious heritages through the Protestant Reformation, it would nevertheless be a mistake to overlook the role Protestants have played in advancing the principle of equality. It would also be a mistake to overlook the religious, racial, and sexual hatreds that religious leaders inflamed over the course of American history and still inflame today, especially in the context of fears of sexual freedom and Islamic terrorism.

If Protestantism is defined in a way that includes these expressions of hatred, then it is certainly not finished. On the other hand, if Protestantism is defined in terms of divine monarchy and absolutism, then it may be finished except among fundamentalists and Pentecostals who embrace the language of monarchy and absolutism with respect to God and morality. Yet these groups are more post-Protestant than Protestant in their reactionary stance against modernism and science, which earlier Protestants did so much to promote and, in the case of Pentecostals, in their enthusiasm for miracles of healing and other gifts of the Spirit rejected in classical Protestant theology.

If Protestantism is defined in terms of the priesthood of all believers and the history of ideas leading up to the principle of equality, as this chapter has suggested, then Protestantism has come to its end insofar as that principle has become fully independent of the religious tradition that nurtured it. The principle of equality that emerged through Milton, Locke, Paine, the founding fathers of the United States, and then developed, through the insights of people from a variety of different religious backgrounds, into an affirmation of religious pluralism, is no longer a Protestant principle although it started out that way; the principle of equality developed through Protestant thought now belongs to everyone. If there is no longer anything distinctively Protestant about equality, Protestantism has come to a good end.

What, then, should we call the Americans who trace their religious heritage through the Protestant Reformation and, in doing so, embrace equality as a core value that shapes their perceptions of human beings and informs their activities in the world? Do American Baptists, Disciples, Episcopalians, Lutherans, Methodists, Presbyterians, Quakers, Unitarian Universalists, members of the United Churches of Christ, the African Methodist Episcopal Church, and other churches in the United States who share this heritage have anything in common with one another in terms of their outlooks and ways of being in the world? If members of these churches have moved beyond Protestantism for any or all of the ways listed above, they have hardly let Christianity go. Indeed, if Christianity supports the relinquishment of prejudice and the trajectory of ideas from the priesthood of all believers to affirmations of racial and sexual equality and appreciation of religious pluralism as a key component of social justice and civic virtue, then the post-Protestants who follow this trajectory may be all the more Christian for doing so.

Not coincidentally, many Christians in the United States who trace their religious heritage through the Protestant Reformation respect historical and scientific evidence and have been willing to criticize and reconceptualize their own religious thinking in light of that evidence. Many clergy and lay people know a great deal about historical criticism of the Bible and regularly employ insights from that criticism in their Bible reading, religious teaching, and pastoral work. Many of these Christians also understand the basic principles involved in the scientific theory of evolution on which so much of biological science is based and are familiar with important discoveries in astronomy and the geological sciences as well. Few if any of these Christians take the Bible literally to mean that the earth is the center of the universe or that the earth was created six thousand years ago. For these Americans, Christianity is not about defending religious faith against scientific and historical evidence. That evidence may be challenging and even frightening; it is also part of the real world to which these liberal Christians are religiously committed.

Liberal Christians may not be the loudest religious voices in the United States today but the strengths of their position with respect to the institutions of American society are considerable. The political aspect of liberal Protestantism has been so successful that it is no longer connected to Protestant Christianity in any exclusive or possessive way. The principle of equality at the core of Protestantism has eroded the anti-Catholicism that gave earlier movements and churches within Protestant history a distinctive Protestant form. With respect to its contribution to the development of the principle of equality, we might even say that Protestantism has been a victim of its own success.

Notes

1. Provocative expressions of individualism in social protest, music, art, fashion, and spirituality faced off against more conservative demands for assent to social order and respect for tradition and authority. In many cases, the tension between freedom of expression and respect for social order emerged in confrontations between Americans on the political left versus those on the right. No less frequently, however, the same tensions appeared within individuals and groups across the political spectrum. In dress, behavior, and religious preferences, hippies and New Agers at one end of the spectrum expressed their individualism, nonconformity, and resistance to the institutions of mainstream society while at the same time espousing communal harmony and organic philosophies that connected the food on your table and the clothes on your back to the global economy and international politics. They were as conservative, in their own organic way, as the defenders of flag and country at the other end of the spectrum who resisted provocative displays of art and sex as threats to public morality and family values. Flag-waving conservatives were just as much proponents of personal liberty, in their own way, and just as distrustful of government bureaucracies as hippies and environmentalists, often defending the individual's right to bear arms and regarding social welfare programs with suspicion.

2. John Milton, *The Tenure of Kings and Magistrates: A Defence of the People of England* (1649) in John Milton, *Political Writings*, ed. Martin Dzelzinis, trans.

Claire Gruzelier (Cambridge: Cambridge University Press, 1991); John Locke, "An Essay on Toleration" (1667) in John Locke, *Political Essays*, ed. Mark Goldie (Cambridge: Cambridge University Press, 1997), quotations from pp. 142, 136; also see Goldie, "Introduction," in *Political Essays*, xviii.

3. John Locke, "Religion" (1681) in Locke, *Political Essays*, quotations from pp. 278–279; Locke, "Essay on Toleration," quotations from p. 138, italics mine.

4. Thomas Paine, *Common Sense*, ed. Isaac Kramnick (New York: Penguin Books, 1986), quotations from p. 76.

5. For example, James Madison (1751–1836) argued against democracy and for republicanism in Federalist Paper #10 but also drafted the First Amendment guaranteeing freedom of religion, which was an implicit endorsement of the principle of equality.

6. Gordon S. Wood, *The Radicalism of the American Revolution* (New York: Random House, 1991).

7. Jerome Huyler, *Locke in America: The Moral Philosophy of the Founding Era* (Lawrence: University Press of Kansas, 1995).

8. James Madison, "To the Honorable General Assembly of the Commonwealth of Virginia, A Memorial and Remonstrance" (1785), reprinted in *James Madison on Religious Liberty*, ed. Robert S. Alley (Buffalo: Prometheus Books, 1985), quotations from pp. 56–60.

9. Locke, "Essay on Toleration," quotations from p. 139.

10. Catherine A. Brekus, *Strangers & Pilgrims: Female Preaching in America, 1740–1845* (Chapel Hill: University of North Carolina Press, 1998), quotation from p. 82.

11. Albert J. Raboteau, *Slave Religion: The "Invisible Institution" in the Antebellum South* (New York: Oxford University Press, 1978), quotations from pp. 291–292.

12. Ruth H. Bloch, *Visionary Republic: Millennial Themes in American Thought, 1756–1800* (Cambridge: Cambridge University Press, 1985), quotations from p. 79.

13. Sidney Mead, *The Lively Experiment: The Shaping of Christianity in America* (New York: Harper & Row, 1963). Also see Martin Marty, *Righteous Empire: The Protestant Experience in America* (New York: Harper & Row, 1970); and Mark A. Noll, *America's God: From Jonathan Edwards to Abraham Lincoln* (New York: Oxford University Press, 2002).

14. William R. Hutchison, *The Modernist Impulse in American Protestantism* (New York: Oxford University Press, 1976); William R. Hutchison, ed., *Between the Times: The Travail of the Protestant Establishment in America, 1900–1960* (Cambridge: Cambridge University Press, 1989).

15. John Dewey, *A Common Faith* (New Haven: Yale University Press, 1934), quotations from pp. 80, 84.

16. Tim LaHaye and Jerry B. Jenkins, *The Remnant: On the Brink of Armageddon* (Wheaton, IL: Tynedale House Press, 2002).

17. Wade Clark Roof, *Spiritual Marketplace: Baby Boomers and the Remaking of American Religion* (Princeton: Princeton University Press, 1999).

18. Thomas Tweed, *The American Encounter with Buddhism, 1844–1912* (Bloomington: Indiana University Press, 1992).

19. Ralph Waldo Emerson, "Self-Reliance" (1841), in *Essential Writings of Emerson*, ed. Bruce Atkinson (New York: Modern Library, 2000), quotations from pp. 146, 145.

20. Dennis C. Dickerson, *Church History: Studies in Christianity and Culture* 74: 2 (June 2005) pp. 217–235.

21. D. T. Suzuki, "Satori," in *A Zen Life: D. T. Suzuki Remembered* (New York: Weatherhill, 1986), quotations from pp. 27–28, 43.

22. Amanda Porterfield, *The Transformation of American Religion: The Story of a Late-Twentieth-Century Awakening* (New York: Oxford University Press, 2001), pp. 125–162.

23. Amanda Porterfield, *Healing in the History of Christianity* (New York: Oxford University Press, 2005).

24. *Lived Religion in America: Toward a History of Practice*, ed. David Hall (Princeton: Princeton University Press, 1997).

25. Increase Mather, *The Necessity of Reformation with the Expedients Subservient Thereunto, Asserted* (Boston, 1679).

26. Nevertheless, Protestants often understood that acceptance of divine providence entailed acceptance of suffering, and that repentance and self-scrutiny were means to this acceptance, not means to a cure. For example, at eighty-six years of age, the famous American evangelist Billy Graham spoke of his infirmities as blessings, and compared himself to the Apostle Paul: "He prayed several times that he might be released from these physical problems. But God didn't answer it that way," Graham explained in 2005. "He said no, and Paul finally decided that the reason he had it was to keep him humble." Graham thought God directed his life in a similar way. "I've had a lot of illnesses and sicknesses and operations and hospital stays, and I've rejoiced in all of it. When I fell and broke my hip a little over a year ago, I was very happy because I knew the Lord was working." Billy Graham, "The Words of a Preacher," *New York Times*, Sunday, June 12, 2005, quotation from A25. In this interview, Graham expressed his admiration for how Pope John Paul II handled his suffering and death. "I didn't agree with him on everything theologically," Graham said, but he also stated that John Paul II "was teaching us how to suffer, and he taught us how to die."

27. Philip Jenkins, *The Next Christendom: The Coming of Global Christianity* (New York: Oxford University Press, 2002), quotations from p. 8.

28. For example, among acquaintances of this author, Khaled Ksaibati, an Engineering Professor at the University of Wyoming and an immigrant from Syria, commented after 9/11 that he could practice Islam in the United States as he thought it should be practiced, and that he could not do that in his country of birth. Shirin Rahimi, an immigrant from Iran and owner of a hair salon in Florida, supported George W. Bush in the 2004 Presidential election, and his efforts to bring democracy to the Middle East. On the other hand, Zubaida Ula, the daughter of immigrants and President of the Islamic Student Association at

the University of Wyoming in 2002, began wearing the headscarf in high school as a sign of her religious identity and commitment to strong religious principles. Like many Muslims around the world, Zubaida strongly opposed George Bush and his policies in the Mideast.

29. Annemarie Schimmel, *Mystical Dimensions of Islam* (Chapel Hill: University of North Carolina Press, 1975), quotations from p. 193.

30. R. M. Mukhtar Curtis, "Urban Muslims: The Formation of the Dar ul-Islam Movement," in *Muslim Communities in North America*, ed. Yvonne Yazbeck Haddad and Jane Idleman Smith (Albany: SUNY Press, 1994), pp. 51–53.

31. Elijah Muhammad's son Wallace Deen Muhammad took over the movement after his father's death in 1975, renamed the organization the American Muslim Mission, and brought it more in line with the teachings of the World Muslim Council. While a splinter group led by Louis Farrakhan adopted the old name, Nation of Islam, and preserved some of the beliefs and practices associated with the earlier Nation, the larger American Muslim Mission strengthened its involvement in the international aspects of Sunni Islam and developed connections with Muslim immigrant communities in the United States. In many masjids in the United States today, Muslims from African American backgrounds worship and study with Muslims who came to the United States from Asian or African countries, as well as with white converts from European backgrounds.

32. Marxism played no less of an influential role in the historical development of radical Islam. During the cold war, Marxist ideology contributed to critiques of modern liberalism and western (especially American) capitalism as well as to hopes of a revolutionary uprising against these forces that would lead to social justice and relief from poverty. Disappointment with Marxist ideology and with the moral and economic failures of Soviet regimes contributed to the resurgence of religious zealotry in the Islamic world, as did the revolutionary and utopian character of that ideology itself.

Working in an intellectual context of German universities strongly influenced by liberal Protestant theology and romantic philosophies of history, the secular Jew Karl Marx developed a theoretical understanding of the relationship between ideology and ownership of the means of economic production that exerted enormous influence on religion and politics around the world. In Islamic countries, the fundamentalist movement emerged in the wake of Marxist influence, partly as a repudiation of the secularism of Marxist thought and its critical view of religion, and partly as a rejection of the political, economic, and religious philosophies of modern liberalism and disappointment at their failure to relieve oppression and exploitation.

33. Religious donors to the Islamic Wahabite movement, centered in Saudi Arabia, poured millions of dollars into religious education in the United States, funding religious training and schools, and forming organizations for the publication and distribution of religious books, pamphlets, and periodicals. Sometimes compared to Puritanism, the Wahabism is a conservative movement within Sunni Islam aimed at confronting the moral evils of modern society with

the purity of Islam and through adherence to clear and conservative interpretations of Islamic law. With respect to its impact on American society, Wahabism is a post-Protestant phenomenon insofar as it offers Islam as the solution to the problems of American society that Protestant Christianity has not only failed to solve but also created, at least insofar as American society is a product of the garbled versions of true religion reflected in Protestant Christianity.

34. For discussion of secularity versus secularism, see Talal Asad, *Formations of the Secular: Christianity, Islam, Modernity* (Stanford: Stanford University Press, 2003).

35. Quoted in Laurie Goodstein, "An Ailing Evangelist Prepares to Come Down from Mountain," *New York Times*, Sunday, June 12, 2005, A25.

36. Gabriel A. Almond, R. Scott Appleby, and Emmanuel Sivan, *Strong Religion: The Rise of Fundamentalisms around the World* (Chicago: University of Chicago Press, 2003); Martin E. Marty and R. Scott Appleby, eds., *Fundamentalism Observed* (Chicago: University of Chicago Press, 1991).

37. H. Richard Niebuhr, *The Kingdom of God in America* (New York: Harper & Row, 1937), quotations from p. 198.

38. See, for example, Rosemary Radford Ruether, *Sexism and God-Talk: Toward a Feminist Theology* (Boston: Beacon Press, 1993; orig. 1984).

39. Carols M. N. Eire, *War Against the Idols: The Reformation of Worship from Erasmus to Calvin* (Cambridge: Cambridge University Press, 1986).

40. Huyler, *Locke in America*, quotations from pp. xi, 308.

41. Will Herberg, *Protestant-Catholic-Jew: An Essay in American Religious Sociology* (Chicago: University of Chicago Press, 1983; orig. 1955), quotation from p. 239; also see pp. 179–198. Liberal interpretations of equality have not always appealed to Jewish intellectuals or to Christian intellectuals either. In American academic circles, Marxist critiques inform many theoretical undertakings and interpretations of religion. Skepticism with regard to human reason is widely prevalent in American society, not only among religious fundamentalists who point to the necessity for obedience to a higher law, but also among cultural critics influenced by Marxist theory. The prevalence of this skepticism about reason highlights the idea that faith in reason is just that.

Bibliography

Abrams, Meier H., *The Mirror and the Lamp: Romantic Theory and the Critical Tradition* (New York: Oxford University Press, 1953).

Abrams, Meier H., *Natural Supernaturalism: Tradition and Revolution in Romantic Literature* (New York: W. W. Norton, 1971).

Ahlstrom, Sydney E., *A Religious History of the American People*, rev. ed. (New Haven: Yale University Press, 2000).

Albanese, Catherine L., *America: Religions and Religion*, 3rd ed. (Belmont: Wadsworth Publishing, 1999).

Albanese, Catherine L., *Sons of the Fathers: The Civil Religion of the American Revolution* (Philadelphia: Temple University Press, 1976).

Alvis, Joel L., Jr., *Religion and Race: Southern Presbyterians, 1946–1983* (Tuscaloosa: University of Alabama Press, 1994).

Ammerman, Nancy Tatom, *Baptist Battles: Social Change and Religious Conflict in the Southern Baptist Convention* (New Brunswick: Rutgers University Press, 1990).

Ammerman, Nancy Tatom, *Bible Believers: Fundamentalists in the Modern World* (New Brunswick: Rutgers University Press, 1987).

Andrews, Dee E., *The Methodists and Revolutionary America, 1760–1800: The Shaping of an Evangelical Culture* (Princeton: Princeton University Press, 2000).

Asad, Talal, *Formations of the Secular: Christianity, Islam, Modernity* (Stanford: Stanford University Press, 2003).

Backman, Milton V., Jr., *Christian Churches of America: Origins and Beliefs*, rev. ed. (New York: Charles Scribner's Sons, 1983).

Baer, Hans A., *The Black Spiritual Movement: A Religious Response to Racism* (Knoxville: University of Tennessee Press, 1984).

Bailyn, Bernard, *The Ideological Origins of the American Revolution* (Cambridge: Harvard University Press, 1967).

Bainton, Roland H., *The Reformation of the Sixteenth Century* (Boston: Beacon Press, 1952).

Baird, Robert, *Religion in America* (New York: Harper & Row, 1970; orig. 1856).

Balmer, Randall H., *Mine Eyes Have Seen the Glory: A Journey into the Evangelical Subculture of America* (New York: Oxford University Press, 1993).

Balmer, Randall H., *A Perfect Babel of Confusion: Dutch Religion and English Culture in the Middle Colonies* (New York: Oxford University Press, 1989).

Balmer, Randall H., *Religion and Public Life in the Middle Atlantic Region: Fount of Diversity* (Lanham: Alta Mira Press, 2006).

Balmer, Randall H., and Lauren F. Winner, *Protestantism in America* (New York: Columbia University Press, 2002).

Baltzell, E. Digby, *The Protestant Establishment: Aristocracy and Caste in America* (New Haven: Yale University Press, 1964).

Bannister, Robert C., *Social Darwinism: Science and Myth in Anglo-American Thought* (Philadelphia: Temple University Press, 1979).

Barbour, Hugh, et al., eds., *Quaker Crosscurrents: Three Hundred Years of Friends in the New York Yearly Meetings* (Syracuse: Syracuse University Press, 1995).

Barkun, Michael, *Crucible of the Millennium: The Burned-Over District of New York in the 1840s* (Syracuse: Syracuse University Press, 1986).

Barlow, Philip, ed., *Religion and Public Life in the Midwest: America's Common Denominator?* (Lanham: Alta Mira Press, 2004).

Bednarowski, Mary Farrell, *The Religious Imagination of American Women* (Bloomington: Indiana University Press, 1999).

Behney, J. Bruce, and Paul H. Eller, *The History of the Evangelical United Brethren Church*, ed. Kenneth W. Krueger (Abingdon: Nashville, 1979).

Bellah, Robert N., ed., *Habits of the Heart: Individualism and Commitment in American Life* (Berkeley: University of California Press, 1985).

Bendroth, Margaret Lamberts, *Fundamentalism and Gender, 1875 to the Present* (New Haven: Yale University Press, 1993).

Bendroth, Margaret Lamberts, *Growing Up Protestant: Parents, Children, and Mainline Churches* (New Brunswick: Rutgers University Press, 2002).

Bendroth, Margaret Lamberts, and Virginia Lieson Brereton, eds., *Women in Twentieth-Century Protestantism* (Urbana: Univeristy of Illinois Press, 2002).

Benedict, Philip, *Christ's Churches Purely Reformed: A Social History of Calvinism* (New Haven: Yale University Press, 2002).

Bennett, James B., *Religion and the Rise of Jim Crow in New Orleans* (Princeton: Princeton University Press, 2005).

Bercovitch, Sacvan, *The American Jeremiad* (Madison: University of Wisconsin Press, 1978).

Bercovitch, Sacvan, *The Puritan Origins of the American Self* (New Haven: Yale University Press, 1975).

Berlin, Ira, and Ronald Hoffman, eds., *Slavery and Freedom in the Age of the American Revolution* (Urbana: University of Illinois Press, 1986; orig. 1983).

Best, Wallace D., *Passionately Human, No Less Divine: Religion and Culture in Black Chicago, 1915–1952* (Princeton: Princeton University Press, 2005).

Billington, Ray Allen, *The Protestant Crusade, 1800–1860: A Study of the Origins of American Nativism* (Chicago: Quadrangle Books, 1964; orig. 1938).

Blassingame, John W., *The Slave Community: Plantation Life in the Antebellum South*, rev. ed. (New York: Oxford University Press, 1979).

Bloch, Ruth H., *Visionary Republic: Millennial Themes in American Thought, 1756–1800* (Cambridge: Cambridge University Press, 1985).

Blumhofer, Edith L., *Aimee Semple McPherson: Everybody's Sister* (Grand Rapids: William B. Eerdmans, 1993).

Blumhofer, Edith L., *Restoring the Faith: The Assemblies of God, Pentecostalism, and American Culture* (Urbana: University of Illinois Press, 1993).

Boller, Paul F., Jr., *George Washington and Religion* (Dallas: SMU Press, 1963).

Bonomi, Patricia U., *Under the Cope of Heaven: Religion, Society, and Politics in Colonial America* (New York: Oxford University Press, 1986).

Boone, Kathleen C., *The Bible Tells Them So: The Discourse of Fundamentalism* (Albany: SUNY Press, 1989).

Boorstin, Daniel, *The Lost World of Thomas Jefferson* (New York: Henry Holt, 1948).

Bordin, Frances, *Frances Willard: A Biography* (Chapel Hill: University of North Carolina Press, 1986).

Bowden, Henry Warner, ed., *A Century of Church History: The Legacy of Philip Schaff* (Carbondale: Southern Illinois University Press, 1988).

Bowden, Henry Warner, *Dictionary of American Religious Biography*, rev. ed. (Westport: Greenwood, 1993).

Boyer, Paul, *When Time Shall Be No More: Prophecy Belief in Modern American Culture* (Cambridge: Harvard University Press, 1992).

Boyer, Paul, and Stephen Nissenbaum, *Salem Possessed: The Social Origins of Witchcraft* (Cambridge: Harvard University Press, 1974).

Boylan, Anne M., *Sunday School: The Formation of an American Institution 1790–1880* (New Haven: Yale University Press, 1988).

Bozeman, Theodore Dwight, *The Precisionist Strain: Disciplinary Religion & Antinomian Backlash in Puritanism to 1638* (Chapel Hill: University of North Carolina Press, 2004).

Bozeman, Theodore Dwight, *To Live Ancient Lives: The Primitivist Dimension in Puritanism* (Chapel Hill: University of North Carolina Press, 1988).

Brantley, Richard E., *Coordinates of Anglo-American Romanticism: Wesley, Edwards, Carlyle & Emerson* (Gainesville: University of Florida Press, 1993).

Brantley, Richard E., *Locke, Wesley, and the Method of English Romanticism* (Gainesville: University of Florida Press, 1984).

Braude, Ann, *Radical Spirits: Spiritualism and Women's Rights in Nineteenth-Century America* (Boston: Beacon Press, 1989).

Breitwieser, Mitchell Robert, *American Puritanism and the Defense of Mourning: Religion, Grief, and Ethnology in Mary White Rowlandson's Captivity Narrative* (Madison: University of Wisconsin Press, 1990).

Brekus, Catherine A., *Strangers & Pilgrims: Female Preaching in America 1740–1845* (Chapel Hill: University of North Carolina Press, 1998).

Brereton, Virginia Lieson, *From Sin to Salvation: Stories of Women's Conversions, 1800 to the Present* (Bloomington: Indiana University Press, 1991).

Breslaw, Elaine G., *Tituba, Reluctant Witch of Salem: Devilish Indians and Puritan Fantasies* (New York: New York University Press, 1996).

Brown, Candy Gunther, *The Word in the World: Evangelical Writing, Publishing, and Reading in America, 1789–1880* (Chapel Hill: University of North Carolina Press, 2004).

Brown, Elisabeth Potts, and Susan Mosher Stuard, eds., *Witnesses for Change: Quaker Women Over Three Centuries* (New Brunswick: Rutgers University Press, 1989).

Bushman, Richard L., *From Puritan to Yankee: Character and the Social Order in Connecticut, 1690–1765* (Cambridge: Harvard University Press, 1967).

Bushman, Richard L., *Joseph Smith: Rough Stone Rolling* (New York: Knopf, 2005).

Butler, Jon, *Awash in a Sea of Faith: Christianizing the American People* (Cambridge: Harvard University Press, 1990).

Caldwell, Patricia, *The Puritan Conversion Narrative: The Beginnings of American Expression* (Cambridge: Cambridge University Press, 1983).

Calhoon, Robert M., *Evangelicals and Conservatives in the Early South, 1740–1861* (Columbia: University of South Carolina Press, 1988).

Cameron, Euan, *The European Reformation* (Oxford: Oxford University Press, 1991).

Capps, Walter H., *The New Religious Right: Piety, Patriotism, and Politics* (Columbia: University of South Carolina Press, 1990).

Carnett, Daniel R., *Contending for the Faith: Southern Baptists in New Mexico 1938–1995* (Albuquerque: University of New Mexico Press, 2002).

Carwardine, Richard J., *Evangelicals and Politics in Antebellum America* (Knoxville: University of Tennessee Press, 1997).

Cashdollar, Charles D., *The Transformation of Theology, 1830–1890: Positivism and Protestant Thought in Britain and America* (Princeton: Princeton University Press, 1989).

Cayton, Mary Kupiec, *Emerson's Emergence: Self and Society in the Transformation of New England 1800–1845* (Chapel Hill: University of North Carolina Press, 1989).

Chambers-Schiller, Lee Virginia, *Liberty a Better Husband: Single Women in America: The Generations of 1780–1840* (New Haven: Yale University Press, 1984).

Chase, Richard, *Emily Dickinson* (New York: Dell, 1965; orig. 1951).

Chaves, Mark, *Congregations in America* (Cambridge: Harvard University Press, 2004).

Cherry, Conrad, *Hurrying Toward Zion: Universities, Divinity Schools, and American Protestantism* (Bloomington: University of Indiana Press, 1995).

Cherry, Conrad, *Nature and Religious Imagination: From Edwards to Bushnell* (Philadelphia: Fortress Press, 1980).

Chmielewski, Wendy E., Louis J. Kern, and Marlyn Klee-Hartzell, eds., *Women in Spiritual and Communitarian Societies in the United States* (Syracuse: Syracuse University Press, 1993).

Clark, Stuart, *Thinking with Demons: The Idea of Witchcraft in Early Modern Europe* (New York: Oxford University Press, 1997).

Clebsch, William A., *American Religious Thought: A History* (Chicago: University of Chicago Press, 1973).

Clebsch, William A., *England's Earliest Protestants, 1520–1535* (New Haven: Yale University Press, 1964).

Coalter, Milton J., John M. Muder, and Louis B. Weeks, *The Confessional Mosaic: Presbyterians and Twentieth-Century Theology* (Louisville: John Knox Press, 1990).

Coalter, Milton J., John M. Muder, and Louis B. Weeks, *The Mainstream Protestant "Decline": The Presbyterian Pattern* (Louisville: John Knox Press, 1990).

Cohen, Charles Lloyd, *God's Caress: The Psychology of Puritan Religious Experience* (New York: Oxford University Press, 1986).

Cohn, Norman, *The Pursuit of the Millennium: Revolutionary Messianism in Medieval and Reformation Europe and Its Bearing on Modern Totalitarian Movements* (New York: Harper & Row, 1961; orig. 1957).

Cole, Phyllis, *Mary Moody Emerson and the Origins of Transcendentalism: A Family History* (New York: Oxford University Press, 1998).

Collinson, Patrick, *The Elizabethan Puritan Movement* (Oxford: Oxford University Press, 1967).

Como, David R., *Blown by the Spirit: Puritanism and the Emergence of an Antinomian Underground in Pre-Civil-War England* (Stanford: Stanford University Press, 2004).

Conforti, Joseph A., *Samuel Hopkins and the New Divinity Movement: Calvinism, the Congregational Ministry, and Reform in New England Between the Great Awakenings* (Grand Rapids: William B. Eerdmans, 1981).

Conkin, Paul K., *American Originals: Homemade Varieties of Christianity* (Chapel Hill: University of North Carolina Press, 1997).

Conkin, Paul K., *Cane Ridge: America's Pentecost* (Madison: University of Wisconsin Press, 1990).

Corrigan, John, *Business of the Heart: Religion and Emotion in the Nineteenth Century* (Berkeley: University of California Press, 2002).

Corrigan, John, *The Prism of Piety: Catholick Congregational Clergy at the Beginning of the Enlightenment* (New York: Oxford University Press, 1991).

Cross, Whitney R., *The Burned-Over District: The Social and Intellectual History of Enthusiastic Religion in Western New York, 1800–1850* (Ithaca: Cornell University Press, 1950).

Davis, Gerald L., *I Got the Word in Me and I Can Sing It, You Know: A Study of the Performed African-American Sermon* (Philadelphia: University of Pennsylvania Press, 1985).

Dayton, Donald W., *Theological Roots of Pentecostalism* (Peabody: Hendrickson, 1987).

Dayton, Donald W., and Robert K. Johnston, *The Variety of American Evangelicalism* (Knoxville: University of Tennessee Press, 1991).

DeLattre, Roland André, *Beauty and Sensibility in the Thought of Jonathan Edwards* (New Haven: Yale University Press, 1968).

Delbanco, Andrew, *Melville: His World and Work* (New York: Alfred A. Knopf, 2005).

Demos, John, *A Little Commonwealth: Family Life in Plymouth Colony* (New York: Oxford University Press, 1970).

Dorgan, Howard, *Giving Glory to God in Appalachia: Worship Practices of Six Baptist Subdenominations* (Knoxville: University of Tennessee Press, 1987).

Dorrien, Gary, *The Making of American Liberal Theology: Idealism, Realism, and Modernity 1900–1950* (Louisville: Westminster John Knox Press, 2003).

Dorrien, Gary, *The Making of American Liberal Theology: Imagining Progressive Religion 1805–1900* (Louisville: Westminster John Knox Press, 2001).

Douglas, Ann, *The Feminization of American Culture* (New York: Alfred A. Knopf, 1977).

Eire, Carlos M. N., *War Against the Idols: The Reformation of Worship from Erasmus to Calvin* (Cambridge: Cambridge University Press, 1986).

Elliott, Emory, *Power and the Pulpit in Puritan New England* (Princeton: Princeton University Press, 1975).

Elliott, Emory, ed., *Puritan Influences in American Literature* (Urbana: University of Illinois Press, 1979).

Ellwood, Robert S., *1950: Crossroads of American Religious Life* (Louisville: Westminster John Knox Press, 2000).

Engelhardt, Tom, *The End of Victory Culture: Cold War America and the Disillusioning of a Generation* (New York: HarperCollins, 1995).

Epstein, Barbara Leslie, *The Politics of Domesticity: Women, Evangelism, and Temperance in Nineteenth-Century America* (Middletown: Wesleyan University Press, 1981).

Epstein, Daniel Mark, *Lincoln and Whitman: Parallel Lives in Civil War Washington* (New York: Random House, 2004).

Evans, Christopher H., *The Kingdom Is Always Coming: A Life of Walter Rauschenbusch* (Grand Rapids: William B. Eerdmans, 2004).

Evensen, Bruce J., *God's Man for the Gilded Age: D. L. Moody and the Rise of Modern Mass Evangelism* (New York: Oxford University Press, 2003).

Fett, Sharla M., *Working Cures: Healing, Health, and Power on Southern Slave Plantations* (Chapel Hill: University of North Carolina Press, 2002).

Fiering, Norman, *Moral Philosophy at Seventeenth-Century Harvard: A Discipline in Transition* (Chapel Hill: University of North Carolina Press, 1981).

Fliegelman, Jay, *Prodigals and Pilgrims: The American Revolution Against Patriarchal Authority 1750–1800* (Cambridge: Cambridge University Press, 1982).

Foster, Lawrence, *Religion and Sexuality: The Shakers, the Mormons, and the Oneida Community* (Urbana: University of Illinois Press, 1984).

Foster, Stephen, *The Long Argument: English Puritanism and the Shaping of New England Culture, 1570–1700* (Chapel Hill: University of North Carolina Press, 1991).

Fox, Richard Wrightman, and James T. Kloppenberg, *A Companion to American Thought* (Cambridge: Blackwell, 1995).

Frey, Sylvia R., and Betty Wood, *Come Shouting to Zion: African American Protestantism in the American South and British Caribbean to 1830* (Chapel Hill: University of North Carolina Press, 1998).

Fulop, Timothy E., and Albert J. Raboteau, eds., *African-American Religion: Interpretive Essays in History and Culture* (New York: Routledge, 1997).

Garber, Marjorie, and Rebecca L. Walkowitz, eds., *One Nation Under God? Religion and American Culture* (New York: Routledge, 1999).

Garrow, David J., *Bearing the Cross: Martin Luther King, Jr., and the Southern Christian Leadership Conference* (New York: William Morrow, 1986).

Gaustad, Edwin Scott, *Dissent in American Religion* (Chicago: University of Chicago Press, 1973).

Gaustad, Edwin Scott, *Faith of the Founders: Religion and the New Nation 1776–1826* (Waco: Baylor University Press, 2004).

Gaustad, Edwin Scott, *Sworn on the Altar of God: A Religious Biography of Thomas Jefferson* (Grand Rapids: William B. Eerdmans, 1996).

Gaustad, Edwin Scott, and Leigh Schmidt, *The Religious History of America: The Heart of the American Story from Colonial Times to Today* (San Francisco: Harper San Francisco, 2002).

Gaustad, Edwin Scott, Philip L. Barlow, and Richard W. Dishno, *New Historical Atlas of Religion in America* (New York: Oxford University Press, 2000).

Gedge, Karin E., *Without Benefit of Clergy: Women and the Pastoral Relationship in Nineteenth-Century American Culture* (New York: Oxford University Press, 2003).

Genovese, Eugene D., *Roll, Jordan, Roll: The World the Slaves Made* (New York: Random House, 1974; orig. 1972).

Giggie, John M., and Diane Winston, eds., *Religion and the Rise of Urban Commercial Culture* (New Brunswick: Rutgers University Press, 2002).

Gilbert, James, *Redeeming Culture: American Religion in an Age of Science* (Chicago: University of Chicago Press, 1997).

Gitlin, Todd, *The Sixties: Years of Hope, Days of Rage*, rev. ed. (New York: Bantam Books, 1993).

Goff, Philip, and Paul Harvey, eds., *Themes in Religion and American Culture* (Chapel Hill: University of North Carolina Press, 2004).

Grant, Jacquelyn, *White Women's Christ and Black Women's Jesus* (Atlanta: Scholars' Press, 1989).

Green, Elizabeth Alden, *Mary Lyon and Mount Holyoke: Opening the Gates* (Hanover: University Press of New England, 1979).

Greene, Jack P., *The Reinterpretation of the American Revolution 1763–1789* (New York: Harper & Row, 1968).

Greene, Jack P., and William G. McLoughlin, *Preachers & Politicians: Two Essays on the Origins of the American Revolution* (Worcester: American Antiquarian Society, 1977).

Greven, Philip, *The Protestant Temperament: Patters of Child-Rearing, Religious Experience, and the Self in Early America* (New York: New American Library, 1977).

Griffith, R. Marie, *Born Again Bodies: Flesh and Spirit in American Christianity* (Berkeley: University of California Press, 2004).

Gunn, Giles, ed., *The Bible and American Arts and Letters* (Philadelphia: Fortress Press, 1983).

Gunn, Giles, *Thinking Across the American Grain: Ideology, Intellect, and the New Pragmatism* (Chicago: University of Chicago Press, 1992).

Gura, Philip F., *A Glimpse of Sion's Glory: Puritan Radicalism in New England, 1620–1660* (Middletown: Wesleyan University Press, 1984).

Hackett, David G., ed., *Religion and American Culture* (New York: Routledge, 1995).

Hackett, David G., *The Rude Hand of Innovation: Religion and Social Order in Albany, New York, 1652–1836* (New York: Oxford University Press, 1991).

Hall, David D., *The Faithful Shepherd: A History of the New England Ministry in the Seventeenth Century* (New York: W. W. Norton, 1972).

Hall, David D., ed., *Lived Religion in America: Toward a History of Practice* (Princeton: Princeton University Press, 1997).

Hall, David D., *Worlds of Wonder, Days of Judgment: Popular Religious Belief in Early New England* (Cambridge: Harvard University Press, 1989).

Haller, William, *The Rise of Puritanism* (Philadelphia: University of Pennsylvania Press, 1972; orig. 1938).

Hambrick-Stowe, Charles E., *The Practice of Piety: Puritan Devotional Disciplines in Seventeenth-Century New England* (Chapel Hill: University of North Carolina Press, 1982).

Hamm, Thomas D., *The Transformation of American Quakerism: Orthodox Friends, 1800–1907* (Bloomington: Indiana University Press, 1988).

Hammond, Phillip E., *Religion and Personal Autonomy: The Third Disestablishment in America* (Columbia: University of South Carolina Press, 1992).

Handy, Robert T., *A Christian America: Protestant Hopes and Historical Realities*, rev. ed. (New York: Oxford University Press, 1984).

Haroutunian, Joseph, *Piety Versus Moralism: The Passing of the New England Theology* (New York: Henry Holt, 1932).

Harrell, David Edwin, Jr., *All Things Are Possible: The Healing and Charismatic Revivals in Modern America* (Bloomington: Indiana University Press, 1975).

Harrell, David Edwin, Jr., *Oral Roberts: An American Life* (Bloomington: Indiana University Press, 1985).

Harris, Paul William, *Nothing But Christ: Rufus Anderson and the Ideology of Protestant Foreign Missions* (New York: Oxford University Press, 1999).

Hatch, Nathan O., *The Democratization of American Christianity* (New Haven: Yale University Press, 1989).

Hein, David, *Noble Powell and the Episcopal Establishment in the Twentieth Century* (Urbana: University of Illinois Press, 2001).

Heitzenrater, Richard P., *Wesley and the People Called Methodists* (Nashville: Abingdon Press, 1995).

Hendershot, Heather, *Shaking the World for Jesus: Media and Conservative Evangelical Culture* (Chicago: University of Chicago Press, 2004).

Henretta, James A., *The Evolution of American Society, 1700–1815* (Lexington: D. C. Heath, 1973).

Herberg, Will, *Protestant-Catholic-Jew: An Essay in American Religious Sociology* (Chicago: University of Chicago Press, 1983; orig. 1955).

Heyrman, Christine Leigh, *Southern Cross: The Beginnings of the Bible Belt* (New York: Knopf, 1997).

Higham, John, *Strangers in the Land: Patterns of American Nativism 1860–1925* (New York: Atheneum, 1970).

Hill, Christopher, *The World Turned Upside Down: Radical Ideas During the English Revolution* (New York: Penguin Books, 1975; orig. 1972).

Hill, Samuel S., Jr., ed., *Encyclopedia of Religion in the South* (Macon: Mercer University Press, 1984).

Hill, Samuel S., Jr., *The South and the North in American Religion* (Athens: University of Georgia Press, 1980).

Hillerbrand, Hans J., ed., *The Encyclopedia of Protestantism*, 4 vols. (New York: Routledge, 2004).

Hoffer, Peter Charles, *The Devil's Disciples: Makers of the Salem Witchcraft Trials* (Baltimore: Johns Hopkins University Press, 1996).

Hofstadter, Richard, *Social Darwinism in American Thought* (Boston: Beacon Press, 1955; orig. 1944).

Holifield, E. Brooks, *The Covenant Sealed: The Development of Puritan Sacramental Theology in Old and New England, 1570–1720* (New Haven: Yale University Press, 1974).

Holifield, E. Brooks, *Theology in America: Christian Thought from the Age of the Puritans to the Civil War* (New Haven: Yale University Press, 2003).

Honour, Hugh, *Romanticism* (New York: Harper & Row, 1979).

Hopkins, Dwight N., and George Cummings, *Cut Loose Your Stammering Tongue: Black Theology in the Slave Narratives* (Maryknoll: Orbis Books, 1992).

Howard-Pitney, David, *The Afro-American Jeremiad: Appeals for Justice in America* (Philadelphia: Temple University Press, 1990).

Hudson, Winthrop S., *American Protestantism* (Chicago: University of Chicago Press, 1961).

Hudson, Winthrop S., and John Corrigan, *Religion in America*, rev. ed. (Upper Saddle River: Prentice Hall, 1999).

Hughes, Richard T., ed., *The American Quest for the Primitive Church* (Urbana: University of Illinois Press, 1988).

Hunter, James Davidson, *Culture Wars: The Struggle to Define America* (New York: HarperCollins, 1991).

Hutchison, William R., *American Protestant Thought in the Liberal Era* (New York: University Press of America, 1968).

Hutchison, William R., ed., *Between the Times: The Travail of the Protestant Establishment in America, 1900–1960* (Cambridge: Cambridge University Press, 1989).

Hutchison, William R., *Errand to the World: American Protestant Thought and Foreign Missions* (Chicago: University of Chicago Press, 1987).

Hutchison, William R., *The Modernist Impulse in American Protestantism* (New York: Oxford University Press, 1976).

Hutchison, William R., *Religious Pluralism in America: The Contentious History of a Founding Ideal* (New Haven: Yale University Press, 2003).

Huyler, Jerome, *Locke in America: The Moral Philosophy of the Founding Era* (Lawrence: University Press of Kansas, 1995).

Isaac, Rhys, *The Transformation of Virginia, 1740–1790* (Chapel Hill: University of North Carolina Press, 1982).

James, Janet Wilson, *Women in American Religion* (Philadelphia: University of Pennsylvania Press, 1980).

Jorstad, Erling, *Holding Fast/Pressing On: Religion in America in the 1980s* (New York: Praeger, 1990).

Kammen, Michael, *A Machine That Would Go of Itself: The Constitution in American Culture* (New York: Alfred Knopf, 1986).

Kammen, Michael, *A Season of Youth: The American Revolution and the Historical Imagination* (Ithaca: Cornell University Press, 1978).

Karlsen, Carol F., *The Devil in the Shape of a Woman: Witchcraft in Colonial New England* (New York: W. W. Norton, 1987).

Kaufman, Peter Iver, *Prayer, Despair, and Drama: Elizabethan Introspection* (Urbana: University of Illinois Press, 1986).

Kaul, A. N., *The American Vision: Actual and Ideal in Nineteenth-Century Fiction* (New Haven: Yale University Press, 1963).

Kennedy, David M., *Birth Control in America: The Career of Margaret Sanger* (New Haven: Yale University Press, 1970).

Kerber, Linda K., *Women of the Republic: Intellect & Ideology in Revolutionary America* (Chapel Hill: University of North Carolina Press, 1980).

Ketcham, Ralph, *Presidents Above Party: The First American Presidency, 1789–1829* (Chapel Hill: University of North Carolina Press, 1984).

Kibbey, Ann, *The Interpretation of Material Shapes in Puritanism: A Study of Rhetoric, Prejudice, and Violence* (New York: Cambridge University Press, 1986).

Kling, David W., *A Field of Divine Wonders: The New Divinity and Village Revivals in Northwestern Connecticut 1792–1822* (University Park: Pennsylvania State University Press, 1993).

Knight, Louise W., *Citizen: Jane Addams and the Struggle for Democracy* (Chicago: University of Chicago Press, 2005).

Koerner, Joseph Leo, *The Reformation of the Image* (Chicago: University of Chicago Press, 2004).

Kolodny, Annette, *The Land Before Her: Fantasy and Experience of the American Frontiers, 1630–1860* (Chapel Hill: University of North Carolina Press, 1984).

Kuklick, Bruce, *Churchmen and Philosophers: From Jonathan Edwards to John Dewey* (New Haven: Yale University Press, 1985).

Lacey, Michael J., ed., *Religion and Twentieth-Century American Intellectual Life* (Cambridge: Cambridge University Press, 1989).

Laderman, Gary, *The Sacred Remains: American Attitudes Toward Death, 1799–1883* (New Haven: Yale University Press, 1996).

Lasch, Christopher, *The Culture of Narcissism: American Life in an Age of Diminishing Expectations* (New York: W. W. Norton, 1979).

Lawless, Elaine J., *Handmaidens of the Lord: Pentecostal Women Preachers and Traditional Religion* (Philadelphia: University of Pennsylvania Press, 1988).

Lazareth, William H., *Christians in Society: Luther, the Bible, and Social Ethics* (Minneapolis: Fortress Press, 2001).

Lears, T. J. Jackson, *No Place of Grace* (New York: Pantheon, 1983).

Leites, Edmund, *The Puritan Conscience and Modern Sexuality* (New Haven: Yale University Press, 1986).

Leverenz, David, *The Language of Puritan Feeling: An Exploration in Literature, Psychology, and Social History* (New Brunswick: Rutgers University Press, 1980).

Lewis, R.W.B., *The American Adam: Innocence, Tragedy, and Tradition in the Nineteenth Century* (Chicago: University of Chicago Press, 1955).

Lincoln, C. Eric, ed., *The Black Experience in Religion* (New York: Doubleday, 1974).

Lindberg, David C., and Ronald L. Numbers, eds., *When Christianity and Science Meet* (Chicago: University of Chicago Press, 2003).

Lindsey, William, ed., *Religion and Public Life in the Southern Crossroads: Showdown States* (Lanham: Alta Mira Press, 2004).

Lippy, Charles H., *Being Religious American Style: A History of Popular Religiosity in the United States* (Westport: Praeger, 1994).

Lippy, Charles H., *Do Real Men Pray? Images of the Christian Man and Male Spirituality in White Protestant America* (Knoxville: University of Tennessee Press, 2005).

Lippy, Charles H., *Seasonable Revolutionary: The Mind of Charles Chauncey* (New York: Burnham, 1981).

Lippy, Charles H., and Peter W. Williams, eds., *Encyclopedia of the American Religious Experience: Studies in Traditions and Movements*, 3 vols. (New York: Scribner's, 1988).

Lockeridge, Kenneth A., *Literacy in Colonial New England: An Enquiry into the Social Context of Literacy in the Early Modern West* (New York: W. W. Norton, 1974).

Lockeridge, Kenneth A., *Settlement and Unsettlement in Early America: The Crisis of Political Legitimacy Before the Revolution* (Cambridge: Cambridge University Press, 1981).

Loving, Jerome, *Walt Whitman: The Song of Himself* (Berkeley: University of California Press, 1999).

Lowance, Mason I., *The Language of Canaan: Metaphor and Symbol in New England from the Puritans to the Transcendentalists* (Cambridge: Harvard University Press, 1980).

Lucas, Paul, *Valley of Discord: Church and Society along the Connecticut River, 1636–1725* (Hanover: Dartmouth University Press, 1976).

Lundén, Rolf, *Business and Religion in the American 1920s* (Westport: Greenwood Press, 1988).

Mallinson, Jeffrey, *Faith, Reason, and Revelation in Theodore Beza* (Oxford: Oxford University Press, 2003).

Manis, Andrew Michael, *Southern Civil Religions in Conflict: Black and White Baptists and Civil Rights, 1947–1957* (Athens: University of Georgia Press, 1987).

Marietta, Jack D., *The Reformation of American Quakerism, 1748–1783* (Philadelphia: University of Pennsylvania Press, 1984).

Marsden, George, ed., *Evangelicalism and Modern America* (Grand Rapids: William B. Eerdmans, 1984).

Marsden, George, *Fundamentalism and American Culture: The Shaping of Twentieth-Century Evangelicalism 1870–1925* (New York: Oxford University Press, 1980).

Marsden, George, *Jonathan Edwards: A Life* (New Haven: Yale University Press, 2003).

Marsden, George, *Religion and American Culture*, rev. ed. (Belmont: Wadsworth, 2001).

Marsden, George, *Understanding Fundamentalism and Evangelicalism* (Grand Rapids: William B. Eerdmans, 1991).

Marsden, George M., and Bradley J. Longfield, eds., *The Secularization of the Academy* (New York: Oxford University Press, 1992).

Marshall, Peter, and Alec Ryrie, eds., *The Beginnings of English Protestantism* (Cambridge: Cambridge University Press, 2002).

Marty, Martin E., ed., *Modern American Protestantism and Its World: Historical Articles on Protestantism in American Religious Life* (New York: K. G. Saur, 1985–1995).

Marty, Martin E., *Modern American Religion: The Irony of It All, 1893–1919* (Chicago: University of Chicago Press, 1986).

Marty, Martin E., *Pilgrims in Their Own Land: 500 Years of Religion in America* (New York: Penguin, 1984).

Marty, Martin E., *Righteous Empire: The Protestant Experience in America* (New York: Harper & Row, 1970).

Marx, Leo, *The Machine in the Garden: Technology and the Pastoral Ideal in America* (New York: Oxford University Press, 1964).

Matheson, Peter, *The Imaginative World of the Reformation* (Minneapolis: Fortress Press, 2001).

Mathews, Donald G., *Religion in the Old South* (Chicago: University of Chicago Press, 1977).

Matthiessen, F. O., *American Renaissance: Art and Expression in the Age of Emerson and Whitman* (New York: Oxford University Press, 1941).

May, Henry F., *The Enlightenment in America* (New York: Oxford University Press, 1976).

May, Henry F., *Protestant Churches and Industrial America* (New York: Harper & Row, 1949).

McCoy, Drew R., *The Last of the Fathers: James Madison and the Republican Legacy* (Cambridge: Cambridge University Press, 1989).

McDannell, Colleen, *The Christian Home in Victorian America, 1840–1900* (Bloomington: Indiana University Press, 1986).

McDannell, Colleen, *Picturing Faith: Photography and the Great Depression* (New Haven: Yale University Press, 2004).

McGann, Jerome, *The Romantic Ideology: A Critical Investigation* (Chicago: University of Chicago Press, 1983).

McLoughlin, William G., *Revivals, Awakenings, and Reform* (Chicago: University of Chicago Press, 1978).

Mead, Sidney E., *The Lively Experiment: The Shaping of Christianity in America* (New York: Harper & Row, 1963).

Meinig, Donald W., *The Shaping of America: A Geographical Perspective on 500 Years of History*, 4 vols. (New Haven: Yale University Press, 1986–2004).

Middlekauff, Robert, *The Mathers: Three Generations of Puritan Intellectuals, 1596–1728* (New York: Oxford University Press, 1971).

Miller, Perry, *Errand into the Wilderness* (New York: Harper & Row, 1964; orig. 1956).

Miller, Perry, *Jonathan Edwards* (Amherst: University of Massachusetts Press, 1981; orig. 1949).

Miller, Perry, *The New England Mind: From Colony to Province* (Cambridge: Harvard University Press, 1953).

Miller, Perry, *The New England Mind: The Seventeenth Century* (Boston: Beacon Press, 1961; orig. 1939).

Miller, Timothy, *The Hippies and American Values* (Knoxville: University of Tennessee Press, 1991).

Miller, William Lee, *The Business of May Next: James Madison and the Founding* (Charlottesville: University Press of Virginia, 1992).

Miller, William Lee, *The First Liberty: Religion and the American Republic* (New York: Alfred A. Knopf, 1985).

Mitchell, Lee Clark, *Witnesses to a Vanishing America: The Nineteenth-Century Response* (Princeton: Princeton University Press, 1981).

Moore, James R., *The Post-Darwinian Controversies: A Study of the Protestant Struggle to Come to Terms with Darwin in Great Britain and America 1870–1900* (Cambridge: Cambridge University Press, 1979).

Moore, R. Laurence, *Religious Outsiders and the Making of Americans* (New York: Oxford University Press, 1986).

Moran, Gerald F., and Maris A. Vinovskis, *Religion, Family, and the Life Course: Explorations in the Social History of Early America* (Ann Arbor: University of Michigan Press, 1992).

Morgan, Edmund S., *The Puritan Dilemma: The Story of John Winthrop* (Boston: Little, Brown, 1958).

Morgan, Edmund S., *The Puritan Family: Religion and Domestic Relations in Seventeenth-Century New England* (New York: Harper & Row, 1966; orig. 1944).

Morgan, Edmund S., *Visible Saints: The History of a Puritan Idea* (New York: New York University Press, 1963).

Mulder, John M., and John F. Wilson, *Religion in American History: Interpretive Essays* (Englewood Cliffs: Prentice-Hall, 1978).

Mullin, Robert Bruce, *Episcopal Vision/American Reality: High Church Theology and Social Thought in Evangelical America* (New Haven: Yale University Press, 1986).

Mullin, Robert Bruce, *Miracles and the Modern Religious Imagination* (New Haven: Yale University Press, 1996).

Mullin, Robert Bruce, *The Puritan as Yankee: A Life of Horace Bushnell* (Grand Rapids: William B. Eerdmans, 2002).

Nash, Roderick, *Wilderness and the American Mind*, rev. ed. (New Haven: Yale University Press, 1973).

Newman, Kim, *Apocalypse Movies: End of the World Cinema* (New York: St. Martin's Press, 2000; orig. 1999).

Niebuhr, H. Richard, *Christ & Culture* (New York: Harper & Row, 1951).

Niebuhr, H. Richard, *The Kingdom of God in America* (New York: Harper & Row, 1937).

Niebuhr, H. Richard, *The Social Sources of Denominationalism* (New York: New American Library, 1957; orig. 1929).

Noll, Mark A., *America's God: From Jonathan Edwards to Abraham Lincoln* (New York: Oxford University Press, 2002).

Noll, Mark A., *A History of Christianity in the United States and Canada* (Grand Rapids: William B. Eerdmans, 1992).

Noll, Mark A., ed., *Religion & American Politics: From the Colonial Period to the 1980s* (New York: Oxford University Press, 1990).

Noll, Mark A., David W. Bebbington, and George A. Rawlyk, eds., *Evangelicalism: Comparative Studies of Popular Protestantism in North America, the British Isles, and Beyond 1700–1990* (New York: Oxford University Press, 1994).

Nord, David Paul, *Faith in Reading: Religious Publishing and the Birth of Mass Media in America* (New York: Oxford University Press, 2004).

Norton, Mary Beth, *Liberty's Daughters: The Revolutionary Experience of American Women* (Boston: Little, Brown, 1980).

Norwood, Frederick A., *The Story of American Methodism* (Nashville: Abingdon Press, 1974).

Numbers, Ronald L., *Darwinism Comes to America* (Cambridge: Harvard University Press, 1998).

Numbers, Ronald L., and Jonathan M. Butler, eds., *The Disappointed: Millerism and Millenarianism in the Nineteenth Century* (Bloomington: Indiana University Press, 1987).

Nuttall, Geoffrey F., *The Holy Spirit in Puritan Faith and Experience* (Oxford: Blackwell, 1946).

Old, Hughes Oliphant, *Worship: Reformed According to Scripture*, rev. ed. (Louisville: John Knox Press, 2002).

O'Leary, Stephen D., *Arguing the Apocalypse: A Theory of Millennial Rhetoric* (New York: Oxford University Press, 1994).

Ostrander, Rick, *The Life of Prayer in a World of Science: Protestants, Prayer, and American Culture 1870–1930* (New York: Oxford University Press, 2000).

Ozment, Steven, *Protestants: The Birth of a Revolution* (New York: Doubleday, 1992).

Ozment, Steven, *When Fathers Ruled: Family Life in Reformation Europe* (Cambridge: Harvard University Press, 1982).

Paris, Peter J., *Black Religious Leaders: Conflict in Unity* (Louisville: Westminster John Cox, 1991).

Parker, Gail Thain, *Mind Cure in New England: From the Civil War to World War I* (Hanover: University Press of New England, 1973).

Pettit, Norman, *The Heart Prepared: Grace and Conversion in Puritan Spiritual Life* (New Haven: Yale University Press, 1966).

Piper, John F., Jr., *The American Churches in World War I* (Athens: Ohio University Press, 1987).

Pope, Robert G., *The Half-Way Covenant: Church Membership in Puritan New England* (Eugene: Wipf and Stock Publishers, 1969).

Popper, Karl R., *Conjectures and Refutations: The Growth of Scientific Knowledge* (New York: Harper & Row, 1965; orig. 1962).

Porterfield, Amanda, *Female Piety in Puritan New England: The Emergence of Religious Humanism* (New York: Oxford University Press, 1992).

Porterfield, Amanda, *Feminine Spirituality in America: From Sarah Edwards to Martha Graham* (Philadelphia: Temple University Press, 1980).

Porterfield, Amanda, *Healing in the History of Christianity* (New York: Oxford University Press, 2005).

Porterfield, Amanda, *Mary Lyon and the Mount Holyoke Missionaries* (New York: Oxford University Press, 1997).

Porterfield, Amanda, *The Transformation of American Religion: The Story of a Late-Twentieth-Century Awakening* (New York: Oxford University Press, 2001).

Prichard, Robert W., *A History of the Episcopal Church*, rev. ed. (Atlanta: Morehouse Group, 1999).

Pullum, Stephen J., *"Foul Demons, Come Out!" The Rhetoric of Twentieth-Century American Faith Healing* (Westport: Greenwood Press, 1999).

Quinn, D. Michael, ed., *The New Mormon History: Revisionist Essays on the Past* (Salt Lake City: Signature Books, 1992).

Rabinowitz, Richard, *The Spiritual Self in Everyday Life: The Transformation of Personal Religious Experience in Nineteenth-Century New England* (Boston: Northeastern University Press, 1989).

Raboteau, Albert J., *Slave Religion: The "Invisible Institution" in the Antebellum South* (New York: Oxford University Press, 1978).

Rajan, Tilottama, and Arkady Plotnitsky, eds., *Idealism without Absolutes: Philosophy and Romantic Culture* (Albany: SUNY Press, 2004).

Reis, Elizabeth, *Damned Women: Sinners and Witches in Puritan New England* (Ithaca: Cornell University Press, 1997).

Reis, Elizabeth, ed., *Spellbound: Women and Witchcraft in America* (Wilmington: Scholarly Resources, 1998).

Richardson, Robert D., Jr., *Emerson: The Mind on Fire* (Berkeley: University of California Press, 1995).

Richey, Russell E., *Early American Methodism* (Bloomington: Indiana University Press, 1991).

Robert, Dana L., *American Women in Mission: A Social History of Their Thought and Practice* (Macon: Mercer University Press, 1997).

Roof, Wade Clark, ed., *Religion and Public Life in the Pacific Region: Fluid Identities* (Lanham: Alta Mira Press, 2005).

Roof, Wade Clark, *Spiritual Marketplace: Baby Boomers and the Remaking of American Religion* (Princeton: Princeton University Press, 1999).

Rose, Anne C., *Transcendentalism as a Social Movement, 1830–1850* (New Haven: Yale University Press, 1981).

Rose, Anne C., *Victorian America and the Civil War* (Cambridge: Cambridge University Press, 1992).

Rose, Anne C., *Voices of the Marketplace: American Thought and Culture, 1830–1860* (New York: Macmillan, 1995).

Ruse, Michael, *The Evolution-Creation Struggle* (Cambridge: Harvard University Press, 2006).

Russett, Cynthia Eagle, *Darwin in America: The Intellectual Response, 1865–1912* (San Francisco: W. H. Freeman, 1976).

Sandeen, Ernest R., *The Roots of Fundamentalism: British and American Millenarianism, 1800–1930* (Chicago: University of Chicago Press, 1970).

Sarna, Jonathan, ed., *Minority Faiths and the American Protestant Mainstream* (Urbana: University of Illinois Press, 1998).

Satter, Beryl, *Each Mind a Kingdom: American Women, Sexual Purity, and the New Thought Movement, 1875–1920* (Berkeley: University of California Press, 1999).

Schmidt, Leigh Eric, *Consumer Rites: The Buying and Selling of American Holidays* (Princeton: Princeton University Press, 1995).

Schmidt, Leigh Eric, *Hearing Things: Religion, Illusion, and the American Enlightenment* (Cambridge: Harvard University Press, 2000).

Schmidt, Leigh Eric, *Holy Fairs: Scottish Communions and the American Revivals in the Early Modern Period* (Princeton: Princeton University Press, 1989).

Schneider, A. Gregory, *The Way of the Cross Leads Home: The Domestication of American Methodism* (Bloomington: Indiana University Press, 1993).

Seager, Richard Hughes, *The World's Parliament of Religions: The East/West Encounter, Chicago, 1893* (Bloomington: Indiana University Press, 1995).

Sears, John F., *Sacred Places: American Tourist Attractions in the Nineteenth Century* (New York: Oxford University Press, 1989).

Senn, Frank C., ed., *Protestant Spiritual Traditions* (New York: Paulist Press, 1986).

Sensbach, Jon F., *Rebecca's Revival: Creating Black Christianity in the Atlantic World* (Cambridge: Harvard University Press, 2005).

Shepard, Robert S., *God's People in the Ivory Tower: Religion in the Early American University* (Chicago: University of Chicago Press, 1991).

Shibley, Mark A., *Resurgent Evangelicalism in the United States: Mapping Cultural Change since 1970* (Columbia: University of South Carolina Press, 1996).

Shipps, Jan, *Mormonism: The Story of a New Religious Tradition* (Urbana: University of Illinois Press, 1985).

Shipps, Jan, ed., *Religion and Public Life in the Mountain West: Sacred Landscapes in Transition* (Lanham: Alta Mira Press, 2004).

Shuffelton, Frank, *Thomas Hooker, 1586–1647* (Princeton: Princeton University Press, 1987).

Silk, Mark, *Spiritual Politics: Religion and America Since World War II* (New York: Touchstone, 1989).

Slotkin, Richard, *Regeneration Through Violence: The Mythology of the American Frontier 1600–1860* (Middletown: Wesleyan University Press, 1973).

Smith, Christian, *American Evangelicalism: Embattled and Thriving* (Chicago: University of Chicago Press, 1998).

Smith, Henry Nash, *Virgin Land: The American West as Symbol and Myth* (Cambridge: Harvard University Press, 1950).

Smith, John E., *The Spirit of American Philosophy* (New York: Oxford University Press, 1963).

Smith, John E., *Themes in American Philosophy: Purpose, Experience and Community* (New York: Harper & Row, 1970).

Smith, Timothy L., *Revivalism and Social Reform: American Protestantism on the Eve of the Civil War* (New York: Abingdon Press, 1957).

Sobel, Mechal, *Trabelin' On: The Slave Journey to an Afro-Baptist Faith* (Princeton: Princeton University Press, 1988).

Sobel, Mechal, *The World They Made Together: Black and White Values in Eighteenth-Century Virginia* (Princeton: Princeton University Press, 1987).

Spurgin, Hugh, *Roger Williams and Puritan Radicalism in the English Separatist Tradition* (Lewiston: Edwin Mellen Press, 1989).

Stannard, David, ed., *Death in America* (Philadelphia: University of Pennsylvania Press, 1974).

Stannard, David, *The Puritan Way of Death: A Study of Religion, Culture, and Social Change* (New York: Oxford University Press, 1977).

Stavely, Keith W. F., *Puritan Legacies: Paradise Lost and the New England Tradition, 1630–1890* (Ithaca: Cornell University Press, 1987).

Stein, Stephen J., *The Shaker Experience in America: A History of the United Society of Believers* (New Haven: Yale University Press, 1992).

Stevenson, Louise L. *Scholarly Means to Evangelical Ends: The New Haven Scholars and the Transformation of Higher Learning in America, 1830–1890* (Baltimore: Johns Hopkins University Press, 1986).

Stone, Lawrence, *The Family, Sex and Marriage in England 1500–1800* (New York: Harper & Row, 1977).

Stout, Harry S., *The Divine Dramatist: George Whitefield and the Rise of Modern Evangelicalism* (Grand Rapids: William B. Eerdmans, 1991).

Stout, Harry S., *The New England Soul: Preaching and Religious Culture in Colonial New England* (New York: Oxford University Press, 1986).

Stout, Harry S., *Upon the Altar of the Nation: A Moral History of the American Civil War* (New York: Viking, 2006).

Stout, Harry S., and Jon Butler, *Religion in American History* (New York: Oxford University, 1998).

Stout, Jeffrey, *Democracy and Tradition* (Princeton: Princeton University Press, 2004).

Stowe, David W., *How Sweet the Sound: Music in the Spiritual Lives of Americans* (Cambridge: Harvard University Press, 2004).

Strout, Cushing, *The New Heavens and Earth: Political Religion in America* (New York: Harper & Row, 1974).

Sweet, Leonard I., ed., *The Evangelical Tradition in America* (Macon: Mercer University Press, 1984).

Sweet, William Warren, *American Culture and Religion* (Dallas: SMU Press, 1951).

Tannenbaum, Rebecca J., *The Healer's Calling: Women and Medicine in Early New England* (Ithaca: Cornell University Press, 2002).

Taves, Ann, *Fits, Trances, and Visions: Experiencing Religion and Explaining Experience from Wesley to James* (Princeton: Princeton University Press, 1999).

Thomas, Keith, *Religion and the Decline of Magic: Studies in Popular Religious Beliefs in Sixteenth and Seventeenth Century England* (New York: Scribner's, 1971).

Tichi, Cecelia, *New World, New Earth: Environmental Reform in American Literature from the Puritans through Whitman* (New Haven: Yale University Press, 1979).

Tise, Larry E., *Proslavery: A History of the Defense of Slavery in America, 1701–1840* (Athens: University of Georgia Press, 1987).

Todd, Margo, *Christian Humanism and the Puritan Social Order* (Cambridge: Cambridge University Press, 1987).

Toulouse, Mark G., and James O. Duke, eds., *Makers of Christian Theology in America* (Nashville: Abingdon Press, 1997).

Trollinger, William Vance, Jr., *God's Empire: William Bell Riley and Midwestern Fundamentalism* (Madison: University of Wisconsin Press, 1990).

Turner, James, *Without God, Without Creed: The Origins of Unbelief in America* (Baltimore: Johns Hopkins University Press, 1985).

Tyler, Alice Felt, *Freedom's Ferment: Phases of American Social History from the Colonial Period to the Outbreak of the Civil War* (Minneapolis: University of Minnesota Press, 1944).

Ulrich, Laurel Thatcher, *Good Wives: Image and Reality in the Lives of Puritan Women in Northern New England, 1650–1750* (New York: Oxford University Press, 1980).

Upham, Charles W., *Salem Witchcraft: With an Account of Salem Village and a History of Opinions of Witchcraft and Kindred Subjects* (Mineola: Dover Publications, 2000; orig. 1867).

Vidich, Arthur J., and Stanford M. Lyman, *American Sociology: Worldly Rejections of Religion and Their Directions* (New Haven: Yale University Press, 1985).

Wacker, Grant, *Heaven Below: Early Pentecostals and American Culture* (Cambridge: Harvard University Press, 2001).

Walsh, Andrew, ed., *Religion and Public Life in New England: Steady Habits Changing Slowly* (Lanham: Alta Mira Press, 2004).

Walters, Kerry S., *The American Deists: Voices of Reason & Dissent in the Early Republic* (Lawrence: University Press of Kansas, 1992).

Walzer, Michael, *The Revolution of the Saints: A Study in the Origins of Radical Politics* (New York: Atheneum, 1971).

Wandel, Lee Palmer, *The Eucharist in the Reformation: Incarnation and Liturgy* (Cambridge: Cambridge University Press, 2006).

Warner, Wayne E., *The Woman Evangelist: The Life and Times of Charismatic Evangelist Maria B. Woodworth-Etter* (Metuchen: Scarecrow Press, 1986).

Watson, Justin, *The Christian Coalition: Dreams of Restoration, Demands for Recognition* (New York: St. Martin's, 1997).

Watson, Patricia Ann, *The Angelical Connection: The Preacher-Physicians of Colonial New England* (Knoxville: University of Tennessee Press, 1991).

Weber, Donald, *Rhetoric and History in Revolutionary New England* (New York: Oxford University Press, 1988).

Weber, Max, *The Protestant Ethic and the Spirit of Capitalism* (London: George Allen and Unwin, 1930).

Weisberger, Bernard A., *They Gathered at the River: The Story of the Great Revivalists and Their Impact upon Religion in America* (Boston: Little, Brown, 1958).

Weisbrot, Robert, *Father Divine: The Utopian Evangelist of the Depression Era Who Became an American Legend* (Boston: Beacon Press, 1983).

Welch, Claude, *Protestant Thought in the Nineteenth Century Vol. 1, 1799–1870* (Westford: Bross Foundation, 1972).

Welch, Claude, *Protestant Thought in the Nineteenth Century Vol. 2, 1870–1914* (New Haven: Yale University Press, 1985).

West, Cornel, *Democracy Matters: Winning the Fight Against Imperialism* (New York: Penguin Press, 2004).

Westbrook, Robert B., *John Dewey and American Democracy* (Ithaca: Cornell University Press, 1991).

Westerkamp, Marilyn J., *Women and Religion in Early America, 1600–1850: The Puritan and Evangelical Traditions* (New York: Routledge, 1999).

White, James F., *Christian Worship in North America, a Retrospective: 1955–1995* (Collegeville: Order of St. Benedict, 1997).

White, James F., *The Sacraments in Protestant Practice and Faith* (Nashville: Abingdon Press, 1999).

White, Ronald C., Jr., *Liberty and Justice for All: Racial Reform & the Social Gospel* (New York: Harper & Row, 1990).

White, Ronald C., Jr., and C. Howard Hopkins, *The Social Gospel: Religion and Reform in Changing America* (Philadelphia: Temple University Press, 1974).

Wiebe, Robert H., *The Search for Order, 1877–1920* (New York: Hill and Want, 1967).

Williams, Daniel Day, *The Andover Liberals: A Study in American Theology* (New York: Octagon Books, 1970).

Williams, Peter W., *America's Religions: From Their Origins to the Twenty-first Century* (Urbana: University of Illinois Press, 2002).

Williams, Peter W., ed., *Perspectives on American Religion and Culture* (Malden: Blackwell, 1999).

Williams, Peter W., *Popular Religion in America: Symbolic Change and the Modernization Process in Historical Perspective* (Urbana: University of Illinois Press, 1989).

Wilmore, Gayraud S., *Black Religion and Black Radicalism: An Interpretation of the Religious History of Afro-American People*, rev. ed. (Maryknoll: Orbis Books, 1983).

Wilson, Charles Reagan, *Baptized in Blood: The Religion of the Lost Cause, 1865–1920* (Athens: University of Georgia Press, 1980).

Wilson, Charles Reagan, *Religion and Public Life in the South: In the Evangelical Mode* (Lanham: Alta Mira Press, 2005).

Wilson, John, *Religion in American Society: The Effective Presence* (Englewood Cliffs: Prentice-Hall, 1978).

Wilson, Robert J., III, *The Benevolent Deity: Ebenezer Gay and the Rise of Rational Religion in New England, 1696–1787* (Philadelphia: University of Pennsylvania Press, 1984).

Wind, James P., and James W. Lewis, eds., *American Congregations*, 2 vols. (Chicago: University of Chicago Press, 1994).

Winship, Michael P., *Making Heretics: Militant Protestantism and Free Grace in Massachusetts, 1636–1641* (Princeton: Princeton University Press, 2002).

Winston, Diane, *Red-Hot and Righteous: The Urban Religion of The Salvation Army* (Cambridge: Harvard University Press, 2000).

Wrightson, Keith, *English Society, 1580–1680* (New Brunswick: Rutgers University Press, 1982).

Wuthnow, Robert, *The Restructuring of American Religion: Society and Faith Since World War II* (Princeton: Princeton University Press, 1988).

Wyatt-Brown, Bertram, *The Shaping of Southern Culture: Honor, Grace, and War, 1760s–1880s* (Chapel Hill: University of North Carolina Press, 2002).

Zakai, Avihu, *Jonathan Edwards's Philosophy of History: The Reenchantment of the World in the Age of the Enlightenment* (Princeton: Princeton University Press, 2003).

Ziegler, Valarie H., *The Advocates of Peace in Antebellum America* (Bloomington: Indiana University Press, 1992).

Ziegler, Valarie H., *Divine Julia: The Public Romance and Private Agony of Julia Ward Howe* (Harrisburg: Continuum, 2003).

Zwiep, Mary, *Pilgrim Path: The First Company of Women Missionaries to Hawaii* (Madison: University of Wisconsin Press, 1991).

Index

About the Author

AMANDA PORTERFIELD is the Robert A. Spivey Professor of Religion at Florida State University and co-editor of *Church History: Studies in Christianity and Culture*. She has written books on New England Puritans, Protestant women missionaries in the 19th century, the transformation of American religion after 1960, and healing in the history of Christianity.